# WEST SOMERSET
# IN THE NEWS

## Jeff Cox

ryelands

First published in Great Britain in 2010

British Library Cataloguing-in-Publication Data
A CIP record for this title is available from the British Library

ISBN 978 1 906551 09 4

**RYELANDS**
Halsgrove House,
Ryelands Industrial Estate,
Bagley Road, Wellington, Somerset TA21 9PZ
Tel: 01823 653777    Fax: 01823 216796
email: sales@halsgrove.com

Part of the Halsgrove group of companies
Information on all Halsgrove titles is available at: www.halsgrove.com

Printed and bound in Great Britain by J F Print Ltd., Sparkford, Somerset

# Contents

There is a natural curiosity in the mind of man to become acquainted with the history of the neighbourhood in which he first drew his breath or has fixed his residence.

*James Savage, History of the Hundred of Carhampton, 1830.*

Many of the things chronicled in local journals may appear very small, but life is made up of small things…

*Charles Dickens on local journalism, January 5th 1861.*

# Acknowlededgments

This book has only been possible thanks to the unquestioning love and support of my wife Jan, who gave me the time and freedom to develop and realise the project; and of my mother Pat Hill, and late stepfather John, who provided bed, lodging and regular hot meals in Minehead, while I researched the material.

The Editor of the *Free Press*, Gareth Purcell and General Manager, David Tucker, gave me generous access to the back files of the paper at Williton, as did the staff at British Library (Newspaper Section) at Colindale.

Many have advised me on the accuracy of the text: for this, I thank Gareth Purcell, Lady Gass, Julian Luttrell, Isabel Richardson, Rachel Thomas, Bernard Dru, William Hancock, Maurice Chidgey, Dr Glyn Court, Ian Coleby and Kate Barlow. But any mistakes are, of course, mine alone.

Photographs did not appear regularly in the *Free Press* until the 1930s; I have sought to uncover new photographs, to illustrate the early years, but make no apology for reprinting some well-known images, especially from those wonderful local photographers James Date, H.H. Hole and Alfred Vowles, whose visual power so effectively illustrate some of the stories from the earlier editions of the *Free Press*.

I am indebted to many kind people for permission to use photographs held either by their local organisations or in their personal collections. In particular, Peggy Anderson at the West Somerset Rural Life Museum at Allerford and Jan Ross at the Heritage Centre in Dulverton, gave me generous and unlimited access to their wonderful collections of photographs, and in Dulverton, John Deering helped me clarify details involving the Michael Deering Exmoor Photographic Archive.

Steve Guscott kindly gave me permission to reprint many of his news photos which have appeared in the *Free Press* over the past decade, as did John Atkins for his photos from the 1990s.

Other photographs have been kindly provided by Oliver Davies, Hilary Binding, Lady Gass, Julian Luttrell, William Hancock, Holly Wright, Ian Coleby, Peter Lockwood, David Worthy (Friends of Coleridge), Joan Astell, Dr Glyn Court, Maurice & Joyce Chidgey, Keith Towells, Graham Haw, Dennis Corner, Freddie Huxtable, Dick Lloyd, Chris Nelder, Sue Farrington, Nigel Hester, (Holnicote Estate), Sir Robin Dunn, Mike Chilcott, Daphne McCutcheon, Laetitia Kelly (Friends of Quantock), Kate Barlow, Jef Brooks, Peter Downer, Frank Clatworthy, Rob Wilson-North and Heike Bernhardt and Tim Parish (all of the Exmoor National Park Authority), Hinkley Point A & B press departments, Mary Miles, Nick Thompson, Tim Auty, Linda Edge, Philip White, Vernon Stone, Old Cleeve Village Hall, and the South Molton and District Museum.

The photographs of Auberon Herbert on page 79 are reproduced from his biography, *The Man Who Was Greenmantle*, by Margaret Fitzherbert, with the kind permission of Emily Fitzherbert.

The marine artist, Mark Myers, kindly allowed me to reproduce his painting 'The *Louisa* off the Holms', portraying the Lynmouth lifeboat rescuing the Forrest Hall in Porlock Bay 1899.

I have tried to confirm and clear copyright for all the photographs used, but apologise now if I have inadvertently failed to contact everyone.

And finally, thanks to the editors of the *West Somerset Free Press*. It is some tribute to the paper and the readership it serves that over the 150 years, the paper has had just seven editors:

  Samuel Cox 1860-1881
  Herbert Cox 1881-1922
  Frank Cox 1922-1964
  Norman Cox 1964-1970
  Jack Hurley 1970-1980
  Bob Alwyne 1980-1982
  Gareth Purcell 1982-

                                                                    Jeff Cox

# Introduction

IN JULY 1860, when Samuel Cox, a printer based in Williton, published his first edition of the *West Somerset Free Press*, the district was on the verge of a rapid and exciting transformation. For generations before then, progress had been glacial, but all this was to change.

In 1860, as in the decades gone by, transport was slow and arduous, along rutted roads by foot, horse, or cart, blocked by tollgates every few miles; most worked on the land, on the farms and smallholdings, and most of their children were denied any real education by the over-riding need to earn money for the family. Homes at night were lit by flickering oil lamps, and woodfires fended off the winter cold or, for the wealthy, coal, shipped across from South Wales. There was no gas for light nor for warmth; gas was still a luxury for the urban elite, and electricity was just a scientific curiosity, a trick of the laboratory.

In 1860, there were no local councils to provide essential services – public health, education, transport. There *were* no local services, beyond the last-resort lifeline for the destitute and the lost in the harsh and unforgiving Poor Law workhouses at Williton and Dulverton. There was no safety net for families hit by illness, unemployment, accident or natural disaster.

In hard times, many relied on the generosity of the landed gentry – the Luttrells of Dunster, the separate branches of the Acland family at Stogursey and at Holnicote, the Wyndhams at Williton and the Trevelyans at Nettlecombe; they were the main employers, and the main benefactors. There was a settled nature to the old order; there hadn't been the need for a parliamentary election for more than twenty years, as no-one had come forward to challenge the local Tory dominance.

But all this was about to change; progress was in the air, the pulse of life was quickening. The great advances of Victorian Britain were finally starting to make an impact on the district.

The appetite of Britain's expanding industries had already kick-started some new enterprises: on the Brendon Hills, the iron mines started in 1851 were expanding, and the first trains on the Mineral Line were carrying the ore down to Watchet; here, the harbour was about to be extended to handle the increased shipments of ore across to the furnaces of South Wales.

And the Mineral Line was about to be dwarfed by the genius of Isambard Kingdom Brunel. His company had already surveyed the route for a broad gauge railway to link the Bristol & Exeter lines at Taunton to the coast at Watchet; Brunel had been commissioned by the West Somerset Railway Company, formed in 1856 and chaired by one of the enlightened gentry, Sir Peregrine Acland of Stogursey.

Up on Exmoor, by 1860 Frederick Knight was finally making progress with his father's grand project to reclaim the ancient Royal Forest for agriculture; farms had been established, grazing land was being won from the hard moors and new strains of sheep were beginning to thrive. Frederick Knight was even considering his own railway, from Simonsbath to Porlock, hoping he, too, could mine iron ore from the moors and deliver supplies to the shore.

On the coast, Minehead had declined steeply from its sea-trading glories of the early eighteenth century; it was also still recovering from the disastrous fire in 1791 that had destroyed much of the town. In 1832, as a symbol of its decline, Minehead had lost its right to send two MPs to Parliament. But now, thirty years later, the town was showing the first signs of a resurgence, as a clean and attractive destination for that new phenomenon created by the growing wealth of the nation – the tourist.

It was this sense of excitement and optimism along the coast and on the moors of West Somerset that Samuel Cox hoped to tap into; he wrote in the first edition of the *West Somerset Free Press* on July 28th 1860, that his ambition for the new paper was...

'...*to keep pace with the advancing spirit of the age.*'

He promised

'...*that trust, fairness, and impartiality shall be the characteristics of its pages... its tone shall be cheerful without levity. . .in short, to all classes of readers. . .our design is to make the Free Press a paper for the people.' July 28th 1860.*

THE ONLY NEWSPAPER PUBLISHED WITHIN A CIRCUIT OF NEARLY TWENTY MILES OF WILLITON.

# THE WEST SOMERSET FREE PRESS,
SATURDAY, JULY 28th, 1860.

## OUR ADDRESS.

IN presenting the first number of a new weekly newspaper for the district of "WEST SOMERSET" generally, we may naturally be expected to place before our readers the principal reasons for entering on so bold and onerous an undertaking, and to trace out the course we intend to pursue.

We believe that it is only expressing the feeling of the inhabitants of this neighbourhood, when we say, that a journal, published in our own vicinity, has long been considered a desideratum. We do not undervalue the various county and district papers which circulate among us, some of which are conducted with considerable ability, but still there are local interests, manifestly growing from year to year, of sufficient importance to occupy far more than a few short paragraphs occasionally appearing in the provincial press. To meet this want the WEST SOMERSET FREE PRESS has been originated, and puts forward its claim for support and patronage.

The rapid approach to completion of a Railway, to connect this district with the Bristol and Exeter lines, coupled with the increasing prospects of a new Harbour, Pier, and Quay, at Watchet,—to keep pace with the advancing spirit of the age,—and the fact of the greater portion of the public business of the neighbourhood being conducted in Williton,—all tend to justify us in making this place the centre of operations. Whilst at the same time, arrangements have been made by which Minehead, Dunster, Stogumber, &c., will secure a weekly report of the news of their own localities.

In the columns of the *Free Press* will be

But it wasn't easy. Many influential people felt threatened by the growing enlightenment that a new newspaper would bring to its readership – in particular, to the working classes who could read

of the wages and conditions enjoyed by workers elsewhere, and who could use the *Free Press* as a forum for complaint against perceived injustices.

For the first few months, Samuel Cox struggled to establish the *Free Press*, threatened with a boycott not only of his new paper but also of his printing and bookselling business in Williton, by 'influential figures' who opposed the project. But he stuck to his guns.

And from those first uncertain weeks, and for the past 150 years, the *West Somerset Free Press* has published every week without fail, faithfully reporting the events and the characters that have shaped the present-day district of West Somerset.

# 1860s: The 'advancing spirit'

Brother Prince was rarely seen outside the high walls of the Abode.

WHEN A newspaper proprietor launches a new title he dreams of a good juicy news story to grab his readers. Samuel Cox had the beginner's luck; after all, he had been only a printer for the past dozen years; this was his first attempt at journalism. For his first edition, he had a local story on his doorstep which was gripping not just West Somerset, but the whole of England: Fleet Street was chasing this one.

Across the Quantocks at Spaxton, a Church of England deacon Henry James Prince, exiled from his parish by the Bishop of Bath and Wells for his radical teachings, was living in scandalous luxury in a secretive commune he called Agapemone, or the Abode of Love. Brother Prince had declared himself the Messenger of God, sent to warn the world of the impending Apocalypse at Spaxton he surrounded himself with those he termed the Righteous – wealthy, impressionable, and for the most part, female followers.

But Prince's fleecing of his gullible flock was being challenged. The very first edition of the *West Somerset Free Press* reports that a court had ordered Prince to return more than £11,000 – an enormous sum in those days – to four daughters of a respectable gentleman who had handed over this fortune to Prince; three of the women had also been forced into marriages in the commune.

The scandals emanating from the reclusive Abode of Love at Spaxton were to run and run, and some sixty years later were to make Ecclesiastical Church history. But, of course, the activities of a self-styled prophet did not reflect the usual activities of West Somerset in 1860, as reported in the columns of Samuel Cox's new paper.

❖

The bustling port of Watchet was the thriving centre of the district's import and export of essential supplies: it had long ago overtaken Minehead, where the town's shipping was a poor shadow of its former great days.

The first edition of the *Free Press* lists all the vessels coming in and out of Watchet during the previous week; the vast majority arrive with coal from

## STORMING THE AGAPEMONE.

### DESPERATE ATTEMPT TO RESCUE MRS. PRICE.—THE "ABODE OF LOVE" IN DANGER.

On Tuesday evening last, the Rev. Lewis Price, one of the latest seceders from the Agapemone, assisted by a party of nearly a hundred men, made a bold and daring attempt at that building to rescue his wife, who, it will be remembered, is a sister of the late Miss Nottidge, and possessed a fortune of £6,000, which was made over to Mr. Prince. The Rev. Mr. Price quitted the loving abode at the beginning of the year, since which time he has made several unsuccessful efforts to gain possession of his spouse, one of which we reported last week.

On the evening in question, the volunteers who had engaged to assist in the undertaking, which had been previously made known, met on the Spaxton road, about six o'clock, and proceeded to the spot, headed by Mr. Price, and several other gentlemen. When they had travelled some distance, and were nearing the scene of action, Mr. Price alighted, and, addressing his companions, explained that the present attempt was made solely to obtain the restoration of that which belonged to him. He urged them to resort to no means of violence, to do no damage, and to strike no blow without they were themselves attacked, and then only in self-defence. On arriving at the Agapemone, they found that intelligence of their contemplated visit had reached the Princeites, for the brethren were in a great state of excitement, and running about in all directions.

## NOTICE.
### CHEAP TRIP TO BRISTOL.

The fast-sailing steamer IRON DUKE, (D. Apperley, commander,) has been engaged for a Trip from

WATCHET TO BRISTOL AND BACK,

On WEDNESDAY next, July 24th,

(Wind and weather permitting,) leaving Watchet punctually at 6 o'clock in the morning, and returning from the Cumberland Basin, Bristol, at quarter-past 5 in the evening to the minute.

The inhabitants of this neighbourhood have never before had such an opportunity as will be offered on Wednesday next, of going to Bristol and back by water on the same day; being allowed about eight hours to visit the ancient City with its numerous attractions; also the romantic scenery of the River Avon, the Clifton Suspension Bridge, Zoological Gardens, Durdham Downs, &c. &c.; whilst at the same time the merchant and tradesman may combine business with pleasure.

FARES—Saloon, 4s. 6d.; Fore-Cabin, 3s.; Children under 12, half-price.

The Iron Duke will arrive at Watchet from Cardiff on Tuesday evening, the 23rd, and make a trip to Minehead and back the same evening, leaving Watchet at quarter-past 7, and returning about 9 o'clock.—Fares Saloon, 9d.; Fore Cabin, 6d.; children half-price. Refreshments may be obtained on board.

The steamer will leave for Cardiff on Thursday morning, the 25th inst.—For further information and for tickets, apply to Mr. R. S. DATE, Watchet.

## A TREAT FOR THE MILLION.
### STEAM EXCURSION
from WATCHET and MINEHEAD, TO ILFRACOMBE AND BACK.

JENNY JONES

The largest, fastest, and most commodious passenger steamer ever seen in Watchet, the JENNY JONES, (D. Howe, commander,) has been engaged at a great expense for a pleasure-trip to Ilfracombe,

On WEDNESDAY, JUNE 26th, 1861,

(wind and weather permitting,) leaving Watchet at 8 o'clock and Minehead at 9 a.m., and starting from Ilfracombe at ¼-past 5, thus allowing Excursionists about six hours to view the delightful scenery in that neighbourhood.

The Steamer will also call off PORLOCK on her way to and fro.

FARES.—Saloon, 4s. 6d.; Fore-Cabin, 3s.; children half-price. Tickets may be had of Mr. J. Chichester, and Mr. R. S. Date, Watchet; Mr. Cox, Williton; and Mr. John Stoate, Minehead;

THE MONKSILVER BRASS BAND will be in attendance.

The Jenny Jones having for several years plied between Bristol and Cardiff, is well known for her excellent accommodation, having saloons for both Ladies and Gentlemen, and is one of the fastest steamers in the Bristol Channel.

Refreshments may be obtained on board.

Newport and Cardiff, and depart destined for the same ports loaded with iron ore from the Brendon Hill mines.

Trading vessels pack into Watchet harbour in this early James Date photo.

---

The first editions also reflect what was then, and remains today, very much part of the district's life – sport, and in particular, cricket... and some of its associated temptations.

Reporting an early fixture between Dunster and St Decuman's, the paper says that Dunster...

'...were first to handle the willow, which they used in prime style (scoring 106) but the bowling on either side did not appear up to the mark... and St Decuman's fielding was poor.' August 4th 1860.

But there may have been a reason for this.

'We would remark, en passant, that if less attention were paid to the shrine of Bacchus and more to this noble manly English game it would remove the stigma which is upon it.'

A GRAND TEMPERANCE MEETING will be held on TUESDAY, AUGUST 7th, 1800, at the Mines on BRENDON HILL, (under the patronage of Sir Walter C. Trevelyan, Bart.,) when ADDRESSES will be delivered by the Rev. H. GALE, B.C.L., Rector of Treborough; Rev. H. KING, of Tiverton; Mr. G. JARVIS, Farmer, of Kilmington; Mr. JOHN PERRY, the Teetotal Blacksmith, of Yeovil, and other Gentlemen.

Tea will be provided in a tent (50 yards long,) at Four o'clock, p.m. Tickets, One Shilling each.— Children under 12, half-price.

☞ A good Band will be in attendance.

The Iron-Mines Company have kindly arranged to run a special Engine to the Hill, leaving Watchet at 3 o'clock precisely, and returning at 9 o'clock, when clean Trucks will be at the service of parties wishing to avail themselves of this mode of conveyance.

*Clergymen, Ministers of the Gospel, Sabbath-School Teachers, &c., are respectfully invited.*

In 1860, the dangers of intoxication were at the heart of a powerful Temperance movement in West Somerset.

That first edition of the paper carried a front page advert with details of the annual 'Teetotal Meeting at the Mines on Brendon Hill,' arranged by Sir Walter Calverley Trevelyan of Nettlecombe Court, who was the first president of the national temperance organisation, the United Kingdom Alliance, 'for the suppression of liquor traffic'.

The rally was held at the top of the steep Comberow Incline, one of the wonders of its time. The West Somerset Mineral Line had allowed passengers to ride in the empty iron-ore trucks up onto the ridge, where 'thousands partook the cup that cheers but not inebriates'; they listened to speeches from temperance missionaries, (including Mr John Perry, the teetotal blacksmith from Yeovil) and enjoyed the scenery below and beyond.

A boy rests on his climb about one third his way up the incline, circa 1870.

*'It is beautiful — grand — magnificent — majestic — sublime. Richly wooded hills and dales, golden-headed fields of corn, with an occasional reddish-looking piece of tillage, land skirted by the sea and backed by the mountainous Welsh coast — all stand in bold relief to our gaze.*

*'About half past eight the train was again in readiness and left with 800 persons. Some hearty cheers were given on arriving at Watchet.' August 10th 1860.*

Construction had by now started on the West Somerset Railway, surveyed and designed by the greatest engineer of the age, Isambard Kingdom Brunel. But following Brunel's death a year earlier, the project was now in the hands of his chief assistant engineer, Mr R.P. Brereton.

In September 1860, the *Free Press* covered the annual general meeting of the West Somerset Railway Company, held at the Pattinsons Hotel in Taunton, chaired by Sir Peregrine Acland of Fairfield House, Stogursey. It is a reflection of the simple journalism of the time that this significant event, a progress report on perhaps the most important single development in the district, warrants just one paragraph in the paper, concluding;

*'A report was read and adopted and it was said that the line was progressing very satisfactorily — upwards of thirteen miles being at present railed off.' September 29th 1860.*

In an editorial the following week, Samuel Cox, offered his readers a little more, with a detailed description of the twists and turns of the route of the new railway, adding;

*'Our railway, we are pleased to state, is fast progressing, and at present there seems to be nothing to prevent it being opened at the stated time in July next... The scenery throughout the line between Watchet and Taunton is of the most picturesque and enchanting description – at almost every mile, it gradually changes, between hill and dale, while fresh beauties are seen on every hand. It may also be stated that there are no tunnels to pass through.' October 8th 1860.*

———————— ❖ ————————

The expansion of Watchet harbour, the terminus of the new railway, is also about to start;

*'It will provide an invaluable boon to vessels bound from Burnham or Bridgwater westward, by proving a refuge of shelter and safety when overtaken by storms or gales, prevented from reaching Minehead, and now compelled to return, at a perilous hazard, back to the river (Parrett).' December 15th 1860.*

And by early 1861, good progress is apparently being made

The scenery throughout the line between Watchet and Taunton is of the most picturesque and enchanting description—at almost every mile it gradually changes, between hill and dale, while fresh beauties are seen on every hand. It may also be stated that there are no tunnels to pass through.
We cannot refrain from expressing our gratification at the highly satisfactory progress of the work, notwithstanding the immense quantity of rain and consequent hindrances during the past summer. Among numerous others we joyfully anticipate its opening, feeling sure that great benefits will immediately accrue to the whole population through the district it passes,—as a means of affording increased communication with other and larger towns, and the transit of crops to the market from this productive neighbourhood, as well as merchandise and coal from the port of Watchet.—[Our thanks are due to an official on the line, for his readiness to give us any information needed.]

*'...daily, at low water, several gangs of men may been seen actively engaged in blasting rocks, raising stones and other necessary requisites. The areas of harbour, when complete, will be ten acres; and a vessel will be able to enter at half-flood or half-ebb tide, which will prove of great advantage.' February 2nd 1861.*

And despite sustained rain in early 1861, in his next report to the WSRC board, R.P. Brereton is optimistic that the new line will open by late summer 1861. The costs have risen above the original estimate of £120,000, and the WSRC is now negotiating for the Bristol and Exeter Railway Company to lease the line and to run the trains.

There were, of course, unforeseen delays; the late 1861 deadline was missed, and an idea to open the line just to Williton was soon rejected.

The first trial passenger train was delayed by an accident involving construction workers at Crowcombe Heathfield, but finally, on March 29th 1862, the *Free Press* reports that the first passengers have travelled on the line; the weather was poor, which kept the crowds down, but this failed to depress their exuberant welcome:

Watchet Station prepares to welcome the first train.

*'Watchet, being the terminus of the line, presented a very gay and animated appearance. For days the inhabitants have been very busy decorating the streets with arches and garlands... About three o'clock three carriages attached to an engine arrived at Watchet, bringing several of the directors and those connected with the Bristol & Exeter line.*

*'On its arrival, however, it was received with a shout, as Englishmen like to give, and when the directors alighted, they were hailed with a cheer. At the entrance to the station, a triumphal arch was erected and amidst a bevy of evergreens and flags we noticed a motto "Welcome ye friends of progress."*

*'The pier and ships were gaily decorated with flags. Men women and children all seemed to wear a holiday aspect and although the weather was unpropitious, it did not appear to dampen the ardour of the public, for all were determined to do their best in giving a cheer for the railway.' March 29th 1862.*

One of the first trains on the new line, a B & E.R broad gauge saddletank no 68, circa 1862.

The formal opening to the public followed on Monday April 1st. The first public service was the 10.35 from Taunton, but the real crowds arrived on the next service, where passengers had to stand in rows two deep in the carriages.

*'All things passed off most pleasantly..... and hundreds, many of whom had in all probability never seen a railed engine before, availed themselves of the opportunity of seeing the "monster" as it made its appearance, screaming and hissing like a serpent of the deep.' April 5th 1862.*

But again the weather tested their enthusiasm of those waiting at the Watchet terminus:

*'The town was the scene of much joy, but. . . from the incessant rains of the two previous days, the roads and pavements were completely gutted and mud lay inches deep. It was indeed a sorry sight to witness that state of the pantaloons and nether garments of the pedestrians, who seemed quite indifferent, so determined were they to have their fill of pleasure.'*

❖

No sooner had the West Somerset Railway given new access to the Bristol Channel than there was talk of another new rail venture in the area – what was to become the Devon & Somerset Railway. Surveyors, land agents and solicitors had been visiting North Devon.

*'It will branch off from the Bristol & Exeter Railway near Taunton, passing through Wiveliscombe, Bampton, and Dulverton, through the Anstey Valley, close by the villages of Bishopsnympton and Molland and the hitherto neglected Southmolton and thence to Barnstaple – bringing Lynton within a short hour's ride by coach – and termination at Ilfracombe, the future packet station for South Wales, Ireland and Liverpool.' September 13th 1862.*

And by the end of the year, there was some excitement that Watchet might not be the end of the West Somerset line:

### BRISTOL AND EXETER RAILWAY.
### OPENING OF THE WEST SOMERSET RAILWAY.
### TAUNTON TO WATCHET.

ON MONDAY, 31st March, this Line will be Opened for

### PASSENGER TRAFFIC

and the following Trains will run:—

#### DOWN TRAINS.

| Leaving | Class 1 & 2. A.M. | Class 1, 2, 3. P.M. | Class 1 & 2. P.M. | Class 1, 2, 3 P.M. |
|---|---|---|---|---|
| | | 5. 0 | | 7.30 |
| Taunton | 9.50 | 2. 5 | 5.14 | 7.44 |
| Bishop's Lydeard | 10. 5 | 2.19 | 5.28 | 7.58 |
| Crowcombe Heathfield | 10.19 | 2.33 | 5.35 | 8. 5 |
| Stogumber | 10.26 | 2.40 | 5.44 | 8.14 |
| Williton | 10.35 | 2.49 | 5.50 | 8.20 |
| Watchet (Arrival) | 10.40 | 2.55 | | |

#### UP TRAINS.

| | A.M. | P.M. | P.M. | P.M. |
|---|---|---|---|---|
| | 8.45 | 12.30 | 3.30 | 6.15 |
| Watchet | | | 3.36 | 6.21 |
| Williton | 8.52 | 12.36 | 3.49 | 6.34 |
| Stogumber | 9. 5 | 12.49 | 3.56 | 6.41 |
| Crowcombe Heathfield | 9.12 | 12.56 | 4. 5 | 6.50 |
| Bishop's Lydeard | 9.22 | 1. 5 | 4.18 | 7. |
| Taunton (Arrival) | 9.35 | 1.18 | | 7. |

This Line will open a direct Route to LYNTON, PORLOCK. MINEHEAD, &c., and well regulated Coaches will run from Williton in connection with the Expresses and Third Class Trains.

*'Minehead has been the scene of some excitement this past week in consequence of reports touching on the long wished-for railway. It was reported that active steps were being taken for the extension of the line from Watchet to Minehead and that land was being measured for that purpose.' December 6th 1862.*

But this optimism was to be ill-founded; the extension to Minehead was to take another twelve years.

The last contested Parliamentary election for the two MPs who then represented the West Somerset constituency (formally called the Somerset Western) had been almost thirty years earlier, back in 1837. Since then a series of Conservative candidates had been returned unopposed.

(The Somerset Western constituency was just one of two non-borough constituencies in Somerset, stretching from Yeovil in the east to Porlock in the west and including Bridgwater, Chard, Crewkerne, Minehead, Wellington, Ilminster, Street, Watchet and Wiveliscombe)

When a by-election was called in

> WEST SOMERSET ELECTION.
>
> This election took place on Friday at the Shire Hall, Taunton. It seemed to excite very little interest, and not above a hundred persons were present at any stage of the proceedings.
> The HIGH SHERIFF (Sir J. H. G. Smyth, Bart.) having stated the object for which this meeting was held,
> E. J. ESDAILE, Esq., proposed the re-election of Sir Alexander Acland Hood, Bart., and the motion was seconded by G. WARRY, Esq.
> M. FENWICK-BISSETT, Esq., proposed the re-election of W. H. P. G. Langton, Esq., and T. HOSKINS, Esq., seconded the nomination.
> No other candidate appearing, Sir A. A. Hood and Mr. Langton were declared duly elected.

July 1865, there was still no great election fever for the *Free Press* to report. Again there was no challenge to the sitting member up for re-election, Sir Alexander Acland-Hood, of St Audries, son-in-law of Sir Peregrine Acland.

*'Booting' the Hobby Horse's victim in Minehead, 1870.*

Some old West Somerset customs persisted, but in the eyes of the *Free Press's* correspondent, maybe for not much longer:

*'On Friday week, the 1st of May, the ceremony called the "hobby horse" was witnessed in Dunster. It consists of a quasi-horse, covered with housings of carpet reaching to the ground, and decorated with gay trappings of ribbon.*

*'This effigy is balanced on the shoulders of a bearer whose head finds vent through the spine of the horse, and who, as best he may to the beat of a drum, imitates the curvilings and prancings of the real quadruped, a long tail trailing on the ground completing this grotesque figure.*

*'The spectators are treated to a ceremony called "booting," which consists of stretching a victim on the ground and treating him to a certain amount of playful flagellation.' May 9th 1863.*

The report goes on to say that the origin professes to be

*'...in commemoration of the wreck of a vessel at Minehead in remote times, or of the advent of a sort of phantom-ship which entered the harbour without captain or crew. Once the custom was encouraged but now it is much neglected and perhaps will soon fall into desuetude. The same thing is reported to have obtained in Padstow.'*

Minehead's sea front
was still undeveloped,
still waiting for the
railway.

By the end of 1864, construction had started on the Devon & Somerset Railway; the promoters had been thwarted in their original intention to drive the line through to Ilfracombe, but the first sod had been cut on the line that was to connect Taunton and Barnstaple.

> *'The engineering difficulties, we are told, are not very great. There will be two tunnels, one in the neighbourhood of Wiveliscombe, over half a mile long; the other at Memridge Wood near Castle Hill which will be under a quarter of a mile.*
>
> *There will be a viaduct at Castle Hill under 100ft high and some others of less magnitude. The broad gauge will be adopted and the Bristol & Exeter have entered into an agreement to work the line.'* October 22nd 1864.

And there is still optimism that the West Somerset Railway may soon be extended to Minehead – and make a profit for its investors.

> *'We understand that in all probability, application will be made to Parliament at the ensuing session for an Act to authorise the extension of the West Somerset Railway to Minehead. The eminent engineer, Mr Brereton, has been recently on the spot arranging the route to be adopted; and we believe he is favour of a line by Washford and Marshwood as being the best and cheapest.*
>
> *The landed proprietors in the district will no doubt support the undertaking which will considerably improve their property, besides being a long needed public convenience. The great natural beauties of Minehead, Dunster, and Cleeve Bay, when more accessible by railway, will be much appreciated by tourists and doubtless become very favourite watering places.'* November 12th 1864.

This Bill finally received Royal Assent the following July 1865 but it was still to be another seven years before work finally started on the line.

———— ❖ ————

In August 1865, a meeting was held in the Market House in Watchet of great importance to the householders of Watchet and Williton – domestic gas was on its way. Some streets and homes in Taunton, Wiveliscombe and Milverton were already lit by gas; as yet there were no plans for gas for Minehead or the west of district, but the residents of Watchet and Williton were about to see the light.

TO GAS ENGINEERS, CONTRACTORS, AND OTHERS.

THE SAINT DECUMAN'S GAS and COKE COMPANY (Limited), are prepared to receive PLANS and SPECIFICATIONS of the necessary works, and TENDERS for the execution of the same, for Lighting the towns of WATCHET and WILLITON, in the county of Somerset, containing about three thousand inhabitants.
   Watchet is the terminus of the West Somerset Railway, and distant from Taunton seventeen miles.
   Further particulars can be obtained on application, either personally or by letter, to the SECRETARY, to whom the Plans, Specifications, and Tenders, are to be delivered or sent on or before the 3rd day of NOVEMBER next.
   The Directors do not pledge themselves to accept the lowest or any other tender, or to adopt either of the plans, which will be returned to the parties.
                            W. L. COPP, Secretary.
   Watchet, Somerset, 3rd October, 1865.

> *'In these days of progress, it surely cannot be deemed necessary for the journalist to descant upon the advantages or disadvantages to be derived from having our streets and business premises, as well as our dwelling-houses, lighted during the winter months with the best and most economical substitute for natural light at present obtainable and which is so much required for our comfort and convenience.*
>
> *'Surely we have been in 'darkness' long enough and in danger of serious collisions in dark nights; and now, having our railway and telegraph, what is to hinder us in obtaining the gas?'* August 12th 1865.

The 'Rowcliffe' engine pulls an early passenger train into Comberow station, circa 1866 .

After months of development, the first gas lights were turned on in Watchet and Williton, in February 1867.

WEST SOMERSET MINERAL RAILWAY.

WATCHET to the BRENDON HILLS.

THE following TRAINS will run, until
further notice:—

| | 1,2,3 | 1,2,3 | 1, 2 | FARES. | | |
|---|---|---|---|---|---|---|
| Leaving | A.M. | A.M. | P.M. | 1st | 2nd | 3rd |
| Watchet | 6.20 | 11. 0 | 3.30 | | | |
| Washford | 6.40 | 11.10 | 3.40 | 0 4 | 0 3 | 0 2 |
| Roadwater | 6.52 | 11.22 | 3.52 | 0 8 | 0 6 | 0 4 |
| Coombe Row | 7.10 | 11.40 | 4.10 | 1 0 | 0 9 | 0 6 |
| Leaving | | | | | | |
| Coombe Row | 7.50 | 11.45 | 6.30 | | | |
| Roadwater | 8. 5 | 11.55 | 6.45 | 0 4 | 0 3 | 0 2 |
| Washford | 8.20 | 12. 5 | 7. 0 | 0 8 | 0 6 | 0 4 |
| Watchet | 8.30 | 12.15 | 7.10 | 1 0 | 0 9 | 0 6 |

BY ORDER.

*Watchet, 28th August, 1865.*

In September 1865, the *Free Press* reported another long-awaited new railway service – the opening of a passenger service on the seven-mile West Somerset Mineral Line, from Watchet to the Comberow Incline at the foot of the Brendon escarpment.

Three return trains were run from Watchet, all of them packed and the shops in the town closed to let everyone try out the new service.

*'It was our fortune to leave Watchet by the 11 o'clock train which left the station amid the cheers of the large assemblage of spectators and the deafening reports of several guns. The engine "Rowcliffe" had been decorated with flowers and its "floral harness" became it very well, as it wounded up through Vallis Florida to Roadwater...*

*'Here the train received a perfect ovation; for some minutes the cheering was intense and one enthusiastic individual, more daring than the rest, with some description of instrument, struck up "Cheer, boys cheer".' September 9th 1865.*

When the trains finally reached Comberow, the passengers heard the constant detonations of the iron ore miners at work in the hills above. And ahead of them lay one of the construction wonders of the age.

*'Beyond Comberow, the principal attraction is the Brendon Hills incline, which rises vertically to the height of 897 ft and which is beyond a doubt, the grandest piece of work of its kind in the United Kingdom.*

*'It has been constructed for the two-fold purpose of removing the ore etc. from the hills to the valley below and at the same time, taking up any traffic which might be required...the carriages are drawn up and lowered on separate roads by wire ropes, coiling over large drums at the top, one carriage ascending while the other descends.'*

There were as yet no plans for a passenger service up the incline. On this first day, a few hardy passengers climbed the incline, where a double arch of evergreen mosses and flowers had been erected and the message 'Success to the West Somerset Mineral Railway' had been spelt out in letters of moss.

❖

In October 1865, Minehead staged what was to be become a regular, and at times unruly, feature of the summer season – the first of the Horse Races on the sands. A one-mile circuit was laid out, with three flights of hurdles, with associated course-side stalls, offering a variety of refreshments and the opportunity to wager on the races. This had been organised by Mr Thristle, landlord of the Plume of Feathers hostelry in Wellington Square, in order...

*'...to supply the want of amusement which has long and painfully been felt by the inhabitants of the town.*

*'The locale selected for the amusements was, of course, the sands, hard dry and almost level and certainly no better spot could have been chosen...*

*'To the west was the Quay, quietly reposing at the foot of North Hill, which towering high in space, with its fertile slopes parcelled into fields and gardens, seemed like a tessellated mass of verdant mosaics....Southwards were the romantic hills around Dunster and the heights of Brendon and away to the east were the dim blue outlines of the Quantock Hills, the whole forming a grand amphitheatre of mountain scenery.' October 14th 1865.*

SATURDAY, OCTOBER 14, 1865.

MINEHEAD HURDLE RACES.

Those of the good people of Minehead who have any taste for out-door sports must have thoroughly enjoyed themselves on Monday, when, for the first time, they had an opportunity of witnessing the noble and health-giving sport of horse-racing, almost (to use a familiar phrase) close to their very doors. The locale selected for the amusements was of course the sands—hard, dry, and almost level; and certainly no better spot could have been chosen, as those who are at all acquainted with the locality will testify. The coast of Somerset-shire is singularly devoid of beds of sand, of any considerable area, but Minehead may fairly claim exception to this rule, for there the sands are very extensive, and have the additional virtue of being hard and firm. They thus form a natural course, of great beauty, and one which cannot be surpassed in this district. The scenery of the neighbourhood is also of an impressive and picturesque character. To the west was the quay and that portion of Minehead in its immediate vicinity, quietly reposing at the foot of the North Hill, which, towering high in space, with its fertile slopes parcelled into fields and gardens, seemed like a tesselated mass of verdant mosaics. Farther towards the south were the lofty peaks of Dunkery and the hills adjacent; and the effect, during sunset, was extremely pretty, the summits and edges of the various eminences appearing as if fringed with gold. Southwards were the romantic hills around Dunster and the heights of Brendon; and away to the east were the dim blue outlines of the Quantock Hills; the whole forming a grand amphitheatre of beautiful mountain scenery.

Huge crowds packed the sands for the Races: this later picture by Alfred Vowles is from 1895.

As many as 2,000 attended the first Races, which were staged intermittently for the next thirty years.

❖

Construction work was by now well under way on the Devon & Somerset Railway with large numbers of labourers brought in to drive the line through from Taunton to Barnstaple. Tragically, some of them brought with them a deadly disease.

One of the navvies working on the line in1866 was taken ill and brought to Wiveliscombe to be treated by the town's doctors, Dr Edwards and Dr Fowells. The doctors quickly diagnosed one of the most infectious killers of the time – cholera.

Within hours, the navvy had died, followed swiftly by one of his fellow workers, and then one of the town's infants collapsed and died. Her parents had treated her with brandy, unaware that this had quite likely simply hastened the child's death.

Wiveliscombe was facing a serious epidemic but the *Free Press* reports that disaster was averted, thanks mainly to the skill of the two doctors and to the quick thinking of the town's chemist Mr Knight…

> '…for having formed and personally assisted to light pitch fires which were kept burning in every street, particularly the High St, the principal scene of the disease, and also for doses of chlorodene which he gave to all who had come into contact with the infected premises.' September 8th 1866.

Mr William Hancock, the founder of the town's brewing business, gave over a house in the town as a temporary hospital, and all bedding in the affected homes and nearby houses was burnt. But by now the first funerals were being held:

> '…the pitch fires lined the route of the funeral procession…which showed hundreds of faces peering forth from the windows of Church St… (people) too afraid to venture out into the diseased town.'

In all, five died in the town, but it could have been so much worse.

❖

The cholera outbreak highlighted the terrible plight of those who fell ill in the district, but a few weeks later, in December 1866 the *Free Press* reported that finally, the district's first hospital was to open, at Dunster – if you could afford the fees.

> 'We are authorised to inform our readers that the hospital will be opened for the reception of patients on Monday next. An experienced matron and nurse have been engaged, and we have no doubt that this institution will be of great benefit to the poor of the district.
>
> 'At present the hospital contains four beds and an extra one for emergency. Out patients are seen twice a week on Mondays at 1.30pm by Mr Roberts and on Fridays at 10am by Mr Hole.

*'Subscribers of £1 are entitled to recommend one in-patient or two out-patients; subscribers of 10s, one out-patient.' April 6th 1867.*

———————— ❖ ————————

The winter of 1867 saw serious rioting in the South West, as mobs accused bakers and butchers of overcharging for bread and meat. Shop premises were attacked and looted and the *Free Press* carried reports of the army, on occasions with fixed bayonets, taking to the streets to put down riots, firstly in several Devon towns including Exeter and Barnstaple, and then in Taunton, Chard and South Petherton.

Fears of copycat riots reached even into the heart of Exmoor. The local police sergeant in Dulverton was sent letters warning of riots if the town's bakers did not reduce the price of their bread by the following Tuesday.

In anticipation of trouble, the police brought in reinforcements, the district Superintendent from Dunster arrived in a trap and the shops were locked up early.

*'Quite easy it is, now to arouse the alarm of a town and cause all the people to be on the tiptoe of expectation and wait with fear the approach of the dreaded riot.*

*'One of the bakers became so concerned for the safety of his shop that on Monday he had caused bills to be posted all over town stating that he had reduced the price of his bread to 7.5d for the 4lb loaf.' November 30th 1867.*

As it was, the threats of a riot appeared to have been exaggerated: the *Free Press* reports:

*'Here were the police, all ready to be called out, but they and the inhabitants generally were agreeably surprised to find that no appearance of riot or disturbance presented itself, everything passing off quietly'.*

However, the following week, the paper reports that there had been some small disturbance in the town.

*'It appears that a large crowd had assembled, near the bridge and that during the absence of police – gathered in another part of own – a mischievous fellow threw a stone at the window of a poor cottager, no doubt thinking that if, once the 'fun' began others would readily follow. They, however, did not feel so inclined.' December 7th 1867.*

So much for the Great Dulverton Bread Riot.

———————— ❖ ————————

Two years after Watchet and Williton first enjoyed the benefits of gas lighting, Minehead's streets were lit for the first time: the Gas Works were near the Quay. Early in December 1869, the town's residents….

*'…witnessed the first time of lighting up the streets, shops and private residences in the town of Minehead with that excellent commodity, gas… both for the convenience of lighting the public thoroughfares during dark and dreary winter nights…as well as the more cheery aspect it will impart to shops and residences…*

*'The town during the evening presented a somewhat animated appearance on comparing it with that of the previous night; and many persons traversed the streets, viewing the illumination.' December 11th 1869.*

**THE RIOT AT BARNSTAPLE.**

Since the riots at Teignmouth, Exeter, and other places became known at Barnstaple, many of the roughs and discontented of the lower order (not a few women) have been labouring under the delusion that the steps taken by the rioters in the neighbouring town were essential to obtain a reduction in the high price of provisions, and they determined that Barnstaple should not be behind in making a similar demonstration. It was expected that a breach of the peace would take place in the market during Friday. Between seven and eight o'clock in the evening, however, it became apparent from the unusual number of roughs and boys standing about that a disturbance would be attempted. Shortly after eight bands of about fifty men and boys, with a sprinkling of women, marched through Green-lane and Derby, beating up tin kettles, and screaming at the top of their voices. Their numbers were largely augmented, and on their return to the butchers' market it was evident they were bent on mischief. In an incredibly short space of time every butcher's shop was closed, amidst hooting and yelling, and cries of "We want cheap beef and bread," and "Let us have our rights."

**THE INTRODUCTION OF GAS INTO THE TOWN OF MINEHEAD.**

Thursday evening last witnessed the first time of lighting up the streets, shops, and private residences, in the town of Minehead, with that excellent commodity, gas, the need of which had for a long time previously been greatly felt, and the convenience, both with regard to the lighting of public thoroughfares during dark and dreary winter nights, so as to enable persons to traverse them without fear of coming into collision with any objects, or meeting with accidents, as well as the more cheery aspect it will impart to shops and residences, will now be doubly experienced. The town during the evening presented a somewhat animated appearance, on comparing it with that of the previous night; and many persons traversed the streets viewing the illumination. Against the side of the market-house gas was burning brightly in the form of a star; and the Minehead brass band discoursed music in various parts of the town. The gas-works and laying of the main pipes were commenced in August last, George Bowers, Esq., of St. Neots, Huntingdon,

# 1870s: Railways expand as turnpikes close

SOME OF the best writing in the early days of the *Free Press* was to be found in the weekly hunting reports. Nothing quite inspired the hunt report contributors like the annual opening meet of the Devon & Somerset Staghounds.

> *'The day of days to West Somerset and North Devon sportsmen has passed; the huntsman's horn has again awakened the echoes in Porlock Vale and old Horner Woods; many a good stag has raised his head aloft in his shady hiding place; heard to him the unwelcome sound and drawn his nose closer to the earth, that no breath of his shall give the searching hound notice of his whereabouts. On Tuesday the first meet took place at Cloutsham... August 20th 1870.*

But not all had come on horseback to hunt.

> *'The first meet is now looked upon as a good and legitimate time for pic-nicing in this lovely place and about twelve o' clock it was a jolly sight to see the different groups with their provisions spread, and to hear beer bottle and champagne corks giving sharp reports all over the field and ferny ball outside, telling that, though a hunting morning, many had come there fully provided with all creature comforts.'*

Early in 1870, the *Free Press* reported the arrival into the district of the very first road steam locomotive. It caused quite a commotion. It was used to haul iron ore from the Brendon Hill mines down to Minehead for shipping across to South Wales.

'Some speculating genius, who considers steam preferable to horse-flesh, has recently added to his stock in trade a road steam engine ... and on Tuesday last and on the following days, it was engaged conveying iron from Eison Hill mine near Cutcombe to Minehead pier.

'The astonishment of the villagers, and especially the youngsters, as it proceeded on the road by slow and steady pace, drawing a heavy burden and crushing to pieces any uneven substance beneath its ponderous wheels, may be easily imagined.

'On arriving at Minehead, a number of persons were assembled to witness its first transit through the town, down to the quay, with its heavy load, some of them appearing to be greatly puzzled by the facility with which it turned the corners of the streets under the guidance of the pilot.' May 21st 1870.

❖

MINEHEAD RAILWAY.—An application is intended to be made to Parliament in the next session, for an act to incorporate a company, with power to make and maintain a railway, with all proper stations, approaches, works, and conveniences connected therewith, commencing in the parish of Saint Decumans by a junction with the West Somerset railway, at the termination thereof at Watchet station, thence passing through and into the parishes, townships, and places of Watchet, St. Decumans, Old Cleeve, Washford, Bilbrooke, Withycombe, Carhampton, Dunster, Alcombe, and Minehead, and terminating near to the sea-beach and at the south side of the road known as the Station-road.

In November 1870, eight years after the West Somerset Railway reached Watchet, the *Free Press* carried a single paragraph noting that another application was being made to Parliament to extend the line to Minehead. This was to prove the successful application, backed by a local consortium led by George Fownes Luttrell of Dunster Castle, that the line finally opened in 1874.

But within a few months of this, there was more encouraging news of the Devon & Somerset Railway, pushing through from Taunton to Barnstaple: under the heading 'The Long-Expected Railway', the *Free Press* in February 1871 reports that two trains had been arranged to transport shareholders of the new line from Wiveliscombe to the company's half-yearly meeting at Taunton.

THE LONG-EXPECTED RAILWAY. — On Tuesday, great numbers of the inhabitants were gratified with the sight of the first train running from the station at Wiveliscombe to Taunton. The occasion was the half-yearly meeting of the directors and shareholders of the Devon and Somerset Railway. To enable the shareholders resident in this town to attend this meeting, two trains were run to Taunton in the course of the day, and a return conveyed the passengers back to their homes. The Bristol and Exeter Railway Company kindly lent their first-class saloon carriage for the occasion, and afforded every facility for the conveyance of the ladies and gentlemen *direct* from the Wiveliscombe station to the Taunton station. The line was found to be perfectly smooth, and the ride was extremely pleasant; without the least mischief—a happy augury, we hope, of its future success. The distance of eleven miles was easily accomplished in twenty minutes, though no trial of speed was intended,

'On Tuesday, great numbers of inhabitants were gratified with the sight of the first train running from the station at Wiveliscombe to Taunton.

'The Bristol & Exeter Railway Company kindly lent their first-class saloon carriage for the occasion, and afforded every facility for the conveyance of the ladies and gentlemen direct from the Wiveliscombe station to the Taunton station.

'The line was found to be perfectly smooth and the ride was extremely pleasant; without the least mischief – a happy augury, we hope, of its future success.' February 25th 1871.

## OPENING OF THE DEVON AND SOMERSET RAILWAY.

The first section of the Devon and Somerset Railway was opened for passenger traffic on Thursday week. The section extends from Taunton to Wiveliscombe, with an intermediate station at Milverton. The line branches from the main line of the Bristol and Exeter Railway at Norton Fitzwarren, close by the West Somerset junction, and runs through a very picturesque country. This section of the line has been completed for some time, and the inhabitants of the district through which it runs have been greatly disappointed at the delay which has taken place in opening it for traffic. The Bristol and Exeter Company are working the line upon certain terms, and are daily running six trains each way. There was a formal opening ceremony, but a number of the leading inhabitants of Wiveliscombe and Milverton were taken to Taunton in a saloon carriage, and were entertained at luncheon under a marquee erected on the lawn adjoining the residence of Mr. Daniel in North Town. Mr. Ellis and

The trains completed the eleven miles to Taunton in 20 minutes.

This first section of the D & S Railway, from Taunton to Wiveliscombe, passing through Milverton, was formally opened some four months later, in June 1871.

Six trains were to run that day, and each was filled to capacity. But for some reason, the atmosphere in Wiveliscombe itself was strangely muted.

One of the first trains on the Devon & Somerset line at the new South Molton Station.

*'At Wiveliscombe, the affair passed off very tamely. The bells were not rung and although the shops were closed, very few persons could be seen on the streets, many of the inhabitants having gone into Milverton, where the event was being commemorated with great spirit… even the Tolland & Lydeard St Lawrence brass band was drowned up by rival band of local performers…and the result was anything but harmonious.' June 17th 1871.*

## RAILWAY TIME TABLE FOR NOVEMBER, 1873.

### GREAT WESTERN & BRISTOL & EXETER RAILWAYS.

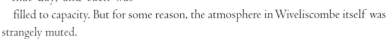

DOWN TRAINS.    WEEK DAYS.    SUNDAYS.

| FROM | 1 & 2 Mail P.M‡ | 1 & 2 Mail A.M | 1 & 2 class A.M | 1,2,3 class A.M | 1 & 2 class A.M¶ | Exp. class A.M‖ | 1 & 2 class A.M | Exp. A.M | 1 & 2 class A.M | 1 & 2 class P.M | Exp. P.M | 1 & 2 class P.M | 1 & 2 Mail P.M | 1,2,3 class A.M | 1 & 2 class A.M |
|---|---|---|---|---|---|---|---|---|---|---|---|---|---|---|---|
| Paddington | 8.10 | | | | 6. 0 | 9. 0 | | 11.45 | 10.30 | 1.50 | 5.10 | | 8.10 | | 10. 0 |
| Swindon (departure) | 10.45 | | | | 9. 0 | 11. 2 | | 1.22 | 1.30 | 4.27 | 7.10 | | 10.45 | | 1.45 |
| Bath | 11.37 | | | 6.45 | 9.48 | 11.50 | | 1.58 | 2.40 | 5.24 | 7.50 | | 11.37 | | 2.49 |
| Bristol (arrival) | 12. 5 | | | 7.20 | 10.15 | 12.15 | | 2.21 | 3. 5 | 5.50 | 8.15 | | 12. 5 | | 3.30 |
| Bristol (departure) | 12.30 | 6.15 | | 8.10 | 10.30 | 12.30 | | 2.26 | 3.15 | 6. 0 | 8.20 | | 12.30 | 6.30 | 3.40 |
| Yatton (for Clevedon) | | | | 8.52 | 10.55 | 12.53 | | | 3.40 | 6.34 | | | | 6.59 | 4. 9 |
| Weston Junction | | 6.43 | | 9.14 | 11. 5 | 1. 9 | | | 3.56 | 6.50 | 8.46 | | | 7.17 | 4.27 |
| Highbridge | | 6.58 | | 9.42 | 11.29 | 1.29 | | | 4.19 | 7.11 | 9. 2 | | | 7.34 | 4.44 |
| Bridgwater | 1.23 | 7.11 | | 10. 4 | 11.44 | 1.42 | | | 4.38 | 7.26 | 9.14 | | 1.23 | 7.49 | 4.59 |
| Durston (for Yeovil) | | 7.24 | | 10.21 | 11.59 | | | | 4.53 | 7.42 | | | | 8. 3 | 5.13 |
| Taunton | 1.48 | 7.37 | 7.40 | 10.43 | 12.14 | 2. 8 | 3.23 | 3.18 | 5. 8 | 8. 0 | 9.33 | | 1.48 | 8.18 | 5.28 |
| **W.S.R.** Taunton | | 8. 0 | | 10.58 | 2.10 | 2.10 | | | 5.10 | 8. 5 | | | | | |
| Norton Fitzwarren | | 8. 5 | | 11. 3 | 2.15 | 2.15 | | | 5.15 | 8.10 | | | | | |
| Bishop's Lydeard | | 8.15 | | 11.10 | 2.21 | 2.21 | | | 5.26 | 8.16 | | | | | |
| Crowcombe H. | | 8.32 | | 11.24 | 2.35 | 2.35 | | | 5.38 | 8.30 | | | | | |
| Stogumber | | 8.41 | | 11.31 | 2.42 | 2.42 | | | 5.44 | 8.37 | | | | | |
| Williton | | 8.52 | | 11.40 | 2.51 | 2.51 | | | 5.52 | 8.46 | | | | | |
| Watchet (arrival) | | 9. 0 | | 11.46 | 2.57 | 2.57 | | | 5.58 | 8.52 | | | | | |
| **C.R.** Taunton | | 8. 0 | | 11. 0 | 2.10 | 2.10 | | | 5.10 | 8.10 | | | | | |
| Thorne | | 8.10 | | 11.10 | 2.20 | 2.20 | | | 5.20 | 8.20 | | | | | |
| Hatch | | 8.25 | | 11.25 | 2.35 | 2.35 | | | 5.35 | 8.35 | | | | | |
| Ilminster | | 8.41 | | 11.41 | 2.51 | 2.51 | | | 5.51 | 8.51 | | | | | |
| Chard | | 8.55 | | 11.55 | 3. 5 | 3. 5 | | | 6. 5 | 9. 5 | | | | | |
| **D.&S.R.** Taunton | | 7.50 | | 10.45 | 12.40 | | | 3.30 | 5.35 | 8.15 | | | | | |
| Norton Fitzwarren | | 7.59 | | 10.52 | 12.49 | | | 3.37 | 5.44 | 8.24 | | | | | |
| Wiveliscombe | | 8.26 | | 11.15 | 1.16 | | | 3.58 | 6.11 | 8.51 | | | | | |
| Morebath | | 8.54 | | 11.40 | 1.44 | | | | 6.39 | 9.19 | | | | | |
| Dulverton | | 9. 6 | | 11.51 | 1.56 | | | 4.27 | 6.58 | 9.31 | | | | | |
| South Molton | | 9.47 | | 12.32 | 2.38 | | | 4.55 | 7.39 | 10.12 | | | | | |
| Barnstaple | | 10.20 | | 1. 5 | 3.10 | | | 5.15 | 8.12 | 10.45 | | | | | |

Sir Peregrine Acland.

That same year, 1871, brought the death of the man who had effectively brought the first railway to West Somerset.

Sir Peregrine Fuller Palmer Acland had in 1856 chaired the first meeting at the Egremont Hotel that lead to the formation of the West Somerset Railway Company. Sir Peregrine was chairman of the rail company up until his death in October 1871, and as the *Free Press* noted, it was

'...*mainly through his untiring efforts, support and influence that this convenient line was built...*'
*October 28th 1871.*

Sir Peregrine died at the age of 81 at home at Fairfield House, Stogursey, where his ancestors had lived since the early 12th century. He was recognised as a friend of the working man, and a liberal employer on his estates; he had both restored St Andrew's Church at Stogursey and rebuilt St Etheldreda's Church at St Audries.

Sir Peregrine's wife Fanny and two of their three children had died of tuberculosis. But, as thanks for the survival of his eldest daughter, Isabel, Sir Peregrine built the school at Stogursey for the children of his estate workers and the villagers.

Clergy and tenants from several parishes were invited to join in the funeral procession, which was led by

'...*ten clergymen, wearing satin hatbands and sashes, and sixteen of the able-bodied oldest workmen on the estate, habited in new suits of mourning, silk hatbands and gloves....*'
*October 28th 1871.*

They took it in turns to carry Sir Peregrine's coffin, followed by relatives, domestic servants, officials and tenants, the one mile from Fairfield House through the village to St Andrew's Church, where the muffled church bells tolled.

The *Free Press* noted that Sir Peregrine never aspired to a career on the national stage, but added that

'...*many years must elapse 'ere the name of this good baronet will be forgotten in West Somerset, for in addition to the memorials of his charity and benevolence in the shape of churches and schools, he will long live in the hearts of his relatives, friends and tenants.*'

Sir Peregrine's surviving daughter, Isabel, had in 1849 married Alexander Hood, a member of the famous naval family, and, taking the name of Acland-Hood, they lived mainly at St Audries House. Alexander – later to become Sir Alexander Acland-Hood – had been MP for West Somerset from 1859-1868.

❖

Within two months of Sir Peregrine's death – and nearly thirty years after it was first proposed – the first steps were taken to extend his West Somerset Railway through to Minehead.

On December 30th 1871, the *Free Press* reports that the first turf was cut in the construction of the eight-mile extension from Watchet.

This time, it was another of the leading local landowners, George Fownes Luttrell, of Dunster Castle, who had encouraged and largely funded the extension of the line, as chairman of the separate Minehead Railway Company. Mr Luttrell had given much of the land over which the track ran, and paid for many of the station buildings. His land agent Thomas

## Death of Sir P. P. F. P. Acland, Bart.

It is with a feeling of profound sorrow, which we are certain will be experienced by a very large number of our readers, that we take upon ourselves the melancholy duty of announcing the death of that venerable and esteemed baronet, Sir P. P. F. P. Acland, which took place at Fairfield-house, Stogursey, on Wednesday morning last, about nine o'clock. For some considerable time, the lamented gentleman has been ailing in health, consequent upon his advanced age, which, even so long ago as last winter, rendered it improbable that he would again gladden the hearts of his friends and tenantry by appearing among them. With the warm weather, however, there came a change for the better, and many, on the occasion of the harvest-home festival at Fairfield-park, about six weeks since, were gratified by a sight of the aged baronet, wheeled in his chair, among the participators in the sports, and rewarding the deserving ones by a lavish expenditure of money prizes. An alteration, however, soon afterwards set in, and once more he was confined to his bed, the result of the attack being his demise. Still, this knowledge that the end must soon come does not in any way diminish the poignant sorrow which is generally felt by all, and more especially by the residents on his estates who have been daily witnesses and in many cases recipients of his unbounded charity, for which his name has become a household word. No man, we believe, ever less courted public notice than he of whom we write, and no man, we may add, ever more despised the florid commendations of unmerited and unnecessary praise, yet, bearing this in mind, we feel it hardly just that one, occupying such a position as Sir Peregrine did, being such a public benefactor, so beloved by high and low, and so worth, a representative of the fine Old English gentleman, living in our midst all his days, should pass away without a word of public testimony to his merits. At the same time, it must be remembered that any attempt to describe his charitable actions and largeness of heart can have but one result—a failure—for these won for him the respect and admiration of all with whom he came in contact, while his conduct towards the poor led them to regard him with a feeling of the deepest affection.

Sir Peregrine was born on November 10th, 1789, and his age therefore is approaching eighty-two

## THE MINEHEAD RAILWAY.

### CUTTING THE FIRST TURF.

The advantages of railway communication to Minehead and the neighbourhood cannot be overestimated ; and, although for nearly thirty years it has been in contemplation, insuperable obstacles were in the way until a recent date, when, through the indomitable perseverance of T. Ponsford, Esq., an Act of Parliament was obtained during the session of 1871. The board of directors include George Fownes Luttrell, Esq. (chairman), James Hole, Esq., and Joseph Gatchell, Esq.; and the engineer is W. Dennis, Esq., of London ; and the solicitors are Messrs. Warden and Ponsford, of Bardon. The contractor for the execution of the works is Mr. Frederick Furniss, of London. The finances requisite for the undertaking have been raised independently of the public.

Ponsford, was credited with 'indomitable perseverance' in successfully lobbying to ensure the Act empowering the new line finally passed into law.

> 'On Thursday morning last, on its becoming known in Minehead that the first sod was to be cut on that day, the principal tradesmen and others were speedily astir and several flags were soon floating from the hotels, bank, shops etc. on the Parade.
>
> 'Although the weather was unfavourable, a large number of persons gathered near the Feathers hotel at noon; and immediately upon the arrival of the Squire's carriage, a procession was formed, headed by several flags and enlivened by the merry strains of the band proceeded on through Station road to the site selected for the terminus of the line of railway.' December 30th 1871.

Cannon had been placed in a meadow nearby, from which were fired several salutes. The nine-year-old son of Squire Luttrell, Master Alexander Fownes Luttrell then

> '…took a new spade handed to him by Mr Furniss (the contractor), cut the first sod, loaded the barrow, wheeled it away and returned, the whole being accomplished in a very workman-like manner, amidst loud applause.'

❖

Dulverton Station was in fact two miles away, at Brushford.

Meanwhile, those thousand or so navvies working on the Devon & Somerset line were progressing through the southern fringes of Exmoor, excavating tunnels, using the spoil to help support embankments, and by the end of 1872, they had pushed the line through from the west to Dulverton.

> 'The benefits of a railway in this district have just been experienced. On Thursday 5th, a train arrived at the Brushford Station on the Devon & Somerset Railway from Barnstaple with a consignment of coal to J A Locke Esq of Northmoor House.
>
> 'On Friday morning, carts and wagons might be seen on the road to Dulverton laden with this valuable article upon which the comfort of all classes so much depends during the cold weather.' December 21st 1872.

The whole length of the Devon & Somerset Railway, the full 43 miles from Taunton to Barnstaple, was finally opened in November 1873, amid great rejoicing, not least in Dulverton. The town was decked with flags and bunting and ceremonial arches, proclaiming 'Success to the Devon & Somerset Railway '… and 'May Dulverton flourish.'

> 'Some of the flags were very large, having to be suspended from poles thirty feet high to prevent their touching the heads of the passers-by.
>
> 'Turning into Church Street, a painting of a huge viaduct with a train passing over it met the gaze, the passengers were waving their hats and the train marked "Express" seemed to be going very fast.' November 8th 1873.

❖

At the end of 1872, the *Free Press* reported plans for yet another railway line in the district; this was indeed the era of Railway Mania. The paper reports that local landowners around the Quantocks were supporting a proposed new line from Bridgwater to Watchet, connecting with Combwich, Stogursey and Nether Stowey.

> "*A glance at the map is sufficient to show that this is the natural route to Watchet and but for unexpected and, it may added, rather unaccountable opposition in certain influential quarters, the provisions would have been made long before the existing branch from Taunton was contemplated.' December 28th 1872.*

This 'unaccountable opposition' was a reference to the intense rivalry between rail companies in the South West – between the Bristol & Exeter, which leased and operated the West Somerset Railway, and its local rivals the Somerset & Dorset Railway.

> '*The line would be a short one, but would traverse a district which is rather thickly populated, and Minehead, Williton and Watchet and the vicinity would be brought into much closer communication with Bristol, the metropolis, and the North of England.*'

There was to be no immediate progress on this proposed route but it was a resilient idea which was still being supported, albeit with important variations, as late as the 1920s.

❖❖

Finally, in July 1874, eight months after the Devon & Somerset Railway had been completed, the first passenger train steamed into Minehead.

The first up train had left for Taunton at 6am. On its return, shortly after nine it brought 200 persons, but the next train, arriving at Minehead at about one o'clock, consisted of fourteen crowded carriages, carrying about 800 passengers.

Among the passengers was George Fownes Luttrell, chairman of the Minehead Railway Company which had sponsored the new line, and several directors of the Bristol & Exeter Railway Company, who would run the services over the new line.

THE MINEHEAD RAILWAY.

On the occasion of the OPENING of the above railway, which is expected to take place early in JULY next, a

LUNCHEON

Will be provided in a marquee erected in a field near the railway terminus at MINEHEAD. The chair will be taken by G. F. LUTTRELL, Esq., of Dunster Castle.

An early application for tickets (4s. 6d. each) is requested, and they may be obtained at S. Cox's, stationer, &c., Minehead.

Further particulars will shortly be announced.

By order of the Committee,
J. MOORE, Hon. Sec.

> '*Minyarders devoted the day to a public holiday, work being entirely suspended. Each train was greeted with salutes from cannon and cheers from human beings, there being all the day a considerable number of persons, to many of whom the railway was a first sight, on the station platform to witness the arrival and departure of each train.' July 18th 1874.*

Thomas Thristle of the Plume of Feathers laid on a lunch in a tent near the station, at which Squire Luttrell made clear that it was now up to Minehead to make the most of this new opportunity.

Minehead Station in the early broad gauge days, with the engine shed on the right, and the Esplanade buildings behind.

## THE MINEHEAD RAILWAY.

### THE OPENING DAY.

The introduction of a railway into any locality is, in these days of progress, commercial activity, and general desire for a quick method of travelling, an undertaking invariably fraught with advantages to all classes of the public ; and never have we heard of an instance in which the effect has been contrary to this. Certainly in some cases there may be a few personal reasons why railway accommodation should not be supplied, but compared with the vast public convenience afforded they sink into utter insignificance. Within the last two or three years a limited revival of "the halcyon days of coaching" has appeared in some parts of England, but pleasure rather than business has been the incentive, and while not despising the past in a neighbourhood where coaching has been for many years almost the only means of public conveyance, it must be acknowledged that the substitution of the new for the old, and the rapid for the slow, is a matter for congratulation. The district

*'If Minehead has had a railway given to it as a present, it must not suppose that it will do to sleep and slumber and think that its fortune and prosperity is already made. Not so; this railway is an opportunity for Minehead and if the inhabitants do not take advantage of it, it may never occur again.'*

Mr Michael Casetyle, one of the directors of the Great Western Railway (who ran joint services with the Bristol & Exeter), emphasised the huge boost the Minehead line gave to the growing tourist potential of the district.

*'We have long wanted to get a watering place where the water is a little more blue than it is at Weston-super-Mare and where it is a little nearer the ocean.*

*'When we can carry, without interruption over the same system without any change, a family from Bristol or Bath to Minehead, I can't help thinking that Minehead is only in its infancy and that is going to be a very celebrated watering place.'*

## RAILWAY TIME TABLE FOR JULY, 1874.

### GREAT WESTERN & BRISTOL & EXETER RAILWAYS.

| DOWN TRAINS. FROM | WEEK DAYS. | | | | | | | | | | | | SUNDAYS. | | |
|---|---|---|---|---|---|---|---|---|---|---|---|---|---|---|---|
| | 1 & 2 Mail A.M. | 1 & 2 Mail A.M. | 1 & 2 class A.M. | 1,2,3 class A.M | 1 & 2 class A.M | 1 & 2 class A.M | 1 & 2 class P.M. | Exp. A.M. | 1 & 2 class A.M. | 1 & 2 class P.M | Exp. P.M. | 1 & 2 class P.M. | 1 & 2 Mail A.M. | 1,2,3 class A.M. | 1 & 2 class A.M. |
| Paddington.............. | 8.10 | ... | ... | ... | 6. 0 | 9. 0 | ... | 11.45 | 10.30 | 1.50 | 5.10 | ... | 8.10 | ... | 10. 0 |
| Swindon (departure).... | 10.45 | ... | ... | ... | 9. 0 | 11. 2 | ... | 1.22 | 1.30 | 4.27 | 7.10 | ... | 10.45 | ... | 1.45 |
| Bath......... | 11.37 | ... | ... | 6.45 | 9.48 | 11.50 | ... | 1.58 | 2.40 | 5.24 | 7.50 | ... | 11.37 | ... | 2.49 |
| Bristol (arrival)......... | 12. 5 | ... | ... | 7.20 | 10.15 | 12.15 | ... | 2.21 | 3. 5 | 5.50 | 8.15 | ... | 12. 5 | ... | 3.30 |
| Bristol (departure)...... | 12.30 | 6.15 | ... | 8.10 | 10.30 | 12.30 | ... | 2.26 | 3.15 | 6. 0 | 8.15 | ... | 12.30 | 6.30 | 3.40 |
| Yatton (for Clevedon)... | ... | ... | ... | 8.52 | 10.55 | 12.52 | ... | ... | 3.42 | 6.34 | ... | ... | ... | 6.59 | 4. 9 |
| Weston Junction......... | ... | 6.43 | ... | 9.14 | 11. 5 | 1. 7 | ... | ... | 4. 1 | 6.50 | 8.46 | ... | ... | 7.17 | 4.27 |
| Highbridge........ | ... | 6.58 | ... | 9.42 | 11.29 | 1.26 | ... | ... | 4.27 | 7.11 | 9. 2 | ... | ... | 7.34 | 4.44 |
| Bridgwater............ | 1.23 | 7.11 | ... | 10. 4 | 11.44 | 1.38 | ... | ... | 4.45 | 7.31 | 9.14 | ... | 1.23 | 7.49 | 4.59 |
| Durston (for Yeovil).... | ... | 7.24 | ... | 10.21 | 11.59 | ... | ... | ... | 5. 0 | 7.47 | ... | ... | ... | 8. 3 | 5.13 |
| Taunton ................. | 1.48 | 7.37 | 7. 0 | 10.43 | 12.14 | 2. 8 | 3.23 | 3.18 | 5.19 | 8. 5 | 9.33 | ... | 1.48 | 8.18 | 5.28 |
| Taunton ............. | ... | 7.45 | ... | 11. 5 | ... | 2.25 | ... | * | 5.45 | ... | ... | ... | ... | ... | ... |
| Norton Fitzwarren.... | ... | 7.50 | ... | 11.10 | ... | 2.30 | ... | ... | 5.50 | ... | ... | ... | ... | ... | ... |
| Bishop's Lydeard... | ... | 7.57 | ... | 11.17 | ... | 2.37 | ... | ... | 5.57 | ... | ... | ... | ... | ... | ... |
| Crowcombe H....... | ... | 8.11 | ... | 11.31 | ... | 2.51 | ... | ... | 6.11 | ... | ... | ... | ... | ... | ... |
| Stogumber............ | ... | 8.18 | ... | 11.38 | ... | 2.58 | ... | ... | 6.18 | ... | ... | ... | ... | ... | ... |
| Williton............. | ... | 8.27 | ... | 11.47 | ... | 3. 7 | ...° | ... | 6.27 | ... | ... | ... | ... | ... | ... |
| Watchet............ | ... | 8.35 | ... | 11.55 | ... | 3.15 | ... | ... | 6.35 | ... | ... | ... | ... | ... | ... |
| Washford............ | ... | 8.43 | ... | 12. 3 | ... | 3.23 | ... | ... | 6.43 | ... | ... | ... | ... | ... | ... |
| Blue Anchor........ | ... | 8.52 | ... | 12.12 | ... | 3.32 | ... | ... | 6.52 | ... | ... | ... | ... | ... | ... |
| Dunster............. | ... | 9. 0 | ... | 12.20 | ... | 3.40 | ... | ... | 7. 0 | ... | ... | ... | ... | ... | ... |
| Minehead............. | ... | 9. 5 | ... | 12.25 | ... | 3.45 | ... | ... | 7. 5 | ... | ... | ... | ... | ... | ... |

(W.S.R.)

This well-known James Date photo captures the early unspoilt character of Minehead, circa 1875.

Only two weeks after the opening of the new rail line to Minehead, there was a foretaste of the less attractive face of tourism, when a train brought 800 trippers from the Bristol Waggon Works on the annual works day out.

*'Their conduct was most discreditable and riotous, even after making a very charitable allowance for exuberant spirits. Gardens were despoiled, people were insulted, goods were openly abstracted from premises without payment, fights in the streets were common and all sorts of mischief was committed – much to the annoyance of the residents.'*

A local resident wrote to the *Western Daily Press*.

*'This was rather too much for the patience of the West Somerset "country-bumpkins" and the men and lads of Minehead soon took it up en masse and only waited for a favourable opportunity of repaying the Bristolians for their insults and had it not been for the prompt interference of the police, a general hand-to-hand battle would have been the result...August 1st 1874.*

The writer blamed excess of alcohol...

*'...men and women, boys and girls were actually lying down in the fields and roads – drunk. If such be a fair sample of what may be expected on excursion days from Bristol, the little town, methinks, would rather have their room than their company.'*

Early in 1876, the *Free Press* carried a one paragraph report that touched on a long-standing local grievance and was to lead to a heated campaign for change.

> 'TOLL GATES ABOLISHED: At 12pm on Friday, the tollgates of the Taunton Turnpike Trust were abolished and the highways thrown open to the public.' Jan 8th 1876.

Each district had its own Turnpike Trust. The United Trusts of Minehead had been set up under an Act of George IV, for making and maintaining the road from Minehead to Bampton and also for making roads in the highway districts of Dunster, Watchet, Crowcombe and Nether Stowey. There were nearly 40 toll gates in this area.

The Act allowed the trustees to erect toll gates on the main roads and to charge payments for the upkeep of the roads and for the necessary construction costs and salaries.

The tolls ranged from 6d for a horse drawing a coach or carriage to a farthing for each sheep, calf, or hog. Every laden or unladen horse cost a penny halfpenny, and three-quarters of a penny was charged for an ox or cow.

Soon the cause to abolish the tolls was taken up in letters to the *Free Press*.

The old toll house at Five Bells, between Williton and Watchet.

> 'When are the gates of the Minehead district to be abolished? I believe that no necessity whatever exists for their being continued one single day further and that they ought in fact to be among the obsoletes of the past.
> 'Will the inhabitants of this district allow themselves to be laughed at . . ...by interested parties (who) may think proper to mulct us of as many tolls almost as the number of miles we ride or drive in these beleaguered parts, where the gates are deftly placed to catch at every turn and so cleverly arranged that one seldom clears another in the direct line of road? Signed: A Victim.' February 12th 1876.

By July, a public meeting had been called, at the Egremont Hotel in Williton; it was observed – with outrage – that within a radius of a mile and a half of Five Bells (between Watchet and Williton) there were no less than 14 tollgates and one man estimated that he paid £75 a year in tolls.

Within a fortnight of this meeting at the Egremont there was good news from Westminster; the local West Somerset concern over the turnpikes was very much part of a national campaign, and the House of Lords was now considering the Turnpike Acts Continuance Bill which would abolish the turnpike trusts by the end of the following year.

When in November 1877, the tollgates were finally removed from the roads of West Somerset, a big bonfire was lit on Tower Hill in Williton in celebration, attended by among others a well-known travelling fishmonger called Ikey, who was always at odds with the tollgate keepers.

(Responsibility for the roads in the district was passed onto newly formed local Highways Boards – based on Dunster, Williton, Dulverton and Wiveliscombe, which were to be the fore-runners of the district councils in the twentieth century.)

THE UNITED TRUST OF MINEHEAD ROADS.
NOTICE IS HEREBY GIVEN, that the TOLLS, payable at the several Gates, known by the respective names of
The Alcombe Cross Gate with the side gate
Dunster Gate
Timberscombe Gate with the side gate
Wheddon Cross Gate with the side gate
Chilly Bridge Gate with the side gate
Dulverton Gate with the side gates
Exbridge and Weare Gates
Carhampton Gate
Watchet West Gate
Green Dragon Stop Gate
Washford West Gate
Washford South Gate
Washford Stop Gate
Doniford Gate
Watery Lane Stop Gate
Wibble Lane Gate with the side gate
Putsham Gate
Limekiln Lane Gate
Jackson's Lane Gate
Stowey Gate with the side gate
Five Bells South-east Gate
Five Bells West Gate
Brendon Hill Gate with the side gate
Raglan Castle Gate with the side gate
Tower Hill Gate
Seven Ash Gate
Dull Cross Gate, and
East Coombe Gate with the side gate

The politics of West Somerset had been dominated by the Conservative cause; there had been no challenge at the polls for thirty years now, but early in 1877 there was a notable visitor to the district whom many hoped might lead to change.

The leader of the Liberal party, the Rt Honourable William Gladstone and his wife travelled to Dunster Castle where they were guests of the Luttrell family. Gladstone had been Prime Minister from 1866 until 1874, when the Liberals had lost power to the Conservatives under Benjamin Disraeli. Gladstone was now travelling the country trying to revive his party's fortunes.

While in West Somerset, Gladstone visited Old Cleeve, attended a church service at Dunster and then, with George Luttrell, drove to Holnicote House, the local home of Sir Thomas Acland. Sir Thomas had been a close friend of Gladstone since their student days together at Christ College Oxford and for twenty years had been the Liberal MP for the Devonshire North constituency.

The *Free Press* reports that after lunch at Holnicote, the party took to their carriages and toured Cloutsham, Dunkery Beacon, Bossington and Minehead before returning to Dunster.

But it was the unreported conversations which were later to fascinate the papers; there was widespread expectation of a revival in Liberal fortunes in the area.

---

### THE TELEPHONE IN TAUNTON

'Mr J.B. Saunders of the Laurels, Taunton, has introduced the telephone to the town. Mr Saunders has had one of the instruments fitted up in his billiard room and connected with his office some distance off ...there is no limit to the uses to which it may be applied.

'The telephone is a small instrument something similar in size and construction to a common ear trumpet. Placing it to his mouth, Mr Saunders called to his son in the office and was immediately answered, it being perfectly easy to distinguish the tones of the voice.' November 3rd 1877.

---

After two decades of expansion and development, in 1879 the *Free Press* reports a serious economic downturn in the district. There had been a sudden slump in the prices paid for Brendon Hills iron ore, caused by the re-opening of more easily worked mines in Spain, and the closure of one of the main Ebbw Vale Company blast furnaces. As a result, in May 1879, the *Free Press* reported that all mining on the Brendons had stopped, and that up to 250 miners had lost their jobs.

> 'These are all now thrown out of employ, at a time, too, when there is a general stagnation in all work, and great distress will doubtless be entailed on them.
>
> 'The trading community of the district cannot but feel the withdrawal from circulation of the large amount of money paid by the company in the shape of wages, and the stoppage will also be felt by the shipping interest at Watchet.' May 10th 1879.

Three weeks later, the paper reports that a large proportion of miners, many of them Cornishmen, had already left the mines to seek work elsewhere. And there are already signs of serious deprivation, at a time when there was no systematic relief for the unemployed or the poor, except for the workhouse.

A public appeal for funds was launched and accounts opened at the Williton and Minehead branches of Messrs Stuckey's Bank. Some of the mines did subsequently reopen, working through until 1883.

Life was hard for the Brendon Hill miners.

———— ❖ ————

For a few weeks, there was great excitement when it became known that West Somerset was to receive an important visitor – Queen Victoria's eldest son, the Prince of Wales, Prince Edward, later to become King Edward VIIth.

Prince 'Bertie' was well-known for his playboy lifestyle, having little constitutional role during the long life of his mother, and he was coming to stay with the Luttrells at Dunster – and to hunt with the Devon & Somersets.

The *Free Press* devoted a full page to reporting each and every detail of his stay in West Somerset, observing

> 'It is rather remarkable that an English Prince, who has the reputation of being a good sportsman and a first-rate rider

*to hounds, should not until the present time have visited the only spot in England where the wild red deer still exist, and are still hunted...' August 23rd 1879.*

It was clear that one of the reasons that the Prince had accepted the invitation was the encouragement of the Rev. John 'Jack' Russell, the sporting vicar of Swimbridge in North Devon — by now into his eighties — who had run with hounds for the past fifty years, and had become a frequent guest of the Prince at Sandringham. The Prince arrived at Dunster Station by special train, and was whisked off to the Castle in a procession of carriages, the local tenants following at a gallop, into the village where thousands had gathered.

*'Owing to the rapid pace, the spectators along the line of route had but little opportunity to have a sight of the Prince: but still their loyalty found expression and cheer after cheer was given, His Royal Highness acknowledging same by lifting his hat.'*

Shortly after his arrival at the Castle, the Royal Standard was raised on the tower. The Prince visited the castle stables to check his five hunters (which had arrived the previous day) and visited the church. Hawkcombe Head had been selected as the venue for the meet, on the northern edge of the old Royal Forest of Exmoor, partly because it presented landscape so different to the traditional fox hunting country that the Prince was accustomed to.

*'The combes that have to be sunk, the hills to be climbed, and the character of the ground to be ridden over are all vastly different from these and for this, a coolness of head and a steadiness of hand are indispensable.'*

The Prince travelled from Dunster, accompanied in his carriage by George Luttrell and the Rev. 'Jack' Russell, passing through a succession of decorated arches along the way at Alcombe, Hopcott, Holnicote, Allerford and Porlock.

Eight to ten thousand hunt followers awaited him at Hawkcombe Head, two thousand of them mounted. The weather cleared up after early rain, and after a light lunch, the pack moved across to Oare Common where some deer had been harboured by Mr Snow's men and the pack laid on to a 'warrantable stag'.

*'His Royal Highness was well to the front, his riding being bold and of that kind which won general admiration. The pace was a rattling one, and at Badgworthy the stag took to the water and after going up and down for about ten minutes, stood at bay. The whip was then placed around its neck, and the quarry drawn to land.*

*'The Prince cut its throat, the mort was sounded, and cheers long and loud were given.*

*'According to ancient and irrefragable custom, His Royal Highness was "blooded," Mr John Joyce respectfully performing this most ancient ceremony which consists of sprinkling some of the stag's blood on the novice's face.'*

The chase had lasted just under two hours, at a fast pace; the stag was five years old, but

*'...unfortunately its head (which is no doubt intended to be presented to the royal guest) was rather a bad one. We hear that it had bow, bay and tray on one horn and bow and bay on the other, with nothing atop either.' August 23rd 1879.*

❖

The day after the Prince left, the Conservatives in West Somerset selected the master of the Devon & Somersets, Mr Mourdant Fenwick Bissett as their candidate at the next general election.

And this was to be a proper election: for the first time for 33 years, the Conservative stranglehold was finally being challenged by the Liberals, as suspected, after William Gladstone's recent visit.

The Liberal candidate was to be Charles Acland, son of Sir Thomas Acland of Holnicote; election fever was again in the air. The 1880s were to stage some of the most colourful and lively elections ever witnessed in West Somerset.

Reverend 'Jack' Russell.

His Royal Highness was well to the front, his riding being bold and of that kind which won general admiration. The pace was a rattling one, and at Badgworthy the stag took to the water and after going up and down for about ten minutes stood at bay. A whip was then placed around its neck, and the quarry was drawn to land. The Prince cut its throat, the mort was sounded, and cheers long and loud were given. According to ancient and irrefragable custom, His Royal Highness was "blooded," Mr. John Joyce respectfully performing this most important ceremony, which consists of sprinkling some of the stag's blood on the novice's face. The time from find to finish was about one hour and forty-five minutes, the pace occasionally being very fast. The stag was considered to be about five years old, but, unfortunately, its head (which is no doubt intended to be presented to the royal guest) was a rather bad one. We hear that it had bow, bay, and tray on one horn and bow and bay on the other, with nothing atop of either. About 150 horsemen were in

Fenwick Bissett.

# 1880s: Election fever and the November 5th riot

## THE BALLOT.

Inasmuch as there has been no contested election in the western division of the county of Somerset since the year 1847, it is not surprising that considerable misunderstanding as to the mode of voting, especially as it has been conducted since the passing of the Ballot Act in 1872, should prevail. We therefore propose to give a brief explanation of the Ballot and its operation for the instruction of electors who will on Tuesday next desire to record their votes.

### SECRECY.

The most careful and elaborate provisions are made and are carried out at every polling-station, to ensure the complete secrecy of the vote. Each elector on declaring that he is the person named in the electoral register receives a ballot paper, on the back of which there is an official mark corresponding to one on the counterfoil from which the ballot paper has been torn out. On this counterfoil the voter's number on the register is entered, and the vote can only be traced by finding the ballot paper, comparing it with the counterfoil, and then hunting up the number on the register. But the law makes careful provision against this being done, and it can only by any possibility be done by special order of the House of Commons, or by the direction of a judge, and such order or direction can only be given when the election is disputed, and there is reason to believe that the vote is a fraudulent one. When the voter receives the ballot paper he marks it in secret, folds it up so that no sign of his mark is visible, and so that only the official mark on the back can be seen, and slips it into the ballot box. As soon as the poll is over the counterfoils are sealed up, so that there can be no possibility of comparing the marked ballot papers with them. The ballot papers are then opened face upwards, in the presence of witnesses on behalf of both sides; the presiding officer is bound to see that no person looks at the numbers on the backs, though even those numbers would not give him any information without the key in the sealed-up counterfoil. Any attempt to look at the number on the back of the ballot paper is, in fact, punishable by six months' imprisonment. When the votes have been counted the ballot papers are at once sealed up, and with the register of electors are sent under seal to London. They are there kept in the custody of the Clerk of the

POLLING DAY for West Somerset's first parliamentary election for 33 years was set for Tuesday April 6th 1880. There was huge excitement in the district and the *Free Press*, aware that few of its readers had ever actually voted in an election before, published a special guide for those who actually had the right to vote – all male householders over the age of 21.

The complicating factors were the tricky issues were 'plumping' and 'splitting'. There were still two MPs representing the constituency, so each voter could make two selections from a cast of three candidates – the sitting MP, Vaughan Hanning Lee; the new Conservative candidate, Mourdaunt Fenwick Bissett, the Master of the Devon & Somerset Staghounds; and the new Liberal challenger, Charles Acland, son of Sir Thomas Acland of Holnicote House.

Voters could either 'split' their vote – if you were a Tory supporter, you would split your vote and vote for each of the two Conservative candidates – or if you were a Liberal supporter, you would just 'plump' for Charles Acland, and not make a second selection.

So *Free Press* went to great lengths to explain these various options in its special supplement, but despite this there was still confusion on the day in the minds of those unpractised in the ways of democracy.

Voting on the Tuesday opened at 8am and closed at 5pm – and polling was heavy. Scenes at the polling stations were invariably raucous, with rival crowds of (generally disenfranchised) supporters decked out in party colours – 'old-fashioned blue' for Conservatives, blue and cardinal for Liberals – heckling and cheering the voters: those who actually had the vote were apparently the quieter and better behaved.

*'One voter, enthusiastic in this respect, drove into Williton with his decorated trap and his hat literally covered not only with dark blue and red but yellow and other coloured streamers, and with "Plump for Acland" bills fixed an each side of his conveyance and loud was the laughter and good-humoured the cheers with which he was greeted.' April 7th 1880.*

The streets of Williton were soon crowded, with some overplastering of opponents' placards; three bands enlivened proceedings, and by the afternoon men and boys were pelting with mud anyone who wore the blue Conservative favours:

> '...there were a few fights during the day, but nothing of a serious nature transpired.'

At Wiveliscombe, the Liberal candidate, Charles Acland arrived by train in the morning, and walked to the polling station in the schoolroom, headed by a band and a cheering crowd, declaring that...

> '...so far as he could gather, at Porlock and Williton things were looking very well.'

A reflection of the times was that there was no polling station for Minehead – voters here had to travel to Dunster to vote – nor at Watchet, where voters crossed the hill to Williton.

The result was declared the following day at the Shire Hall in Taunton. The *Free Press* had made arrangements to telegraph the voting figures to Williton, to be published in a Wednesday 'election special' edition.

The large crowd gathered outside the Shire Hall to hear the High Sheriff announce the result of West Somerset's first election for 33 years; the two Conservative candidates had squeezed out their Liberal contender, but their margin of victory was narrow: Lee 3186 votes, Bisset 3136, Acland 2967.

So there was no change to the old Conservative order; the resurgence in Liberal support, sponsored by the two powerful land-owning families, the Aclands and the Luttrells, had just failed to get their man in.

The result was greeted with a loud cheer and a rush to the committee rooms and the telegraph office. Charles Acland said he had been defeated, but he was not beaten, and would fight again if requested. A large crowd of victorious Conservative supporters gathered outside the Castle Hotel; the new MP Mr Bissett, Master of the Devon & Somerset Staghounds, appeared on the balcony and thanked them for confirming the Conservative's generation-long hold on the district.

❖

Early the following year, in April 1881, the *Free Press* published a small column entitled *Notes By the Way*. It was the first article to be signed by its author – and, apart from a few weeks through unavoidable illness or death – these *Notes* have appeared in every edition of the *Free Press* since that first article.

The founding author was Clement Kille, the headmaster of Old Cleeve School who was later to give up teaching to become the *Free Press's* chief reporter. In his first *Notes*, Mr Kille set the tone for the thousands of weekly columns that were to follow.

> 'As an outsider looking on, interested in the various events passing around,
> but more especially in this immediate neighbourhood, I purpose making a few notes
> and remarks from time to time on the people and things which may happen to come under my notice but
> in so doing I trust I may never exceed the bounds of fair criticism, nor overstep the limits of good taste by
> noticing in this column matters which it would have been better to pass by unregarded.' April 30th 1881.

Among the topics Mr Kille addressed in his first column was the decline in the population of West Somerset, as shown in the 1881 census, reflecting the worrying new trend of young people leaving the district to seek work elsewhere.

**VOTE ONLY FOR ACLAND!**

**THE BALLOT BOX IS SECRET!**

To the Liberal Electors of West Somerset.

GENTLEMEN,—If Mr. Acland is to be returned as our member for West Somerset, Liberal Electors must *not give their second* vote either for Mr. Lee or Mr. Bisset. If this be done, we shall be helping the Conservatives to win, viz., by adding our (Liberal) vote to the Conservative ones. I say to all Liberals, vote for Acland ONLY, and we shall return him. Remember the ballot is *safe*. Vote according to your convictions, and promise nothing. No person will ever know for whom you have voted, unless you are simple enough to tell.

A LIBERAL ELECTOR.

**West Somerset Free Press,**

WILLITON, SATURDAY, APRIL 3, 1880.

**THE WEST SOMERSET ELECTION.**

**A SUPPLEMENT,**

Containing reports of the speeches made at the Liberal meetings held at Minehead, Watchet, and Williton, and at the Conservative meeting held at Williton, on Friday, will be issued on Saturday morning, April 3rd, and may be had, gratis, at the Williton and Minehead offices and of the usual agents.

The declaration of the poll will be made by the high sheriff of the county at Taunton on Wednesday next. The result will be telegraphed to this office, and a

**SPECIAL EDITION**

Will be published *immediately*. The price will be one penny, and the paper may be had at the offices and of the agents. Copies will also be sent by post to any persons who may send orders for them.

**NOTES BY THE WAY.**

[It must not be assumed that the opinions of our contributor are identical with our own.—ED.]

As an outside looker on, interested in the various events passing around, but more especially in this immediate neighbourhood, I purpose making a few notes and remarks from time to time on the people and things which may happen to come under my notice, but in doing so I trust I may never exceed the bounds of fair criticism, nor overstep the limits of good taste, by noticing in this column matters which it would have been better to pass by unregarded.

Clement Kille.

A few of West
Somerset's pioneer
golfers; standing in the
middle of the back row
is one of the club's first
professionals, a
Scotsman called Mr
Gair, circa 1890.

*'Agricultural depression is the chief cause assigned now for the lessening numbers but there is also a large number of our country lads and girls who now leave their homes, in or near which in bygone times they will have lived and died, to seek fortunes further afield in our centres of industry…and for those whose fathers would not many years ago have considered Bristol as the uttermost end of the earth, London and other large towns offer a wide field of labour, with easy communications.'*

*Notes By the Way*, under the pen of Mr Kille and his successors, present a fascinating commentary on the rapid changes in West Somerset. Perhaps surprisingly, he is not much struck by the age-old custom of wassailing, or 'singing to the trees,' as he described it:

*'A number of men go around to the principal orchard owners and get their permission to enter the orchards where they sing a quant ditty to the trees, fire off guns and make the air re-echo with hurrahs, all of which is supposed to have some beneficial effect on the apple crop the following season.*

*'It is not, however, often done now, though the custom still lingers here and there; but as the cider cup is expected to be freely passed round at each place they stop at, the party generally return home very much the worse for their perambulation. No one likes to see old customs drop into disuse but this is one we can very well afford to lose, unless it is reformed into something a little more creditable to the parties concerned.' January 7th 1882.*

❖

But Clement Kille did show keen interest in the prospect of a new golf club opening at Minehead; this was a pioneering development – at the time, the *Free Press* reported, there were only six other golf courses in the whole of England, the nearest being at Westward Ho!

A founding meeting was held at the Plume of Feathers and the *Free Press* reports that the mysteries of the new game were explained to those present by a Dr Clark, 'as few of them knew anything about the game.'

*'The speaker then gave a general description of the game, explaining that it was the usual practice to start from the hole nearest the tent and two, three or four might play although in matches it was nearly always two.*

*'Three or four different kinds of club were used according to the manner in which it was*

**FORMATION OF A GOLF CLUB AT MINEHEAD.**

A preliminary meeting for the purpose of forming a golf club was held at the Feathers' hotel, Minehead, on Tuesday afternoon, when several gentlemen interested in the proposal were present. Mr. D. Badcock was called to the chair, and in opening the proceedings said he had hoped that position would have been taken by Mr. G. F. Luttrell, but although he was not present then he (the Chairman) was sure he would take an interest in this proposal, as he did in everything else in the neighbourhood. Their first business was to decide by vote whether they should have a golf club, and he thought the idea a very good one. Perhaps, however, as few of them knew anything about the game, it would be best if Dr. Clark would kindly give them some information concerning it.

The golf pro's house on the left; the low building is the first clubhouse.

*desired to strike the ball. The combatants played alternately and the object was to get the ball into whatever hole you were playing for, the one who did so in the fewest number of strokes winning that hole.*

*'He could assure them that a great deal of excitement attached to the game and old and young thoroughly enjoyed it.' April 8th 1882.*

Mr Luttrell had agreed to let the land on the Warren for annual rent of £7 10s. and a motion was passed to form the Minehead and West Somerset Golf Club.

---

At the end of 1881, the *Free Press* reported that Mr John Clark of West Luccombe had taken delivery from Minehead railway station of a new ten-ton steam traction engine for ploughing and threshing.

Within a few months, this new technology was causing quite a row in Porlock Vale, as evidenced by a letter to the paper the following May.

*'Mr Clark is evidently much concerned about that "diabolical wheelbarrow" of which he is so proud and which we all know would never have invaded our pretty vale, without the assent of his great friend (Sir Thomas Acland).*

*'It is also pretty well known that Mr Blathwayt would have preferred to keep such a death-dealing, money-saving nuisance out of our quiet and lovely lanes and villages...*

The writer is even worried about the impact on the district's early tourism.

*'Is it desirable that residents and visitors (the latter are not attracted to our pretty country by traction engines) should have their daily comfort sacrificed and their lives put in jeopardy by the use of such a monstrosity, to the hindrance also of ordinary traffic?' Signed PROGRESS. May 6th 1882.*

---

November 1882 saw a dramatic development in the West Somerset Railway – the overnight transformation of the entire 21-mile branch line from Taunton to Minehead, from Brunel's old 7ft broad gauge to the more manageable 4ft 8½ins narrow gauge of the main arterial lines now criss-crossing the country.

The West Somerset line was one of the last in the country to remain on the old Great Western Railway standard.

*'The change will be heartily welcomed by everyone who had much to do with goods traffic for the removal of goods in course to transit at Taunton or other places from narrow to broad gauge trucks has hitherto been attended with considerable delay and generally a large amount of damage.*

## ALTERATION OF GAUGE ON THE WEST SOMERSET RAILWAY.

In accordance with announcements previously made, the alteration of the local railway line from the broad to the narrow gauge was successfully effected at the beginning of the present week, the work being carried out, under the superintendence of Mr. Hammett, of Taunton, the chief engineer of the Bristol and Exeter division of the G.W.R., by about 500 men. These were divided into seven gangs of about seventy men, each under the charge of an inspector, who had charge of an average distance of some three miles each. The portion of line altered was from Minehead to Norton Fitzwarren, where it joins the main system, on which, as is well-known, both gauges are in use. After the ordinary trains on Saturday a "special" was run from Minehead about nine o'clock p.m. in order to clear up all broad gauge trucks, luggage, &c., and the work of alteration was then rapidly proceeded with, and, the crossings, where possible, having been previously altered, and everything placed in readiness, before noon on Sunday the shifting of the rails had been so far completed as to allow of a train being run over them. This left Taunton about twelve o'clock, and conveyed the district superintendent, Mr. Campfield, Mr. Hammett, and other officials. The work of packing, &c., was afterwards proceeded with until about five o'clock, when the men retired for the night, sleeping in the company's goods sheds, which had been prepared for the occasion. Work was resumed on Monday morning, and by nine o'clock the task of alteration was practically completed. Only one passenger train each way ran on Monday, but there were others for the conveyance of workmen. On Tuesday the ordinary traffic was resumed. The West Somerset Railway was, we believe one of the last branch lines to retain the old broad gauge, as laid down by Brunel on the Great Western. The difference between the two gauges, as is made apparent by the large space between the double line of rails at Williton, is considerable, the broad gauge being seven feet wide, whilst the width of its successful rival, as regulated by Parliament, is 4ft. 8½in. The work at Williton was watched on Sunday with interest by a considerable number of spectators. The alteration will no doubt be of great convenience, as luggage trains can now be run on to the main line, avoiding the trouble and risk of transferring goods from one train to another. Whilst its economy as regards rolling stock is considerable, the narrow gauge is also undoubtedly of greater utility on short lines like our own, where there are stations at brief intervals, owing to the facility with which speed can be either got up or reduced on the smaller locomotives.

'Henceforth the change will be unnecessary and those who deal in breakable material will derive a great advantage from it being forwarded right through, without having to incur the risk of a hurried transfer, as in times past.' October 28th 1882.

The overnight conversion was completed without a hitch...

'...in very expeditious as well as effective manner. It was an unusual sight for a Sunday to see the gangs of workmen busy on the line, but the heaviest part of the work was got through in the course of the night before. Fortunately, the weather of the night was all that could be desired, and the bright moonlight favoured the operations of the workers.

'The clanking of the metals and the hum of the voices throughout the night were the only sounds to indicated that anything unusual was going on.' November 4th 1882.

❖

## DAILY COACH FROM LYNTON TO MINEHEAD AND BACK.

THE well-appointed fast four-horse coach "LORNA DOONE," leaves the ROYAL CASTLE HOTEL, LYNTON, daily (Sundays excepted) at 8 a.m., arriving at the RAILWAY-STATION, MINEHEAD, in time for the 11.45 up train, and starts on the return journey soon after the arrival of the 3.7 down train, passing through Porlock and Lynmouth, arriving at Lynton about 7 p.m.

On MONDAY, JUNE 28th, another four-horse coach, the "RED DEER," will run between MINEHEAD and LYNTON as last year.

Further particulars may be obtained of the Station-master, Minehead, or of Mr. T. BAKER, Lynton.

The old four-horse coaches still ran the Minehead-Lynton route; here the Red Deer, heading westward awaits another oncoming coach – possibly the Lorna Doone.

❖

By early 1883, a House of Lords select committee was considering the Bridgwater and Watchet Railway Bill, the new rail line first proposed more than ten years earlier.

This proposed line would run for 20 miles through Cannington, Stogursey, Nether Stowey, Kilve and East Quantoxhead before ending at Watchet and had apparently first been considered – and rejected – by Brunel in the 1850s.

Now the idea was being revived. The QC advocating the new line said it was necessary to open up faster connections between West Somerset and Bridgwater, and from there on to Bristol and the Midlands, to avoid the slow service currently provided by the West Somerset Railway via Taunton.

But he acknowledged that while the district through which it would run was very beautiful, it was…

> '…somewhat complicated for railway purposes by the undulating character of the ground and the high lands which intersected it and particularly the hills from the seashore to the eastward of Watchet and which, for the purpose of railway communication, severed the eastward from the westward.' April 14th 1883.

The proposed new line had an unexpected supporter in Sir Alexander Acland-Hood, now chairman of the rival West Somerset Railway. This was doubly significant, for not only would the Bridgwater-Watchet line offer real competition to the WSR, but its route would also cut through Sir Alexander's own estates at Stogursey and West Quantoxhead. Sir Alexander told the committee;

> 'Speaking therefore from a point of view of mere personal convenience, as regards my houses, the line will be very objectionable…as it will cut me off from the sea, and will go through my pleasure grounds. At the same time, I believe it will be of great benefit to the inhabitants of the neighbourhood.'

Sir Alexander said the proposed new line would be better for his tenants wanting delivery of building materials and coal etc. and he believed tourists would use this route to get to Minehead, Porlock, Lynton, Lynmouth, instead of travelling via Taunton.

He regretted that the WSR had become 'stagnant' for want of proper investment by the Great Western Railway (which had merged with the old operator, the Bristol & Exeter Railway Company, in 1876).

(Clement Kille in his *Notes By the Way* was intrigued by the prospect of such a small town as Watchet being served by THREE railway lines – the WSR, the Mineral Line and the proposed new Bridgwater line!)

At a later hearing, the Great Western Railway, which operated the main regional line to Taunton, opposed the proposed new branch line, arguing that the existing railways in the area were losing money, and given the construction costs of £437,000 – twice the cost of building the WSR – the new line could never be expected to make a profit.

The Bridgwater and Watchet Railway Bill finally received Parliamentary approval, but by August 1883, after failing to raise the necessary capital, the promoters admitted the scheme was dead.

Mr Kille, in his *Notes*, hoped that the GWR might be magnanimous in victory and now invest to improve the service on the WSR, hoping:

> '…it might manage to 'hurry on' its trains and endeavour regularly to adhere to the times advertised on its bills, for the trains have not been noted for their extreme punctuality of late.
> 'The journey from Taunton is slow and melancholy to the last degree at all times, but when there is the added uncertainty of getting to the journey's end only within half a hour or so, even more, of the proper time, it becomes still more tedious.' September 1st 1883.

After an absence of more than thirty years, elections followed thick and fast in West Somerset. A by-election was called in April 1884. The Liberals increased their vote, but again failed to loosen the Tory hold on the seat. The by-election had been called following the resignation of the former master of the Devon & Somerset Staghounds, Mr Mordaunt Fenwick Bissett, on grounds of ill-

**BRIDGWATER & WATCHET RAILWAY BILL.**
[SPECIAL REPORT.]
HOUSE OF LORDS, Tuesday.

The Select Committee of the House of Lords appointed to consider the merits of this Bill commenced its proceedings this morning, Lord Romilly presiding. The Bill seeks powers to construct a new railway from the town of Watchet, on the Bristol Channel, where the line will ramify in three directions and also form a junction with the Great Western Railway, to Bridgwater, where it will have three spurs. One will join the Great Western system; the second will form a terminus in the town; and the third a junction with the Bridgwater Railway to Edington, in connection with the Somerset and Dorset Railway.

Mr. Bidder, Q.C., for the promoters, in opening the case, described the character of the proposed line, stating that the distance across country between Bridgwater and Watchet was twenty miles, whereas the present railway was twenty-eight miles in length. All traffic at present had to run on the main line between Bristol and Exeter; it had to be changed, and the time of the trains did not at all approximate, and consequently created delays in the journey—which was very serious indeed. The proposed railway would accommodate a district which was at the present time entirely destitute of railway accommodation, and the people of the district believed it would be a means of developing the resources of that part of the country by giving better communication with the world east of Bridgwater. It would open up a competing district represented by the South-Western and Midland Railways, which, with Parliamentary sanction, had competing powers as owners of the Somerset and Dorset Railway Company. The length of the proposed line from Bridgwater to Watchet would be twenty miles, and with the three spurs in Bridgwater and three in Watchet the total length would be twenty-two miles. The entire cost of the whole line would be £137,000. The line was partly promoted by gentleman who were large owners of property in

Fenwick Bissett.

health. Within three months, Mr Bissett, was dead, greatly mourned in the district, but also celebrated for having revived both the health of the red deer on Exmoor, and also the future of the Devon & Somerset Staghounds.

*'He was not prominent in any political sense, for he cared not for the "babble and turmoil, the endless strife of words" in the British House of Commons; nor in a military sense, for he courted not the bubble reputation at the cannon's mouth, but as a country gentleman, the type of landed nobility now fast dying out in England.*

*'In all manly sports and especially in the chase, he excelled; and it was his intrepidity in the field and his sound judgment that fitted him for the proud position of Master of the Devon & Somerset Staghounds, which he held for 26 years.*

*'At that time, the hunting of the red stag in its native wilds of Exmoor was only carried in a feeble and half-hearted manner and threatened to become extinct. With the advent of Mr Bissett, a new state of things was inaugurated. A taste for the good old sport was revived and after four years of varying fortunes, the pack of staghounds came under the able Mastership of Mr Bissett who improved the hunt to a marvellous degree.' July 12th 1884.*

By November of the following year, 1885, a General Election was called and the local Tories faced the most significant challenge to their hold on the constituency; after more boundary changes, it was now called the Wellington Western Division, Williton having lost a heated campaign to have its name used in the new constituency title.

Sir Thomas Acland of Killerton and Holnicote, the 11th baronet, had first sat as MP for West Somerset from 1837-47 as a Conservative, but he became a convert to the Free Trade polices of the Liberal party, and for the past twenty years had represented North Devon as a Liberal.

Sir Thomas Acland, photographed later in life, circa 1890.

These new constituency changes saw Sir Thomas move across the county boundary and again stand for election in West Somerset, contesting the seat his son Charles narrowly failed to win five years earlier.

And this time, it was head to head; the 1885 Redistribution of Seats Act meant that just one MP now represented the new constituency. Sir Thomas was challenging the incumbent Tory MP Mr Charles Elton, a London lawyer who had won the seat in the previous year's by-election – and had distinguished himself by making no less than three maiden speeches on the day he first rose to his feet in the House of Commons.

After a hard-fought contest, the crowds gathered outside the Shire Hall in Taunton the day after the poll to hear the result. After an extended delay, and in front of a noisy and expectant crowd of at least six hundred supporters, the returning officer Mr Fowler declared that Sir Thomas had broken the Conservative's stranglehold and won the seat for the Liberals with a majority of over five hundred votes.

*'Ringing cheers greeted the announcement. . .there was a general rush to the telegraph office to send the messages away into the country. The news flashed from mouth to mouth "Sir Thomas is in" and a large number made their way to the London hotel where Sir Thomas was staying.' December 5th 1885.*

Sir Thomas, thanked his supporters, in particular the Luttrells of Dunster Castle, but he reserved his real thanks for the newly-enfranchised farm labourers of the district;

o'clock. The crowd grew larger every minute, and at a quarter to one there were not less than six or seven hundred people present. The time was beguiled by the interchange of experiences by those who had taken part in the election, and many "tall stories" were told. In the midst of conversation, as Mr. W. H. Fowler (deputy returning officer), attended by Mr. Elton, Sir A. A. Hood, and other gentlemen, stepped out of the hall on to the portico, there was a sudden hush, and then a cheer, and a man in the crowd bawled out, "Sir Thomas is in! I can see by M——'s face without waiting for the figures—hurrah!" The cheer was taken up vigorously, and after it had subsided, Mr. Fowler read out in clear distinct tones the state of the poll, which was as follows :—

| | |
|---|---|
| Sir THOMAS ACLAND (L) ... ... ... | 4,299 |
| Mr. C. I. ELTON, Q.C. (C) ... ... ... | 3,760 |
| Majority for Acland ... ... ... | 539 |

Ringing cheers greeted the announcement, at the end of which Mr. Elton proposed a vote of thanks to the returning-officer, who had done his duty in a very kind, straightforward, and honourable manner. The cheering having been repeated, there was a general rush to the telegraph office to send messages away into the country. The news flashed from mouth to mouth, "Sir Thomas is in," and a large number of people made for the London hotel, where Sir Thomas was staying. Mr. Charles Acland, M.P. was seen in the crowd

*'The cause owes most of all to the honest artisans and intelligent labourers who have worked among their fellows…..what has given me most pleasure and confidence for the future of England is the temperate, sober, contented and kindly tone of the new electors (cheers)'.*

(Two sons of Sir Thomas also won seats at this election: Charles Acland, who had lost in West Somerset in 1880, won North Cornwall for the Liberals and his younger brother Arthur won Rotherham.)

---

Ten years after the arrival of the trains at Minehead, the town was clearly developing rapidly. Mr W.H. Farrar is now the new author of *Notes By the Way*, and he writes:

*'The North Hill at Minehead seems to be obtaining favour as a building site, as I see certain buildings are now in the course of construction on its slopes. The only wonder is that the beauty has not been seen before. There is a magnificent view of the valley towards Taunton, a sweeping expanse of Channel below and the hills of Exmoor on the other side, like green billow rising one above the other. There are unrivalled opportunities for indulging in the pleasures of the chase and for those that have plenty of money, and experience difficulty in putting it out so as to obtain a good return, with adequate security, no better investment can be met than a building venture on the North Hill.' February 27th 1886.*

---

But Sir Thomas's hold on the seat was short-lived – as indeed were the Liberal Party's fortunes in West Somerset and in the country as a whole.

The Liberals had held power for 18 of the previous 27 years, but in 1886, the party was split over the contentious issue of Home Rule for Ireland.

Sir Thomas supported his life-long friend, the Prime Minster William Gladstone, in advocating Home Rule for the Irish, but a breakaway Unionist wing of the Liberals sided with the Lord Salisbury's Conservatives.

Another general election was called in July 1886 and the Irish question dominated the debate; Liberal party election posters portrayed the blessings of Home Rule, with scenes of comfortable cottages, and well-fed pigs: the Conservative posters warned of evictions and misery.

Polling was reported to be quiet and orderly, and resulted in a dramatic reversal of the Liberal's majority only eight months previously; Charles Elton won back the seat for the Conservatives with a majority of almost nine hundred votes over Sir Thomas.

Mr Elton addressed crowd, draped in the national colours:

*'This is a grand day for the old Union Jack. Conservatives and Liberal Unionists have joined together nobly in defence of their country.'*

---

W.H. Farrar, in his *Notes by the Way*, was always keen to comment on the coming trends. In 1886, it was the telephone:

*'An enterprise is on foot for linking Western towns together in telephonic communication and if the enterprise succeeds, the telegraph will to a great extent be superseded….the great obstacle in its adoption was that telephony was of no use for great distances.*

*'It has, however, been so much improved that messages may be sent by telephone 50 miles without the slightest difficulty…Then the husband at Taunton may communicate with his wife in Williton, if he has a private switch on, and enable her to make preparation when he is about "to take company" home.' August 28th 1886.*

---

The decade of the 1880s ends on a tragically low note, the killing of a young Minehead man in a Bonfire Night riot, and as a result, the removal from the district of a previously-popular policeman.

For the past few years, the celebration of Guy Fawkes night in the town had become rowdy; fireworks had been set off in the streets, stones thrown, and lighted tar barrels rolled down the

# THE FRACAS AT MINEHEAD ON GUY FAWKES' NIGHT.

## DEATH OF A YOUNG MAN.

## THE CORONER'S INQUEST.

The row which occurred at Minehead on Guy Fawkes' night (as described in the last issue of the *West Somerset Free Press*), had a most lamentable result in the death, on Saturday afternoon last, of a young man, named George Hellard, who was struck in the forehead with a policeman's staff. The wildest reports were in circulation in the town and neighbourhood from the time when the fatal termination of the affray became known until the elucidation of the facts before the deputy-coroner and a jury commenced,, it is only right to suspend judgment until the fullest investigation has been made. The blow on Hellard's forehead had not the appearance of a serious one. He was taken to the surgery of Dr. Ollerhead, who attended to the wound, and he was afterwards able to walk to his home in Quay-street. On his arrival home, he was in a very depressed condition, and told his wife that he believed the blow he had received would cause his death. He seemed no better in the morning, and afterwards became delirous. He was attended by Dr. Ollerhead, and Dr. Clark was also called in. The patient, however, seemed unable to get any sleep, and this was a bad sign. On Saturday morning, he was able to get out of bed, and it was hoped that he would pull through. He even noticed from his window P.C. Weeks passing in the street and made a remark upon it. Later in the day, however, he became rapidly worse, and died soon after four o'clock in the afternoon. The receipt of the news in the town caused great consternation and surprise, and the sad event has been the staple topic of conversation ever since. Superintendent Gerity was in Taunton on business on Saturday afternoon, and did not hear of the death of the poor fellow until his return home. He immediately came on to Minehead, and he also telegraphed to Superintendent Durham, of Taunton, who came down and has been in the town since Sunday making enquiries into the facts on behalf of the Chief Constable. On Monday, the Chief Constable himself also came to Minehead. The deceased was 22 years of age, and had for some ears been in the employ of Mr. Thristle, of the Feathers Hotel, where he was an ostler and driver. Acting-Sergeant Broomfield has been very much prostrated since the sad occurrence, and has been suffering from the effects of a blow or kick which he received some time during Tuesday evening. His wife also has been dangerously ill owing to the nervous shock.

Parade. Some youths had even set light to effigies of the town's policeman for the past 15 years, Acting-Sergeant Abraham Broomfield.

So, in anticipation of more trouble, three extra constables joined Sergeant Broomfield on that night of the November 5th 1889; by early evening there were more than a thousand people milling around Wellington Square and The Parade, and quickly things got out of hand, as the police tried to stop fireworks being discharged in the streets.

By ten at night, there appears to have been a full scale riot. Sergeant Broomfield waded into the crowd who had attacked a bystander, one John Fry.

Sergeant Broomfield later told an inquest, held in the Beach Hotel,

*'They were beating him with fists and sticks. I heard them crying out 'Kill the b...' In my effort to rescue the man, I was kicked in the legs several times and received blows on the body by fists and two blows over the head by sticks.*

*'I drew my staff to try to keep back the surging crowd. I threw it round sideways and said "Keep back, keep back."' November 23rd 1889.*

In the melee, it is clear that Sergeant Broomfield had struck the head of a young ostler from the Plume of Feathers, one George Hellard.

*'The blow on Hellard's head had not the appearance of a very serious one. He was taken to the surgery of Dr Ollerhead, who attended to the wound and afterwards, he was able to walk to his home in Quay Street.*

*'On his arrival home, he was in a very depressed state, and told his wife he believed the blow he had received would cause his death. He seemed no better in the morning and afterwards became delirious...'*

The following day, Hellard's condition worsened and by the evening he was dead. At the inquest, Sergeant Broomfield denied that he had struck Hellard deliberately.

*'I did not know that the deceased was struck by me but afterwards I heard so. I had to use my staff in this tumultuous crowd ...but when I used it, I did not strike at any particular person...I considered that my life was in danger...'*

Broomfield denied allegations that he had threatened that he would 'knock the brains out' of the first man that came near him, and accepted that Hellard was not one of ringleaders.

Summing up, the Coroner, Dr George Cordwent said

*'It appears that the people of Minehead wanted to keep up their traditional celebrations but knew they were breaking the law...and that not one of the persons called as witnesses had stated the Broomfield had any animus to, or intended to strike, any individual, but unfortunately there was a blow which undoubtedly caused the death of the deceased.'*

*Up to 300 needy folk could be accommodated in the Williton Workhouse.*

Sadly frequent in the *Free Press* are reports from the police courts of the plight of the travelling poor of the district, the tramps who wandered the lanes looking for work, food and shelter and who often sought refuge in the Williton Workhouse, where they had to labour in return for their minimal comforts.

Sir Alexander Acland-Hood presided over the case of one tramp, Thomas Hartnell, from Brompton Ralph, who refused to do his daily labours.

*'The Master of the Workhouse, Mr Foot, said he gave the accused the usual amount of stones to break, 13cwt and of these he broke only 2cwt, and those in an unsatisfactory manner, as about one half of them would not pass the Surveyor of Highways' examination.*

*He also gave the prisoner some oakum to pick, but he did only about half of it and made an excuse that that kind of work made his fingers sore.*

*'Sir Alexander Acland-Hood said "The Board of Guardians cannot keep you unless you do the requisite amount of work, and as you will not do it, you must go to prison with 14 days hard labour."' October 29th 1887.*

The jury took three quarters of an hour to return a verdict of accidental death and awarded their jury fees of £1 16s to the widow of the deceased. Later, a local public subscription was opened for funds for young widow.

Acting Sergeant Broomfield was transferred to Wincanton the day after the inquest closed.

# 1890s: The Autocar arrives, and an overland launch

More than 3,000 volunteers camped out on North Hill.

THE SUMMER of 1890 saw a massed military invasion of the district that was to become a welcome regular feature, but also a harbinger of future conflicts before the decade was out.

The full-time British Army was supported by Volunteer units, fore-runners to the present-day Territorial Army. These part-time soldiers – riflemen, artillerymen and engineers – regularly gathered for annual training and for the first time, in 1890, North Hill in Minehead was chosen to stage a Volunteer Camp for more than 3,300 citizen soldiers from South Wales, Gloucestershire and Somerset.

Temporary water reservoirs were constructed on North Hill, pipework installed, wagons hauled wood up onto the hill for camp fires, and gorse and bracken was cleared for the tented villages that sprang up on the landward side of North Hill, between the Upper Town and Woodcombe overlooking 'the new road to Porlock.'

On one day in July 1890, steamers, many of them charted from R.S. Date of Watchet, brought 1,800 South Wales Borderers into Minehead harbour, where they mustered before marching through the town and up onto North Hill. The following day, a succession of trains brought into town another 1,100 men for Gloucestershire and members of the Somerset Light Infantry.

Reports in the *Free Press* suggest that many thought that just getting up to the camp was an achievement in itself.

The locals in Moor
Road turned out to
watch the mules haul
the guns up through
Higher Town.

*'(The volunteers) ...arrived in camp hot and perspiring with their steep climb, and looking forward to a
high time of it for the magnificent weather put everybody into the best of spirits. They were preceded by a
detachment of cyclists, who found the hill to the camp a trying piece of work.*

*'Being the first affair of this kind ever held in this neighbourhood, the camp has excited a large amount
of interest, not only at Minehead but round the whole countryside, and the interest has developed into
absolute excitement, as the tents have sprung up day by day and the baggage and store wagons have come
rolling heavily up the hill.*

*'The programme of events will include some night work, the repulse of an imaginary attack from
the sea, also a very interesting experiment in the form of an attack on an improvised fort on the seashore,
the firing to be with ball cartridge.' August 5th 1890.*

West Somerset had never before seen such a gathering of so many people and the Volunteer
Camps – on North Hill and throughout the district – were to be a regular feature for the next fifteen
years. But those trained on these hills would soon to be fighting for real, first in the Boer War, and
later in the First World War.

In May 1891, the first elected local council in the area – the Minehead Local Board – met
under the chairmanship of Thomas Ponsford, Mr Luttrell's influential land agent. And
one of the first improvements under their administration was the introduction of electric
lights to the town.

Watchet and Williton may have been the first with gas lighting, but Minehead had
surged ahead in the intervening years.

The first generator was in the town's tannery where the manager, Mr Evans, had a
2-horse power engine, sufficient to run 200 incandescent lights and was hence

*'...in a position, if required, to supply the electric light to private houses or hotels in
the town at a far cheaper rate than could otherwise be done by persons running dynamos
for themselves. As for brilliancy and safety, the electric light is far superior to gas and ....it
is unquestionably the light of the future.' February 13th 1892.*

The General Election of July 1892 saw the Conservatives consolidate their hold on the constituency
– with a new candidate who was to dominate local politics for the next two decades. Captain
Alexander Acland-Hood was the son of Sir Alexander Acland-Hood, the third baronet, who had
been one of the two constituency MPs from 1859-68.

Sir Alexander had long ago resigned his seat – 'the atmosphere of St Stephens was little to his taste' – and had devoted the remainder of his life to improving his Fairfield and St Audries estates, and the conditions of those working for the estate.

His son, Capt. Alexander, had the previous year returned from two years' diplomatic service in Australia, and the young captain took over as the new Conservative candidate for the seat on the resignation of the sitting MP, the lawyer Charles Elton.

And just six weeks before the election, his father Sir Alexander died, so the baronetcy passed to his son on the eve of the poll; this he comfortably won for the Conservatives with a majority of 885, defeating the Liberal candidate, another London lawyer, Mr W. Latham, QC.

Outside the Castle Hotel, the new MP and the new fourth baronet, Sir Alexander Acland-Hood told the crowd:

*'You have shown those men who have come down here and don't know anything of the country that you intend to stick to a West Somerset man. I was last in coming into the field, and if it had not been for your energy, I should not have won this great victory.' July 9th 1892.*

This was the start of a notable political career that was to see 'Sir Alec' rise to become Government Chief Whip early in the next century.

Sir 'Alec' Acland-Hood with his wife Mildred, at home at St Audries, soon after their marriage.

An extraordinary road race was staged in autumn 1892, across the twenty miles of steep coastal roads from Lynmouth to Minehead and back, for prize money of £15 to the winner, and £10 and £5 to the runners-up. Entries were restricted to runners from Lynmouth and Lynton.

*'A race that excited a great deal on interest in Lynmouth and Minehead came off on Wednesday when 22 competitors started off from the Bridge at Lynmouth to go to Minehead railway station and back, the rules being that they should keep on foot but otherwise please themselves as to pace, resting etc. and that they should travel by the coach road the whole way, making no short cuts by other roads.*

*'And those who know the road will quite understand how much it must have tried the capabilities of the competitors. Alfred Oxenham of Lynmouth led on the outward leg and held the lead to the end finishing in 6hours 30 minutes, 11 minutes ahead of second placed Alfred Balman of Lynton.' September 3rd 1892.*

A prestigious dinner was held at the Memorial Hall, Farringdon St, London, to honour a famous son of Watchet. Mr Thomas Allen was presented with memorial scrolls and 200 guineas in recognition for his pioneering achievements in the art of shorthand writing.

The inventor of the world's first shorthand system, Mr Isaac Pitman, also presented Thomas Allen with an engraved address from the townspeople of Watchet, describing him as 'the premier shorthand writer in the world' and expressing pride that 'Watchet and Watchet alone is able to regard you as her son.'

In his acceptance speech, Mr Allen recalled his schooldays in the town,

*'...where I spent so many delightful hours among the low slippery weed-covered rocks catching crabs and gathering limpets.' November 26th 1892.*

Mr Allen had recently returned from working in India for a government commission into the opium trade, which apparently had fully tested his ability to write at 200 words a minute.

❖

A meeting was held in the Public Hall in Minehead in the summer of 1893, to resolve a long-running and embarrassing town saga; what to do with Queen Anne.

A statue of Queen Anne had been presented to Minehead in 1719 by one of the town's two MPs, Sir Jacob Bancks, but after standing inside St Michael's Church on North Hill for many years, it was now languishing in the basement beneath the Town Hall.

The chairman of the meeting said it was to the shame of the town that

*'...the beautiful statue was now shut up in a box below that room (where they were meeting) covered with filth and dirt. What did they think Sir Jacob Bancks would have said, if he had ever thought that the grand statue which he gave to the parish for ever, would ever descend to that condition.' July 22nd 1893.*

An earlier meeting in 1887 had recommended that the statue be erected in Wellington Square but at the time, many believed the statue to be carved from alabaster and they feared that it would not survive outside in all weathers.

Crowds gathered awaiting Queen Anne's installation in Wellington Square.

The statue was formally opened by George Fownes Luttrell.

However it was finally decided to place Queen Anne in the Square, under an ornate canopy, and ten months later, in May 1894, the statue — now known to be carved from marble — was unveiled in her new home before a large crowd by Mr George Fownes Luttrell who remarked

*'Some time after the statue was presented to the town, the great fire occurred and it was taken into the church (St Michael's) where it remained a long time.*

*'Then came a period where Her Majesty was hidden away for a time in obscurity (laughter) but now that she had again been brought into view, they might hope that it marked a time of prosperity for the town.'*
*May 19th 1894.*

❖

Minehead was developing as a popular resort, but it still lacked a pier.

If Minehead was truly to live up to its ambition to be a premier holiday resort then there was one thing lacking — a pier. Weston-super-Mare's Birnbeck Pier had opened in 1867 and Clevedon Pier in 1869.

THE PROPOSED PIER.—The preparations for the new pier are so far advanced that the prospectus shortly to be issued will be advertised in this paper next week. The pier, which is to be of ironwork, will be situated west of the present jetty, and will be 755 feet long, running out to a point accessible to steamers at nearly all states of the tides. A considerable sum of money is to be laid out on improving the approach; the present "slip" at the harbour will be filled in, to provide for the road to cross on the right of the Pier Hotel, and a new "slip" will be made. The directors of the Minehead Pier Company, Ltd., are Messrs. W. G. Blow, John R. Christie, and John Cory, of Cardiff; John Richards Davis, of Minehead; Philip Froude Hancock, of Wiveliscombe; and Richard Haswell Holman, of London. The tenders of Messrs. Alexander Penney and Co., of Fenchurch-street, London, for the construction of the pier, and Mr. H. W. Pollard, of Bridgwater, for the harbour improvement, have been accepted, and it is intended that the work shall be commenced at once. The share capital of £12,000 is divided into 1,200 shares of £10 each, of which £5,000 is reserved for the directors and their friends. With the construction of the pier so closely in view, the advisability becomes more than ever apparent of the town constructing the proposed sea-wall and otherwise improving the sea front by the formation of an esplanade—an improvement that has already engaged the attention of the Urban District Council, and would undoubtedly be welcome to visitors.

Twenty-five years behind their local rival resorts, in 1894 the town met to hear surveyors commissioned by George Luttrell explain their plans for a pier at Minehead.

To ensure that steamers could use the pier at all tides, there were two options. The most sensible was to locate the pier half a mile west of the harbour, necessitating a pier one thousand feet in length, but many thought this too far from the town to be economically successful.

Others at the meeting lobbied for the pier to be sited at the heart of the sea front, at the bottom of The Avenue. The *Free Press* reports

*'This would undoubtedly be the best place for a promenade pier, but they had to consider whether it would be practicable. A pier from the bottom of the Avenue out to the depth of water proposed by the engineers would have to be more than three quarters of a mile in length, and cost something like £40,000.' August 25th 1894.*

Despite intense lobbying, this seafront option was considered just too expensive, and a compromise was agreed for a site just west of the pier, accepting that a pier at this site might not be accessible in all tides. The construction costs were estimated at around £7,560, and a limited company was formed, with shares at £50, potential investors being assured that most pier companies paid dividends of between nine and 15 per cent.

Wiveliscombe was plunged into mourning just before Christmas 1896, when the death was announced of William Hancock, at the age of 86. Mr Hancock's father (also called William) had founded the family firm, but it was only after his son, the second William

Hancock, had taken over the reins in 1846 that the family's brewing and banking business really took off. He expanded the brewing business into South Wales and developed the family's banks, before selling them to the Wilts and Dorset Banking Company (later absorbed by Lloyds Bank).

Mr Hancock had lived in Wiveliscombe all his life; at least a thousand people lined the streets of the town to witness his funeral.

'Never before was such a largely-attended and imposing funeral seen in Wiveliscombe as that of the late Mr William Hancock ...it is said that previous to his fatal illness, he had scarcely experienced a day's illness during the whole of his long life.

'He was a fine old specimen of an Englishman ...he had for many years been the leading inhabitant of Wiveliscombe, to which he ever proved a faithful friend.

'As a token of respect, the whole of the shops were closed during the funeral, and the blinds of the private residences were pulled down, and the mournfulness of the scene was added to by the muffled peel of the bells of the parish church. Among those present were represented all classes of society, for all combined to show their appreciation of the virtues of the deceased gentleman.' December 12th 1896.

The coffin was carried on bier borne by eight members of the Hancock staff, all from different departments of the business.

For several weeks during the summer of 1897, the *Free Press* carried weekly bulletins on the health of the one man who, outside of the Luttrell family, can be said to have shaped modern-day Minehead.

Thomas Ponsford was born in Cutcombe; after his schooling, he worked as clerk with Messrs Warden and Leigh, a firm of solicitors based at Bardon House, near Washford and in 1867, was appointed steward to the Dunster Castle estate by the new squire, George Luttrell.

Much of Minehead was owned by the Luttrell family estate and the recent rapid development of the town was thanks largely to the ambitious design of the Luttrell family, delivered and managed by Mr Ponsford as steward of their property.

Mr Ponsford moved to Minehead in 1883, and the *Free Press* reports that he was an investor in some of the town's new constructions, being involved in the building of Esplanade lodging houses, the Esplanade Hotel, the Wellington (Temperance) Hotel and the Town Hall among many others.

He later led the new elected council in the town, becoming the first chairman of the Minehead Urban District Council in 1894 and he was still attending meetings, aged 86, when in July 1897, he took a chill. A month later he was dead.

### Death of Mr. Ponsford, of Minehead.

After the paragraphs that have recently appeared in our columns respecting the illness of Mr. T. Ponsford, of Minehead, it will not be a surprise to our readers that we now record his death, which took place at his residence, No. 8, The Avenue, on Thursday evening, at a quarter-to-nine o'clock. Mr. Ponsford, it will be remembered, last attended a meeting of the Minehead Urban District Council, of which he was the chairman, on July 12th. He was much indisposed at the time, having taken a chill, and on the following day peritonitis set in, from which he suffered a severe attack. Although Mr. Ponsford's strong constitution enabled him, under the watchful care of his medical attendant, Dr. F. G. Hayes, of Dunster, to pull through this illness, it left him so weakened that at his age it became a serious question whether he would ultimately recover. His condition fluctuated for several weeks, but it was apparent that he grew weaker, and he was only supported by sustenance of a nourishing and stimulating character. In consequence of the great interest felt in his illness and the many inquiries made, bulletins have been issued daily, but they have never been of a hopeful character, and though his natural vitality was great he continued gradually to sink until Wednesday, when he became unconscious, remaining in a comatose state until Thursday evening, when he passed quietly away.

*'The extension of the railway to Minehead from Watchet was one of the schemes in which Mr Ponsford may be said to have been mainly instrumental in bringing to a successful issue and this did more than anything to lay the foundations for the development of Minehead as a watering hole.*

*'He expended large sums of money in building and in his schemes for the advancement of the town, he had constantly in view the future rather than the present.*

*'His name has become a household word and the course of his business has caused him to be connected with almost everything that has been done, not only in the town, but in a wide area of district for many years past.' August 14th 1897.*

Mr Ponsford was buried at St Decuman's, alongside his wife.

---

There was great excitement on the roads of West Somerset – at Minehead and in Williton especially – caused by the appearance of what the *Free Press* described as the first motor car in the district. Others may dispute this description, as it was clearly little more than a motorised tricycle, but it was undoubtedly a sign of things to come.

A solicitor from Bridgwater, Mr F.W. Bishop, accompanied by a local cycle dealer Mr R. Carver, drove a Boilee Voiturette, manufactured by the Horseless Carriage Co Ltd London at 'a rapid rate' along the rutted lanes to Minehead and he then proceeded to give demonstration rides up and down The Parade and The Avenue.

The *Free Press* reporter could not restrain his scepticism:

*'A combination of the light carriage with the tricycle, it constituted a neat and rapid means of transit for two people. The motor is 2-horse power and is driven by petroleum, the speed obtained being anything within the Government regulations of 14mph.*

*'Mr Carver gave one or two persons an opportunity of testing its speed and comfort, one being our representative who was greatly pleased with the machine, and promptly made up his mind to place an order with Mr Carver, as soon as he has 150 guineas to spare.' October 30th 1897.*

W.H. Farrar, writing in *Notes By The Way* was equally doubtful, as he observed the machine passing through Williton:

*'A droll-looking machine, like a perambulator of the dachshund type, and it has a funny little cough, caused by the oil explosions which furnished the motor power.'*

A MOTOR CAR.—A great deal of interest was shown on Friday afternoon in the appearance of a motor car, the first that has been seen in the town. It sped along at a rapid rate through The Parade and The Avenue, and, returning by North-road and Blenheim-road, made a short stop at the Plume of Feathers Hotel. The gentlemen riding were Mr. F. W. Bishop, solicitor, of Bridgwater, and Mr. R. Carver, the enterprising cycle dealer, of the same place, who were out for a spin from Bridgwater. The machine was under the management and guidance of Mr. Carver, to whom it belonged, and was what is called by the makers—the Horseless Carriage Co., Limited, London, for whom Mr. Carver is agent—the Boilée Voiturette, or, in other words, a motor tricycle. A combination of the light carriage with the tricycle, it constituted a neat and rapid means of transit for two persons. The motor is of 2-horse power and is driven by petroleum, the speed obtained being anything within the Government regulations of 14 miles an hour, while under favourable circumstances this rate can, if necessary, be increased. Mr. Carver gave one or two persons an opportunity of testing its speed and comfort, one being our representative, who was greatly pleased with the machine and promptly made up his mind to place an order with Mr. Carver as soon as he has 150 guineas to spare.

---

❖

---

Two years had gone by since the pier at Minehead had been first proposed, when suddenly there are reports of an unexpected new project that could challenge the pier's prospects and, unusually, also set the district's two biggest land-owning families at loggerheads.

The rumours first surface in an anonymous and spirited letter to the *Free Press* in March 1898, entitled "Minehead-Lynmouth Rail".

*'There is a rumour that a line has been planned, and that plans will be deposited of it, from Minehead to Lynmouth...The course of it is said to be up Hawkcombe, through a tunnel to cost £100,000 to Weir Water, then following the Lyn to Lynmouth.*

*'If this is true, and I believe it is, then goodbye the prosperity of Minehead, which will become a mere wayside station instead of a terminus, goodbye the pick of the staghunting, goodbye to the beauties of Brendon, Rockford, Watersmeet and the Watersmeet Valley.*

*'I hope, sir, that from Minehead to Lynmouth, such a cry will be raised that the scheme, even if people could be found foolish enough to finance it, will be "dapped on the 'ade" at once.' March 2nd 1898.*

Within six weeks, the *Free Press* carried an advert, giving notice under the Light Railways Act of proposals to build two light railways: one from near the Tors Hotel, Lynmouth, via County Gate and Culbone to Minehead, and a second short light railway from Minehead station along the sea front to the site of the proposed new pier, and the terminus for the proposed Lynmouth light railway.

The extraordinary proposal to build a railway line from Minehead-Lynmouth sparked off a heated debate in the *Free Press* between the promoters of the line and its opponents who feared the damage such a line would do to the landscape and environment.

The competing sides of this argument were thrashed out in public by the two most respected land-owning families in the district, the Luttrells of Dunster and the Aclands of Holnicote.

George Luttrell was one of the promoters of the new line, in association with two railway companies across the channel in South Wales, the Vale of Glamorgan Railway Company and the Barry Railway Company

Mr Luttrell wrote to the *Free Press*:

> *'I am fully convinced that it will confer a great benefit on the whole of this district, but more especially on Porlock, if it can get a railway...I have never heard of any town or parish...that does not derive benefit from railway communication, but I know many that suffer from the want of it and Porlock is not an exception to this universal rule...' April 23rd 1898.*

Mr Luttrell's enthusiasm for his scheme was quickly challenged by Charles Acland, son of Sir Thomas Acland, who owned much of the land around Porlock through which the proposed new light railway would have to pass.

Charles Acland responded in a letter to *The Times*, reprinted in the *Free Press*:

> *'It is true that Mr Luttrell is a resident in the neighbourhood but he does not reside in the actual district where the line is actually to run, nor has he any property or interest in the Porlock Valley.*
>
> *'As a resident therefore, he is in no way affected. His property lies outside that valley, though Minehead, where the pier is to be erected, chiefly belongs to him.*
>
> *'He also says that it will not touch Exmoor....the railway will go through some of the most beautiful parts of this wild moorland and woodland and cannot but mar the beauties of it and of the wooded cliffs between Porlock and Lynton.*

A new railway would finally bring to an end the horse-drawn coach traffic across the lonely moors.

## THE LIGHT RAILWAYS ACT, 1896.

### LYNMOUTH AND MINEHEAD LIGHT RAILWAY.

NOTICE IS HEREBY GIVEN that APPLICATION is intended to be made in the month of MAY next to the LIGHT RAILWAY COMMISSIONERS, under the Light Railways Act, 1896, for an Order to incorporate a Company (hereinafter referred to as the Company), and to authorise the Company to make and maintain the Railways hereinafter described, from Lynmouth, in the County of Devon, to Minehead, in the County of Somerset, or some part or parts thereof, together with all necessary sidings, stations, roads, approaches, buildings, works, and conveniences connected therewith or incidental thereto ; that is to say—

### RAILWAY No. 1.

A Railway commencing in the Parish of Countisbury, in the County of Devon, on Countisbury Hill, at or near a point 635 yards east of the Tors Hotel and 100 yards south of the main road leading from Lynmouth to Minehead, and pr ceeding in an easterly direction for a distance of 600 yards, where it crosses the said main road, and then proceeding in a north-easterly direction along the northern boundary of Countisbury Common, crossing Kipscombe Combe 150 yards north of Kipscombe Farmhouse, and passing south cf Chubhill Wood and

*'The only benefit that will be reaped by this scheme, if it is carried out, will be the profit realised by those who are pecuniarily interested in the Cardiff and Minehead piers and steamers, and the fares by those who use the light railway as passengers...' May 14th 1898.*

The arguments were taken up in a packed public meeting in Minehead's Public Hall which, having heard from Mr Luttrell, voted unanimously to back the rail link with Lynmouth.

Many in the town felt that it was a case of Minehead either having a new pier or a new rail line to Lynmouth: W.H. Farrar in his weekly *Notes*, put it best;

*'The air of Minehead palpitates with questions of profound interest. One the new pier; the other, the new railway. Minehead is trying to make up its mind as to which it wants most.*

*'Put shortly, the pier, it is said, will tap (to use a publican's simile) Cardiff, Barry and Bristol. When Taffy knows there is a pier at Minehead, he will come over to this side of the Channel to fish for shrimps and he will come in large numbers.*

*'If the light railway is constructed, people will not stop at Minehead; they will go on to Lynton, probably stopping for a drink at Porlock. Therefore Minehead's interest is in the pier and in the railway does not appear.' May 14th 1898.*

Finally, the matter was resolved in August at an inquiry held in Minehead by the Light Railway Commissioners. After only a few hours of evidence, the commissioners brought the proceedings to a halt, stating

*'The commissioners do not think that any good purpose will be served by prolonging this inquiry. It is clear that the owners of some 18/20ths of the land proposed to be taken are strongly against the scheme, besides which the commissioners have received from residents and others interested in the district representations showing that on various grounds there is strong aversion to it*

*'It was clear that...over a large portion of the line there would be very little local traffic and that the line is intended to serve not so much the local needs as tourist requirements'. August 13th 1898.*

## THE PROPOSED
## LIGHT RAILWAY
### FROM
## LYNMOUTH TO MINEHEAD

### INQUIRY AT MINEHEAD.

On Tuesday, the Light Railway Commissioners commenced, at the Public-hall, Minehead, an inquiry into the application to authorise a light railway from Lynmouth to Minehead. There was a very large attendance, the greatest interest being taken locally in the mat'er for and against the railway. The applicants were Messrs. Robert Forrest and Thomas Roe Thompson, two of the directors of the Barry Railway Company; Mr. Edmund Lyons Evan Thomas, director of the Vale of Glamorgan Railway Company; and Mr. George Fownes Luttrell, of Dunster Castle.

The commissioners were the Right Hon. the Earl of Jersey, G.C.M.G. (chairman); Colonel Boughey, R.E.; and Mr. R. Vesey FitzGerald.

The counsel for the promoters was Mr. Abel Thomas, Q.C., M.P., who was instructed by Messrs. Downing and Handcock (solicitors, of Cardiff) and Messrs. Ponsford, Joyce, and Davis (solicitors, of Minehead), also by Mr. C. Blackford (solicitor, of Minehead) on behalf of several of the inhabitants of Porlock and Lynmouth. Mr. Pember, Q.C., and Mr. Askwith (instructed by Messrs. Radcliffe, Cator, and Hood, solicitors, of London), opposed on behalf of Miss Halliday, Lord Lovelace, Lord Ebrington, Sir Thomas Acland, and other owners of property along the line of route; Mr. A. M. Poynter, secretary of the National Trust for Places of Historic Interest and Natural Beauty, appeared for that society; and Mr. Atherley Jones, Q.C. (instructed by Messrs. Ffinch and Chanter, solicitors to the Lynton and Barnstaple Railway Company), appeared on behalf of that company. There were also present Mr. G. F. Luttrell; Sir James Szlumper, engineer of the proposed line; Mr. Wm. Szlumper; Messrs. Joyce and Davis; Mr. C. Blackford; Mr. H. Acland Hood; Sir Douglas Fox; Mr. J. H. East, General Manager's Department, G.W.R., Paddington; Mr. J. Campfield, district superintendent, G.W.R., Exeter; Mr. William Dunn, clerk to the Somerset County Council; Mr. Willcox, county surveyor, Mrs. Luttrell, Miss Luttrell, Miss B.

Without local support, compulsory purchase orders to acquire the necessary land could not be contemplated and so the scheme collapsed.

As a footnote, a prescient observation was made by one of the many readers who wrote to the *Free Press* about the scheme.

*'It is perhaps worth pointing out that the promotion of a light railway is inopportune at the present time in any district, unless urgently wanted, for the reason that in all probability they will be ultimately superseded by the development of motor-car traffic on ordinary roads.' April 23rd 1898.*

In the midst of the row over the light railway, the death was announced of one of the protagonists – at least in name – Sir Thomas Acland, at his Devon home of Killerton, at the age of 89.

Much was made of the fact that he died in the same week as the funeral of his close friend and former great Liberal Prime Minister, William Gladstone.

As we have already seen, Sir Thomas started his political life as a staunch Conservative, like his father before him, representing West Somerset as a Tory MP from 1837-47, but his opposition to the Corn Laws, and support for Free Trade saw him convert to the Liberal cause.

Sir Thomas's funeral was held at Killerton, with a memorial service at Selworthy. Sir Thomas was succeeded by his son Charles, the former MP for North Cornwall and Launceston, who in turn was immediately addressed by all as 'Sir Thomas', in recognition of his father and the succession of Sir Thomas Aclands before him.

The *Free Press* of December 21st 1898 carried the first published account of one of the most oft-told and inspiring stories of the district – the night-time overland launch of the Lynmouth lifeboat.

Mountainous seas at Lynmouth had prevented the launching of the town's lifeboat late on a Thursday night, called to rescue an iron-hulled full-rigged vessel the *Forrest Hall*, wallowing rudderless off Porlock, in the teeth of the storm.

The tale is by now well-known, but the *Free Press* reporter of the day lived up to the challenge of its first telling; of how the lifeboat, the *Louisa*, was dragged by horse and man over the huge ridge-back cliffs of Countisbury, across County Gate and down Porlock Hill to Porlock Weir.

> **THE LYNMOUTH LIFEBOAT.**
> **A DIFFICULT AND ARDUOUS FEAT.**
> **GALLANT WORK.**
>
> The Lynmouth lifeboat received a call by wire from Porlock on Thursday night. As the hurricane was then at its height, with a tremendous sea breaking over the Esplanade and harbour, a launch at Lynmouth was impossible. The only remaining alternative was a 12 miles journey by the exposed coach road (1,000 feet high) over Exmoor—one of the worst roads in the country. The darkness, gale, and narrowness of route added very considerably to the great difficulty of the task. There are several sharp turns, with long steep descents like the roof of a house. Some dozen or fifteen horses were quickly procured from

*'As the hurricane was then at its height, with a tremendous sea breaking over the Esplanade and harbour, a launch at Lyn was impossible.*

*'The only remaining alternative was a 12 miles journey by the exposed coach road (1,000feet high) over Exmoor — one of the worst roads in the country. The darkness, gale and narrowness of the route added very considerably to the great difficulty of the task.*

*'There are several sharp turns, with long steep descents like the roof of a house. Some dozen or 15 horses were quickly procured by Messrs Jones Bros, and others and supplemented by 100 willing helpers, a start was made with Mr John Crowcombe in command at about 8.30pm.*

*'The stupendous difficulty of the task can be more readily conceived from the fact that the top of Countisbury Hill (one and a half miles from Lynmouth) was not reached till one o'clock. ...*

*'Several portions of the road were only just sufficiently wide to admit the lifeboat carriage and at the narrow Ashford Lane, the boat had to be taken off and hauled through, the carriage being taken round over the moor. Here two hours were lost.*

*'The steep descent to Porlock was finally negotiated in safety and Porlock reached at 5am. The road to Porlock Weir had been washed up by the sea, but the boat was finally launched at 5.30am, after nine hours of the hardest continuous toil man has ever been put to.*

*'The vessel in distress was a full-rigged ship, anchored one and a half miles off Porlock, and in imminent danger of coming ashore. The boat remained alongside to render assistance if necessary and at the request of the captain, several of the (lifeboat) crew went on board the ship and proved of great service in helping to navigate her to Barry Roads, where she arrived on Friday evening after an eventful voyage.*

*'The magnificent feat in transporting the boat from Lynmouth to Porlock in the darkness remains a monument to the pluck, industry and perseverance exhibited by the Lynmouth lifeboat in aid of their fellow-men'.*

'The *Louisa* off the Holms' by Mark Myers captures the Lynmouth lifeboatmen finally approaching the *Forrest Hall* in Porlock Bay.

After delivering the *Forrest Hall* to safety, the lifeboat crew then made for Barry.

*'All the men bore traces of their severe buffeting, having had scarcely anything to eat or drink for 24 hours and some having been on board the lifeboat since she left Porlock and having had an awful experience towing on the weather side of the ship.'*

The Lynmouth lifeboat finally left Barry on Saturday morning in the tow of the SS *Letbury*, bound for Genoa, and they were delivered safely back at Lynmouth before noon, some forty hours after they has set off on that momentous overland ascent.

---

Early in 1899, the *Free Press* marked with sadness the passing of one of the district's most determined petty criminals, whose exploits seemed to have attracted a grudging fondness.

'Miser' Coles, as he was known to all, died at Williton Workhouse, of bronchitis and heart failure, ending a 30-year career of petty poaching, regularly rewarded with sentences of penal servitude.

*'His occupation was that of a labourer, but a greater part of his life having been spent in gaol, very little time was left him, comparatively speaking, even had he felt disposed for work.*

*'He owed his long period of prison life chiefly to an unconquerable penchant for possessing himself of other people's fowls and loud and numerous in days gone by used to be the complaints made to the police of pilfered fowl-houses, whenever Coles was at large.*

*'It may be mentioned that Miser had a liking for fowls, stewed with onions, potatoes and such like and the culinary utensil was generally a stolen bucket, on more than one occasion these buckets having been found with savoury repasts ready prepared within them, which Coles never had the chance to enjoy.' February 11th 1899.*

Miser was released from his last prison sentence only five months earlier, but his health deteriorated, and he died two weeks after entering the workhouse.

After the false-start of the 'motorised tricycle' two years earlier, what was undeniably a proper motor car arrived in the district just before the century was out. The *Free Press* headlined the report simply, An Auto-Car

'*Minehead at present appears to lie out of the track for touring motor cars, possibly because further west the hills become too difficult even for these machines, unless of the first-class type, to negotiate but during the summer, two or three have been seen in the town.*

'*At present there is an autocar belonging to a gentleman staying at the Plume of Feathers which much surpasses anything that has yet been seen here.*

'*It is a Gobron Brillé car built in Paris by the famous firm of Belvalette and is of the most improved type, costing over £800, one speciality being that it is non-vibrating, even if its machinery is still going when the car is at a standstill.' September 23rd 1899.*

The engine was a vertical double cylinder of ten-horse power and carried five passengers, besides the driver.

'*The motive power is petrol, a double-distilled benzoline, with an electric apparatus for the ignition spark. The car is charged with sufficient electricity for a journey of 5,000 miles but the petrol requires renewing after 200 miles. It is capable of running at any speed, from the slowest up to 30mph.*

'*The owner, Mr Clarence Knight Gregson, a gentleman, one of the most enthusiastic auto-carists in England... and by his kindness, a large number of townspeople have enjoyed the novelty of a short trip in the swift and handsome car.*

'*Under the management and guidance of the professional engineer who attends to the car, a great many short runs were made during Tuesday afternoon and evening, mostly along the Parade and Avenue...'*

AN AUTO-CAR.—Minehead at present appears to lie out of the track for touring motor cars, possibly because further west the hills become too difficult even for these machines, unless of first-class type, to negotiate, but during the summer two or three have been seen in the town. At present there is an auto-car belonging to a gentleman staying at the Plume of Feathers Hotel which much surpasses anything that has yet been seen here. It is a Gobron Brillé car, built in Paris by the famous firm of Belvalette, and is of the most improved type, costing over £800, one speciality being that it is non-vibrating even if its machinery is going when the car is at a standstill. The engine is a vertical double cylinder of ten-horse power, and is capable of taking 30cwt. up any ordinary hill. Another point of interest about the car is its improved acetylene lamps. Constructed something after the style of a waggonette, and beautifully appointed in every respect, the car will carry five persons, besides the driver. The motive power is petrol, a double-distilled benzoline, with an electric apparatus for the ignition spark. The car is charged with sufficient electricity for a journey of 5,000 miles, but the petrol requires renewing after 200 miles, and the cost of running is about ¾d. per mile. The vehicle was built to order, and

The motor car quickly became a common sight in West Somerset; this motor car rally at Dunster was held in 1905.

# 1900s: A harbour wrecked, and a defrocking

THE NEW century opened in sombre mood; many young men from West Somerset were fighting for their country thousands of miles from home in South Africa. On paper, the Boer War appeared a mismatch between the might of the Imperial Army set against the untrained Boers. But these tough farmer militias exploited classic guerrilla tactics to undermine the lumbering British forces, and for the first weeks, the British were being forced back by a determined Boer offensive.

But in March, the *Free Press* reported better news. General Sir Redvers Buller VC – a West Countryman, born in Crediton – led British forces in the relief of the Siege of Ladysmith. West Somerset joined in the national celebration, none more so than the people of Williton.

*'Good news, long looked for from the seat of war in South Africa, came this week and was received with profound satisfaction. Ladysmith has been relieved so many times here and elsewhere by telegrams that proved to be mere rumours, that the public could not now feel certain of the news until the* Free Press *telegram was posted.*

*'Young Williton continued to "demonstrate" through the streets, singing "Soldiers of the Queen" for some time and some enthusiastic people showered nuts, sweets and biscuits upon them, bringing*

## AFTER THE SIEGE.

### HOW LADYSMITH WELCOMED BULLER.

Ladysmith was relieved just in time. The garrison could have held out but a few days longer. There were, as may be guessed, joyous scenes in the town when its deliverers appeared. A correspondent who was in Ladysmith throughout the siege writes of the last days:

"There was nothing early in the morning of Wednesday to indicate that the hour of our deliverance was so near at hand. We knew that our men had great fight of Tuesday; we knew that our men had won, but we thought there would be one more sanguinary fight before we saw the head of General Buller's column. That fight everyone said would take place at our own door, and we were nerving ourselves to play our part in the battle. Just an occasional shell—for ammunition was running low—until three o'clock in the afternoon, when we were

CONVOYS ENTERING LADYSMITH.

## THE RELIEF OF MAFEKING

### FIERCE ATTACK REPULSED.

### MANY PRISONERS TAKEN.

Mafeking was relieved on May 18th. Lord Roberts, it may be mentioned, had promised help by that day. The relieving force was a composite column of about 2,300, under Colonel Mahon.

The official account of the relief, and also of the last fighting in which the garrison had taken part, was thus described by Lord Roberts in despatches from Kroonstad:

"Mahon reports having joined Plumer at Jammassibi on May 15th. He was followed by the Boer commando from Maritsani Siding, and turned westward to avoid it. On 13th he was attacked in thick bush, losing five killed, two missing, twenty-four wounded, including: Major Mullens, Imperial Light Horse (dangerously); Captain Maxwell, Kimberley Mounted Corps (severely); Mr. Hands, *Daily Mail* correspondent (dangerously). The Boers lost more than Mahon in killed and wounded.

RUINS OF HOTEL AT MAFEKING.

"Another report has been received from Baden-Powell, dated May 13th, giving the important news

*about a general scramble in which, for a moment, Ladysmith was entirely forgotten. Cannon also were let off and the bells at the church and school were rung for a time.' March 3rd 1900.*

This was but a foretaste of celebrations that greeted the Relief of Mafeking two months later. The *Free Press* carried a full page of reports from around the district; Watchet was first to hear the good news.

*'Watchet may be said to have been in a delirium of joy last weekend when the long-expected and welcome news of the relief of Mafeking was definitely announced...*

*'On hearing the news, the coastguard was immediately informed. This was at 10.5; five minutes later, rockets were being discharged and to make sure that the people should be awakened, the No2 was sent up. The consequence was that long before 10.30pm, the town was alive.*

*'John' went round with the crier's bell to spread the information and the magic word 'Mafeking' sufficed to give the cue to anxious inquirers, who with one accord turned into Swain St which soon became thronged with an excited mass of humanity, some of whom were very scantily attired.*

*'Persons embraced their neighbours in the most affectionate manner, the ladies by no means receiving all the kisses, while in private houses, hospitality was dispensed to a degree never before witnessed.*

*'A party of enthusiastic torch-bearers decided to journey to Williton with the welcome intelligence and ultimately reached home about one or two o clock.' May 26th 1900.*

---

Given the popularity that the Exmoor classic novel Lorna Doone acquired in the twentieth century, it is perhaps surprising that the death of its author R.D. Blackmore, early in 1900, met with little comment in the *Free Press*, and the comment it did attract was, at best, lukewarm.

W.H. Farrar in his *Notes By the Way*, writes:

*'Blackmore, the author of that charming book* Lorna Doone, *is dead but he will not leave any great void in the world of literature, as he had not published anything special for the last twenty years. He was a one-book man and even that one was rejected by about twenty publishers.*

*'After it was published, it fell flat and for years it promised to be a dead loss to the publisher. Very curiously, when the marriage of the Marquis of Lorne to the Princess Louise (Queen Victoria's fourth daughter) was announced, the intelligent public had a suspicion that there was some connection between Lorna Doone and the Marquis of Lorne and began to buy the book. Its own merit afterwards carried it through many editions...'* January 27th 1900.

R.D. Blackmore.

---

Motor cars were becoming more common – even in West Somerset – but they still made the news, not least because of the astonishing speeds they achieved.

Lord Carnarvon, the elder half-brother of Aubrey Herbert of Pixton Park, Dulverton (and the financier of Howard Carter's discovery in the Valley of the Kings of the tomb of Tutankhamun) was called before London magistrates accused of 'furiously driving a motor car to the danger of the public.'

*'PC Tyler, 204J, said that on the day in question he saw a motor car coming towards him at the "flying rate" of 20 miles per hours. He and another constable stepped into the roadway and raised their arms for the car to stop.*

*'A cyclist, H. Scott of Woodford, deposed that he was riding along at about ten miles an hour and the defendant's car passed him 'like a flash of lightning'. . .another witness deposed that the car passed him 'like an express train.' June 9th 1900.*

The Earl was fined of 40s and 11s costs. He was not present in court.

*St Mary Street in Nether Stowey in quieter times; the old toll house is on the left.*

Bridgwater magistrates condemned what they called a 'disgraceful riot' in Nether Stowey after an incident of late-night drinking got out of hand. The *Free Press* reports how the village policeman PC Broomfield and a colleague were called to the Bakers Arms in the village after ten one evening and started taking down the names of those caught drinking illegally after closing time, when

*'...the company made a general rush to clear out of the house. PC Broomfield, who was standing in the kitchen doorway, was speedily knocked over falling on his back in the passage.*

*'The crowd, who had made their exodus, congregated outside the inn and began shouting at the police. The police began a retirement in the direction of Castle Hill but they were followed by the crowd who had developed into an excited state. They yelled out to the police "Go home you ___" and, at length, one of the crowd suggested they should "drive" the police.*

*'Thereupon, the crowd, who numbered thirty to forty persons assailed the police officers with showers of stones, and as a result of the pelting , PC Broomfield was rather badly injured, and the rest of the police were also struck many times, causing blood to flow freely.' May 12th 1900.*

The landlord of the Bakers Arms, William Knight, was fined £3 for allowing drinking after hours, and sentenced to a month's prison with hard labour for assaulting police. Nine others were convicted of illegal drinking and assaulting the police.

❖

A few weeks later, a gentleman from London drove his 16-horsepower Napier motor car all the way to West Somerset for the express purpose of being the first to drive a car up Porlock Hill, one of the steepest and longest ascents in England.

*'The attempt to climb this formidable hill was the outcome of a sporting wager made some months ago when a gentleman visiting Porlock, owning a motor car, essayed the task but failed.*

*'The opinion was then expressed that it was an impossible feat for a motor car but the gentleman stated his determination to have a car which should accomplish it.' August 25th 1900.*

Artists were excited by the idea of cars tackling Porlock Hill.

The Napier – which cost the huge sum of £1,300 – was driven by Roger H. Fuller of Ditton Hill, Surbiton accompanied by Mr S.P. Edge and F.T. Bidlake.

*'The start was made from the Ship Inn, the car carrying the three gentlemen, flying away up the hill at a good pace and reaching Pitcombe Head in the remarkable space of 17 minutes.'*

They chose a Sunday for their successful hill-climb, to lessen their chances of meeting conveyances coming down the hill, not least the horse-drawn stage coach from Lynton.

———————— ❖ ————————

Watchet had been hit by a series of destructive storms in recent decades, but just after Christmas 1900, on the night of December 27th and into the following day, the town and harbour was battered by the worst storm in living memory that appeared to have destroyed Watchet's future as a thriving port.

## REMARKABLE FEAT WITH A MOTOR-CAR.

### CLIMBING PORLOCK HILL.

Considerable interest, not to say excitement, was caused at Porlock on Sunday afternoon when it became known that an attempt was to be made to climb Porlock Hill with a motor-car. The road traversed daily by the Lynton coach and other conveyances rises, as is well known, very steeply, especially for the first mile, and has some sharp bends. The whole distance from the Ship Inn, Porlock, to Pitcombe Head is 3½ miles, and the altitude reached at that point over 1,400 feet, the ascent being one of the longest and steepest in England. The attempt to climb this formidable hill was the outcome of a sporting wager made some months ago, when a gentleman visiting Porlock, owning a motor-car, essayed the task, but failed. The opinion was then expressed that it was an impossible feat for a motor-car, but the gentleman stated his determination to have a car which should accomplish it. Accordingly, on Saturday he came to Minehead from London with a 16-horse-power Napier car, the building of which cost £1,300, and the motive power being petrol. The car remained at Minehead for the night, Sunday being chosen for the attempt for the reason that few conveyances are to be met with that day on the road, and one source of danger would thus be avoided. The gentleman referred to above, Mr. Roger H. Fuller, of Kenley, Ditton Hill, Surbiton, accompanied by Mr. S. P. Edge and Mr. F. T. Bidlake, left Minehead on Sunday morning for Porlock, where, before long, it became known what was about to be attempted. The start was made from the Ship Inn, the car carrying the three gentlemen flying away up the steep road at a good pace, and reaching Pitcombe Head in the remarkable space of 17 minutes. The return was made by the new road through the Porlock Parks to Porlock Ford, a very difficult road, and back to the Ship Inn, the whole journey being finished in 48 minutes from the start.

Watchet harbour shortly before the storm.

The following morning, the destruction of the harbour wall and breakwater was revealed.

The *Free Press* cleared its pages for extensive reports, including for the first time in the paper's history, photographs of the widespread damage.

The fateful storm had started to build on the Thursday night: there were

> '...unmistakable signs of the approach of dirty weather – rain squalls, and an "angry" moon and a strong wind veering more and more from south-west to the westward. In anticipation, the local owners made their craft as snug as possible, especially so as there were, as is usual at holiday times, a very fair number in port...' January 5th 1901.

The storm abated in the early hours of Friday December 28th, but it proved only the prelude to something far more destructive.

> 'With the approach of daylight, it became apparent that the gale was increasing in fury. Out in the Channel a tremendous sea was running and the incoming tide was a scene of awful grandeur, the waves running at great height.
>
> 'By the tide's half-flood, the enormous waves had breached the breakwater reducing it to rubble and damaging the adjoining pier. The vessels in harbour now had no protection from the full force of the storm. Those heavily laden with coals awaiting unloading suffered worst, then three vessels broke adrift, smashing into adjoining craft.
>
> 'Here they lay, grinding against each other, while masts went by the board, bulwarks were stove in like matchwood, sail and gear torn to ribbons and the hulls greatly battered.'

The author of *Notes By the Way*, W.H. Farrar, witnessed the storm at its height and the desperate efforts of the sailors to save their vessels.

> 'All seemed as brothers in misfortune. Side by side they worked at the ropes in an almost futile endeavour to prevent further wreckage. Smothered with mud and lashed in the face by the spiteful gale, grim and silent they stood at the ropes till the fury of the gale abated. No thought of self, no hope of reward, only an Englishman's desire to do his duty to his brother in distress.' January 5th 1901

The gale was unrelenting, blowing throughout the day and into the evening, thwarting any attempts to salvage what vessels remained intact.

Sailors tried to salvage whatever remained from their smashed vessels.

*'The owners and crews were the helpless spectators of another distressing night. . .for hours, groups kept their weary vigil, sheltered behind the steam cranes, with only the light of the moon to locate a falling mast or a crashing of timber.'*

By the following morning, the full extent of the destruction was revealed. The breakwater was totally destroyed, and this had exposed the western wharf to the full fury of the waves with the result that large parts of the wharf had been lifted up and dumped into the harbour.

Inside the harbour, by the Esplanade and at the eastern wharf, there was a terrible tangle of battered vessels, their sterns smashed into adjoining hulls, their masts and rigging strewn across other damaged vessels.

Miraculously, three vessels remained afloat, but they were judged too badly damaged to be worth repairing. And of course, nothing was insured.

*'Late in the afternoon, permission was given to the large crowd of lookers-on to secure any of the smaller pieces of wreckage for use as fuel and men, women and children eagerly availed themselves of this opportunity of thus curtailing their coal consumption. . .wading through the mud of the harbour to gather their booty.'*

Huge crowds visited Watchet to see the full extent of the damage; by then it was clear that past failures to invest in proper sea defences had contributed to the extent of the damage.

At low tide, it was clear the harbour was left defenceless against the next storm.

*'That the breakwater gave way is, after examination, a matter of no great surprise, for many of the larger baulks were practically worthless, having been almost eaten through by the destructive sea-worm.*

*'A peculiar feature of about the work of this little creature is the fact that it attacks the timber from behind, so that while the portion facing the water appears sound, the inner side and centre are gradually being converted to the state of honeycomb.'*

W.H. Farrar, in his *Notes*, summoned up the depth of despair felt by the people of Watchet – and of the wider district:

*'Unless something can be done, Watchet is practically ruined. The damage is roughly estimated at £10,000 and the men who have lost vessels have no means of replacing them.*

*'But of far graver import to the town is the damage to the harbour. There are absolutely no funds to repair it and, left as it is, no vessel could ride in safety in half a gale.*

*'All the district benefits either directly or indirectly through the harbour, as in the case of sea-borne coal, and this and other commodities will probably be increased in price when merchants have to depend entirely on railway transport.'*

The storm of December 1900 was a tragedy, not just for Watchet, but for the whole of West Somerset.

# THE NEW PROMENADE PIER AT MINEHEAD.

## OPENING CEREMONY AND LUNCHEON.

Saturday last was a great day in the history of Minehead, when G. F. Luttrell, Esq., of Dunster Castle, and lord of the manor of Minehead, formally opened the new promenade pier at Minehead. The advisability of having a pier is a subject that has been before the minds of the public of Minehead for years past, and opinion has been sharply divided on the question. Not a few people held that it would vulgarise Minehead and tend to its decline rather than its prosperity, while others held just as strong opinions in the opposite direction. Some of the former have in the course of time come over to the ideas of the latter, but there are still some who look askance at the project and hold aloof from it. Which are right, or which are wrong it would be of no benefit now to discuss; time only will show, for the pier is an accomplished fact, and Minehead, for the summer time at least, is in daily connection with South Wales. When all other watering-places strive their utmost to get a pier and are never content till they have one, it is hardly to be wondered at that the majority of people in Minehead are gratified with the circumstances that have at last brought about what they consider so desirable an adjunct, for it is hardly to be questioned that in this age of strong competition the person or place who does not bid for popularity with the many must fall hopelessly behind in the race for supremacy.

The new pier had a two-level landing stage to receive steamers at varying tides.

Westwards along the coast, Minehead, too, had been battered by the gales but, more protected from the westerlies by the bulk of North Hill, had suffered little by comparison. Construction of the new promenade pier was by now was well under way and there are no reports of the storm damaging the new iron structure.

Indeed, three months later, in April 1901, work was virtually complete and the first docking of a Campbell's steamer was witnessed by a huge crowd given free access to the pier for the occasion.

The *Cambria* brought 500 passengers from Bristol, having earlier called at Clevedon, Cardiff and Penarth.

The pier was formally opened at the end of May by George Luttrell. Constructed of latticed cast iron and steel, it stretched more than 700ft out to sea, was 24 feet wide for most of its length, widening to 76ft at the end of the pier, where there were kiosks and shelters. Along its length there were cast iron railings, wooden hand rails and benches. It was designed to stand 20 feet higher than the highest spring tide.

Opening the pier shortly before the arrival of the first steamer, Mr Luttrell again emphasised the potential benefits to the district of closer links with the industrial and economic powerhouse of South Wales. He said West Somerset

Huge crowds pressed to be among the first to walk along the 700ft long promenade deck.

Some of the early pier staff

'...could not hope to vie with neighbours across the Channel in wealth, enterprise nor industrial or commercial importance, but they could and they did give them a hearty welcome to the enjoyment of the beautiful scenery and if, in their busy lives they could find enjoyment and beauty on that side of the Channel, they should be very pleased.' June 1st 1901.

The opening party then paid their penny admission through the turnstiles and walked on to the pier to welcome the arrival of the *Glen Rosa* from Barry, the first of four steamers that arrived that day, joined later by the *Westward Ho!* from Bristol and the *Waverly* and *Ravenswood* from Cardiff and Weston. At one stage there were three steamers lying abreast the pier.

The cost of the pier was £12,000 and not everyone thought it was money well spent.

'Not a few people held that it would vulgarise Minehead and tend to its decline rather than prosperity, while others held just as strong opinions in the opposite direction...when all other watering-holes strive their utmost to get a pier and are never content until they have got one, it is hardly to be wondered that the majority of people in Minehead are gratified...'

The pier quickly became an important focus for the town's activities; here crowds watch a lifeboat launch.

The Conservative MP, Sir Alexander Acland-Hood, of Fairfield and St Audries, had been returned to Parliament unopposed by the Liberal party for the past 14 years, and in November 1904, had been given one of the highest political honours of the land when he was made a Privy Councillor, in recognition of his service as the Government Chief Whip in Parliament.

Sir 'Alec' celebrated his re-election, by the narrowest of margins, at St Audries House.

The *Daily Mirror* was struck by Sir Alec's military demeanour, recalling his early exploits, fighting for the Grenadiers in 'the Soudan.'

*'He has the fair hair, the fair moustache, blue eyes, tall straight figure – something over 6ft in height - broad shoulders with the pronounced drawl which is always supposed to be the characteristic of a guardsman. And he knows what he is talking about on military matters for he is no carpet knight.' November 12th 1904.*

But early in 1906, the political tide was turning in favour of the Liberal Party, with the Conservatives split over free trade and tariff reforms, and in West Somerset, they once more challenged Sir Alec. Taking advantage of Sir Alec's absence on party duty in the Whip's office at Westminster, the Liberals came close to seizing the seat from Sir Alec; but he prevailed, with a slim majority of just 272.

———————— ❖ ————————

(Left) The ketch, the *Louisa*, was towed across the channel with six three-ton trucks for the Brendon Hills mines on deck as it had been impossible to raise full sail.

(Right) Platelayers linked the West Somerset line with the Mineral Line to receive the 47-ton engine, recently used on the Metropolitan Railway in London, for use in the re-opened mining operation.

Early in 1907, the man who had overseen the reconstruction of Watchet harbour, Mr H. Blomfield Smith, led a business syndicate set up to re-open the Brendon Hills mines, following the recent increase in the price of iron ore. This time, they had hit on a simple way of reducing their costs:

*'The idea is to drive levels into the (side of the) hill rather than mine from the top, thus avoiding much of the expense necessarily entailed in pumping and also in the working of the incline.*

*'Whereas in former days, the industry centred on the top of the Brendons, the principal scene of operations under the present scheme will be in the combes which indent the hillside...it is intended to attack the ore from different points, by means of adits, or tunnels in the side of the hills.' March 16th 1907.*

But after initial encouraging analysis of the purity of the new ores raised, by June 1908 there was another collapse in demand for the ore, as the Ebbw Vale furnaces lay idle. All mining on the Brendons ceased in 1909 and in 1910 the syndicate was wound up and all the stock and machinery sold. The rail track lay idle (apart from a brief, exciting venture in 1912/13) until it was finally sold, along with the station properties, in August 1924.

---

In October 1903, two Porlock farmers had scored a remarkable success at the 25th Brewers Exhibition held at the Agricultural Hall in London.

Thomas Rawle of Court Place was awarded the Championship of the World and 1st and 2nd prizes, for two bushels of Chevalier malting barley he had grown on fields between Porlock and West Porlock. And his near neighbour, R. Ridler, won the Gold medal in the same barley category with his sample of Webb's Kinver Chevalier.

*'It is remarkable that these awards go to one section, and that a very limited one, of the country. The weather in the Porlock district has evidently been more suitable for barley growing or else farmers in that locality were exceptionally fortunate in selecting the right time for planting and harvesting.' October 24th 1903.*

---

❖

---

West Somerset's first 'speed trap' was reported in the *Free Press* in September 1908.

Four local police constables positioned themselves on the outskirts of Williton, at the bottom of St Audries Hill. PC Tomkins stood at the start of a measured mile and when passed by a car, registration LC 3090, driven by a Huddersfield man, Mr Arthur Wakefield, gave the signal to his colleague PC Eno to start his stopwatch.

Williton Petty Sessions was later told that Mr Wakefield was recorded as travelling at 25mph in defiance of the speed regulations of 20mph, and only 10mph in built-up areas. He was fined three pounds, including ten shillings costs.

---

❖

---

Early in 1909, the Church of England finally took legal action against the continuing scandal of the Abode of Love at Spaxton that the *Free Press* had reported intermittently since its very first edition.

Three years after the death of Brother Henry James Prince in 1899, the Rev. John Hugh Smyth-Pigott and his wife moved to Spaxton, fleeing from Clapton in London, where Smyth-Pigott had outraged his congregation by claiming to be the Messiah, the Son of God.

Smyth-Pigott assumed control of the reclusive sect and took the scandal to a new height by his selection of a number of 'soul brides' from within the Abode's community, by whom he later fathered, out of wedlock, two children, named Glory and Power.

This was finally too much for the church to bear. In January 1909, a 'trial unparalleled in the history of the Ecclesiastical Courts'

Rev. Smyth-Pigott, in the centre front-row, with his 'official wife' to his left, and supporters of the Agapemone.

Smyth-Pigott late in life (surrounded by 'heavenly clouds').

opened at Wells Cathedral, where Smyth-Pigott was charged that, during the past five years, he had been guilty of 'immoral acts, immoral conduct and immoral habits'.

> 'Mr B.R. Vachell prosecuting said that, under the guise of so-called religion, they lived a life of blasphemy, fraud and immorality.
>  'Smyth-Pigott claimed to be the Messiah, the Son of God. He claimed that he and the members of this community having received the Sprit of God, were lifted above the ordinary code of morality.' January 23rd 1909.

Mr Vachel said that if the court found Smyth-Pigott guilty

> '...(he) should be cast from the Church of England and that they should not continue to allow this beautiful hamlet at Spaxton to be the centre of a particularly repulsive vice.'

Smyth-Pigott was indeed found guilty but was unrepentant, later saying

> 'We shall go on as if nothing had happened. We have nothing to do with the outside world, which does not understand our beliefs and so cannot enter into the truths of them.'

Seven weeks later, the self-proclaimed Messiah was formally defrocked.

> 'A ceremony, the like of which there is no record in the archives of the diocese of Bath & Wells, took place within the venerable walls of Wells Cathedral on Saturday afternoon when the notorious head of the Agapemone, or Abode of Love, at Spaxton, was publicly degraded from his sacred office of a priest with the Church of England.
>  The ceremony of unfrocking took place at a special service, which was conducted with peculiar solemnity and impressiveness.' March 13th 1909.

Smyth-Pigott died in 1927 and the sect gradually declined until the death of its last member in 1956.

## THE SPAXTON "ABODE OF LOVE."

### J. H. SMYTH PIGOTT UNFROCKED.

### SENTENCE PRONOUNCED IN WELLS CATHEDRAL.

A ceremony, the like of which there is no record in the archives of the diocesan registry for the diocese of Bath and Wells, took place within the venerable walls of Wells Cathedral on Saturday afternoon, when the notorious head of the Agapemone, or "Abode of Love," Spaxton, near Bridgwater, was publicly degraded from his sacred office of a priest of the Church of England. The ceremony of unfrocking took place at a special service, which was conducted with peculiar solemnity and impressiveness. The Bishop of the Diocese was surrounded by his ecclesiastical and lay officers, including the Ven. the Archdeacon of Wells (Archdeacon Brymer), the Chancellor of the Cathedral (Canon Scott Holmes), the Chancellor of the Diocese—or, to use his ecclesiastical designation, the Official Principal and Vicar General—the Worshipful Charles Edward Heley Chadwyck-Healey, C.B., K.C., the Principal of the Theological College (Preb. Goudge), the Bishop's Chaplain (Rev. J. M. Alcock) carrying the pastoral staff, Priest Vicars the Revs. H. J. Green and J. A. Hollis, the Bishop's Secretary (Mr. R. G. Harris), the Diocesan Registrar (Mr. R. Harris), Bishop Stirling and the Bishop of Exeter, who took part in the service. The service was fixed for 2.30, and took place in

# 1910s: Taking to the air, and to the trenches

ARLY IN June 1910, all activity in the village of Dunster came to a halt for the funeral of the one man who, perhaps, had done more than any other for the development and modernisation of that part of West Somerset, George Fownes Luttrell, who had died at the age of 83.

*'Never before perhaps has Dunster Church been filled with such a large congregation and hundreds were unable to gain admission. High and low, rich and poor met at the graveside with but one thought – to honour the memory of him who was gone – and the scene was very striking and impressive.' June 4th 1910.*

George Fownes Luttrell had been squire of the Dunster estates for forty-three years: the *Free Press* carried a tribute from the *Westminster Gazette*, acknowledging the scale of his contribution to the district, and in particular, to his investment in Minehead.

*'The disenfranchised borough, which was little more than a village when it entered into his possession, has under his fostering care grown into a flourishing seaside town, with public buildings and a pier. To him is also largely due the extension of the railway to that place.'*

The *Free Press* paid tribute to his refurbishment of the churches in Dunster, Minehead and East Quantoxhead and also of Dunster Castle itself, where Mr Luttrell had employed architect Anthony Salvin, who had earlier worked on Warwick and Windsor Castles.

*'In the course of the alterations, some of the oldest features of the Castle were opened up, and brought to light, the venerable gatehouse was renovated, with carriage road, with an easy gradient, was constructed round the tor on which the Castle stands.. Mr Luttrell had a great respect for old institutions and whatever he took in hand in this way was carried out in a broad and reverent spirit.'*

And in particular, Mr Luttrell rescued Cleeve Abbey from appalling neglect:

*'He no longer permitted the place to be used as farm buildings, cattle sheds and rick and manure yards, but thoroughly cleansed and restored existed buildings and arrested decay'.*

Two months after Mr Luttrell's death, his successor as squire, Alexander Fownes Luttrell opened one his father's great modernising projects, the first proper water supply for Minehead.

Dunster villagers gather for the funeral of George Fownes Luttrell.

In August 1910, the Countess of Lovelace opened one of the most beautiful, but short-lived, sporting facilities in the district – a new golf course on Porlock Marshes.

The 9-hole course was reached down a rutted Sparkhayes Lane, with a clubhouse in the village, opposite the Castle Hotel.

*'The links are situated on land bordering Porlock Bay and it is safe to say that no more beautiful, breezy and health-inspiring course could be found anywhere and its general position and contour lends itself entirely to this popular recreation.' August 27th 1910.*

*Even before the inundation, water was a hazard on the Porlock Golf Course.*

But sadly, this proximity to Porlock Bay proved the downfall of the short-lived course. Four months later, a violent storm in the Channel caused extensive damage along the West Somerset coastline; at Porlock, the pebble ridge was breached and the marshes inundated.

### PORLOCK GOLF CLUB.

President : The COUNTESS OF LOVELACE.
Vice-Presidents : Sir C. T. D. ACLAND, Bart.;
R. W. BLATHWAYT, Esq.
A GOOD SPORTING COURSE has been OPENED at Porlock. The temporary Club House is in the Village.
Subscription—Two guineas per annum ; Ladies, one guinea. No entrance fee for members joining before August 1st.
Non-playing Members at half fees.
For particulars apply to the Hon. Sec , the Rev. W. H. BOYNE BUNTING.

*'While the gale was at its worst, the sea made a large breach in the ridge, pouring an immense volume of water inland and rendering the low lying land between Bossington and the Weir a lake.*

*'Altogether, over a hundred acres were submerged, the water in some cases being several feet deep, including the golf course greens which (while still submerged) are feared to be covered with large deposits of stones etc which the waves carried with them'. December 24th 1910.*

Two weeks later, the marshes were still under water and the tons of pebbles and debris dumped on the golf course meant an early end to the project.

Responding to the needs of the Motor Age, the newly-tarred roads in the district were proving a bit too smooth for those who still travelled on horseback; there was a flurry of letters to the *Free Press*, from bruised and angry riders whose horses had fallen on the new surface...

*'...my misfortune was entirely due to the slippery asphalt street...the glazed surface of the Minehead streets is an abominable curse to all horse traffic...surely this evil will be remedied by rough grit being laid down before broken necks augment the large lists of accidents which have occurred. It seems such a needless cause for horses' knees being broken, not to mention one's own bones.' R. Corbett The Bank, Alcombe. October 22nd 1910.*

*'As a ratepayer and owner of horses, I consider myself entitled to use the roads without endangering myself or my horses...are the roads only intended for motorists and has the Urban Council no regard for horse owners generally? Personally I should as soon ride on ice as on the tarred roads...' Le Clement de Taintegnies, Cleveland, Minehead. October 22nd 1910.*

Sir Alexander Acland-Hood had again been returned to Parliament unopposed in the General Election of December 1910, and the following year he was elevated to the peerage, taking the title of Lord St Audries, after 19 years as the local MP.

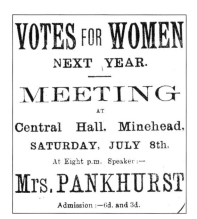

VOTES FOR WOMEN
NEXT YEAR.
—
MEETING
AT
Central Hall, Minehead,
SATURDAY, JULY 8th,
At Eight p.m. Speaker :—
Mrs. PANKHURST
Admission :—6d. and 3d.

The opportunity created by the by-election was seized upon by the most militant political movement of the time as a platform for their radical views; the Suffragettes flooded West Somerset to publicise their national campaign for a woman's right to vote.

In July 1911, the founder of the Suffragettes, Emmeline Pankhurst herself, visited Minehead. She addressed a massed rally held in stiflingly hot conditions in the Central Hall.

Speaking for over an hour, Mrs Pankhurst said that the prosperity of resorts like Minehead relied on the labour of women in the hotels and boarding houses.

*'They were performing the double duties of a citizen – they were both mothering their children and performing the tasks of bread-winning, which men, when they talked about votes for women, seemed to think were exclusively performed by men. Therefore, it was well for a town like Minehead to illustrate the cause for West Somerset.' July 15th 1911.*

She went on to say that there were 10,000 men in West Somerset who on July 21st would vote for a new MP…

*'…whether intelligent or stupid, sober or not sober, whether they were law-abiding or not…and there were also in the constituency probably 1,500 women qualified in the same way as the men, either as owners, householders or lodgers; and women similarly qualified around the country probably numbered about a million and a half.'*

Later, the Suffragettes staged an open air meeting in Wellington Square, advertised by chalking notices on the town pavements, and in the evening they staged a small gathering by the Yarn Market in Dunster.

But not all Suffragette rallies were so orderly; at Wiveliscombe a Suffragette speaker was jeered off her platform, and the following week, there were rowdy scenes in Watchet when both the Conservative and Liberal parties staged political rallies.

SUFFRAGETTES IN WEST SOMERSET.
—
MEETING AT MINEHEAD.
—
ADDRESSES BY MRS. PANKHURST AND MISS JOACHIM.
—
SUPPORT FOR THE UNIONIST CANDIDATE.
—

The entry into the political arena of some of the leading supporters of the movement for Women's Suffrage marks a new departure in West Somerset. The first to enter the field was the Women's Social and Political Union, of which Mrs. Pankhurst is the founder and hon. secretary, and having taken committee-rooms at Wellington they at once proceeded to extend their sphere of influence, Minehead being selected as a sub-centre from which operations will be directed over a considerable part of the division. Here the first indoor gathering at that end of the district was held on Saturday evening, when Mrs. Pankhurst was announced to speak on the subject of "Votes for Women." Although the temperature was then well over 70 in the shade, making it anything but enjoyable indoors, and in addition a charge was made for admission the Central Hall was well filled, the bulk of those present being ladies, many of whom, judging by the frequent applause, cordially supported the speakers' views. All the duties appertaining to the meeting were carried out by ladies, Mrs. Dove-Willcox and Miss Joachim, who are staying for the present at Minehead, supervising. On entering the room, Mrs. Pankhurst, who was accompanied by Miss Joachim, met with a very cordial reception.

ADDRESS FROM THE CHAIR.
Miss Joachim presided, and in explaining the objects of the Women's Social and Political Union said that as the promoters went about the

The Conservative candidate Col Dennis Boles, campaigning in Minehead in support of the Suffragette cause.

Two years later the new
cinema on Minehead's
seafront showed news
reels of the Suffragette
Mrs Davison throwing
herself in front of the
King's horse in the
Derby.

The Conservative candidate Colonel Dennis Boles, the Master of the West Somerset Foxhounds, supported the Suffragette cause, but the Liberal candidate Dudley Ward was still sitting on the fence.

Another national leader of the Suffragettes, Miss Annie Kenney, was addressing a small crowd on Watchet's Esplanade, standing on a lorry used by the Conservative campaign, when a noisy crowd of Liberal supporters, surrounded her, having just ended their own rally nearby.

'Miss Kenney preserved her sangfroid, in spite of persistent interruptions...
the climax was reached, however, when a local lady, apparently taking umbrage at the frequent interruptions, struck a young man across the face with a stick. Miss Kenney implored her friends to leave the crowd to her and not interfere.

'PC Penny promptly quelled the rising disturbance but strong resentment was manifested as to the assault...Had not the wheels of the lorry been chained, it is probable that the ladies would have been given a free ride, but on their perceiving that efforts were being made to shift the vehicle, they evacuated it and the crowd took possession.'
July 22nd 1911.

To the satisfaction of the Suffragettes, Col Boles won the seat for the Conservatives with a comfortable majority.

———————— ❖ ————————

The motor car was by now part of everyday life: August 1911 was to witness the first arrival into the district of the next miracle of the twentieth century – the aeroplane.

'Thursday night saw the advent of the first aeroplane in Minehead. It arrived swiftly, silently, and mysteriously, through the air and alighted as gracefully and lightly as a bird on the meadow near Mr Claridge's Sea-Front Cinema at about 7.30.

'Very few people were "in the know" and though there were hundreds on the Esplanade and the sands, only a very small number realised what was happening until the aeroplane swooped down from mid-air and skimmed along, like a gull, at the height of about thirty feet over the marshes to find its resting place.

'The 7.26 train was just going out of Minehead as the aeroplane flew over the marshes and the windows of the carriages were full of excited cheering people, the machine passing along close by them.'
August 19th 1911.

The intrepid airman was Mr B. C. Hucks, having flown the 25 miles from Burnham on Sea in just 22 minutes,

'...to give demonstrations in flying and to enlighten the Minehead visitors and residents as to the wonderful possibilities of the aeroplane.'

Mr Hucks, an airman with the Blackburn Aeroplane company, had just competed in the *Daily Mail* £10,000 Circuit of Britain race. He stayed in Minehead for six days, giving a series of exhibition flights in his 50 horsepower, seven cylinder Gnome aircraft, complete with map holder and, apparently, room for a Teddy Bear mascot.

Huge and enthusiastic crowds attended each day; bathers on the beach craned their necks to watch the plane soar overhead. But Mr Hucks gave just one complimentary passenger flight – to a black terrier pup belonging to one Mr Claude Forrest.

'The dog, it may be mentioned, behaved very well during the flight, but seemed quite indifferent to the great honour which many may have envied him.'

Mr Hucks and passenger landed on Dunster Lawns, causing the suspension of a polo match, and took tea in the Castle, before returning to the canvas hanger on Minehead sea front.

At the end of his stay, bad weather prevented Mr Hucks from flying to his next destination, so the plane was dismantled and packed onto a train for a rather low-key conclusion to the district's first experience of powered flight.

Huge crowds came to see the district's first ever plane, housed on the marshes on Minehead's sea front.

❖

While travel by train was commonplace, safety standards on the rail network were poor and each year hundreds were killed in train crashes. But new technology was being developed and a stretch of the old Mineral line beween Watchet and Washford was chosen to test a revolutionary new rail safety system, observed by the leading railway engineers from around the world, and hundreds of inquisitive locals alike.

An Australian engineer A.R. Angus had, in great secrecy, leased, relaid and straightened the track; he had bought two former GWR engines from the Swindon works and fitted them with his radical safety equipment, described as an 'electrical brain.'

The plan was to drive the two engines towards each other on the same track, and see if the new system automatically stopped them from a catastrophic collision. Huge crowds turned out to see what would happen, many of them clearly hoping for the worst.

Representatives from all the main British and colonial railway companies, reporters from the British and French newspapers, together with hundreds of spectators gathered on the slopes of Cleeve Hill one Friday morning in July, to watch the series of six runs.

One train set off from the Watchet end of the line, the other a mile away from the Washford end, steaming towards each other...

(Left) Local workmen had worked for six months to prepare the stretch of old Mineral line left abandoned two years earlier.

(Right) The tension grew, as the trains steamed towards each other.

> '...the engines raced towards what seemed certain destruction... There was tense excitement among the onlookers as the distance between the two trains swiftly lessened... each of the two trains automatically gave an emphatic intimation to stop by blowing its danger whistle...

*'As if determined to end their days, the two drivers ignored the warnings but the engines refused to be a party to depriving the Commonwealth of the service of such valued officers, and amid heartfelt applause from the assembled crowd, the trains repeated their warning and then automatically came to a stop, when a couple of hundred yards or more apart.' July 13th 1912.*

The *Free Press* reports that not everyone was impressed at this technological miracle averting the certain destruction of the trains. Some had come 'with the expectation of seeing something of a very "creepy" character'.

*'What I should like to see is a blooming good collision," opined a disappointed one, apparently quite indifferent to the fact that in the event of such a disaster, the whole aim and object of the inventor would have been defeated.'*

But for the railway engineers, the tests proved a huge success. They were repeated the following year, attracting one particular distinguished observer, who arrived at Watchet amidst great secrecy – none other than the Grand Duke Alexander Michaelovitch, uncle of the Czar of all the Russias, President of the Russian Imperial Council.

*There were tense moments as the new motor coaches competed for room on the old roads.*

TELEPHONE, 133.

HARDY & CO.'S
MOTOR
CHAR-A-BANC TRIPS
For the Month of JULY.

All Trips Start from WHITE BROS., 4, The Parade.
Luxurious Private Landaulette, also large and small Touring Cars for Hire at Taxi Prices.
Private Lock-ups for Gentlemen's Cars.

**DAILY—DUNSTER,**
Start 10.30 a.m.; Return Fare 1/-.

**PORLOCK & PORLOCK WEIR,**
Start 2.30 p.m.; Return Fare, 2/6.

**SELWORTHY & HORNER WOODS**
Start 2.30 p.m.; Return Fare, 2/-.

**MONDAY—LYNTON AND LYNMOUTH, AND DOONE VALLEY,**
Via Porlock, Watersmeet, Rockford, and Brendon. Allowing 2 hours at Doone Valley. Start 10.30 a.m.;

The summer of 1914 saw the arrival in the district of the charabanc – the first motorised coaches for taking visitors around the moors and villages. Given the increasing numbers of motor cars, and the continued prevalence of horse-drawn transport – including the stage coaches to Lynton – on the narrow roads, these charabancs were not universally welcomed.

The distinguished cartoonist F. Carruthers Gould, living at Upway at Porlock wrote to the *Free Press* to

'...draw attention to the danger and inconvenience caused to the users of the roads by the introduction of the huge motor char-a-bancs which have recently appeared.

'...if these monstrous machines are going to run over moorland roads, many, indeed most of them narrow and winding, in the summer months...there will be serious trouble and many accidents.' May 2nd 1914.

Salmet pulled out of one attempt to land before finally bumping down safely on the sands.

Three years after B.C. Hucks brought the first aeroplane to West Somerset, there was great excitement at the exploits of another pioneer aviator, a Frenchman called Henri Salmet who flew his Bleriot 90-horsepower monoplane to Minehead, completing the first flight over Exmoor. He was met by local dignitaries and the town's troop of Boy Scouts who immediately ran a protective cordon around his plane.

*'The airman, standing in his seat on the aeroplane, apologised to the crowd for his late arrival, and buffeting his arms vigorously he remarked that he was cold, very cold.' May 9th 1914.*

The town's boy scouts help guard Salmet's plane; the photographer, Alfred Vowles, leans on his bicycle.

The following day, M. Salmet – who was sponsored by the *Daily Mail* – gave exhibition flights, and as thanks to the Boy Scouts, offered a flight to the local Scoutmaster, Mr Murray Hill, who thus became, most likely, the first man from Minehead ever to fly.

After a flight out to sea, involving several steep turns, Mr Hill observed

*'...his flight to have been glorious but the wind at times was so terrific, he could scarcely hold his head up against it.'*

But M. Salmet's is best known for his inauspicious departure from Minehead. With another passenger on board, Mr H. van Trump of Taunton, he set a course for Weston-super-Mare, but there was great consternation among the watching crowds in Watchet when his plane was seen suddenly to lose height and ditch nose-first into the Channel.

Salmet prepares to take off; is this the ill-fated flight, with his passenger H. van Trump of Taunton on board?

*'It sent up a huge column of spray and steam, obliterating all traces of the machine and its occupants and for a few seconds it seems as if both had completely disappeared. A feeling of terror gripped many of those who had witnessed what seemed to be a dive to the death...*

*'...but the tension was momentarily relieved as presently the tail of the machine and gradually the heads and shoulders of two men appeared above the surface.' May 9th 1914.*

The tide was too low for the Watchet lifeboat to launch, so the crew commandeered a local shallow-draught 'hobble' boat and rowed after the stricken plane, which was now drifting down channel on the receding tide.

*'The boat's crew were working like Trojans, never once stopping for a breather...and when, with the swing of their bodies and regular dip of their oars...they eventually swung the boat round and sidled alongside the frame of the machine, a round of cheers sent their echoes across the water to the rescuers and the rescued.'*

Safely onshore, M. Salmet admitted that this was not the first time he had ended up in the sea, and thanked the Watchet lifeboatmen for their heroic efforts. Neither the aviator nor his passenger could swim.

❖

# SHOCKING OCCURRENCE AT PORLOCK.

## MAN FATALLY SHOT IN THE HIGHWAY.

### ASSAILANT ATTEMPTS SUICIDE.

#### COURAGEOUS CONSTABLE FRUSTRATES HIS EFFORTS AND SECURES HIM.

##### A YOUNG WOMAN ALSO WOUNDED.

To say that many of the residents of Porlock were thrown into a state bordering on panic is no exaggeration of the position there on Wednesday evening, when, soon after six o'clock, a report was circulated to the effect that a murder had been committed in Parson's-street. At first, save by those in the immediate vicinity, the tidings were largely discredited. Porlock, like other parts of West Somerset, has so long enjoyed immunity from serious crime that, in spite of what might happen elsewhere, the taking of life was totally unthinkable. Hence the temporary disinclination to credit the story, but rumour in this instance proved to be distressingly accurate and was confirmed by those who were eye-witnesses of a tragedy which has no parallel in the history of the village.

**SCENE OF THE CRIME.**

Abutting on the main road through Porlock

space the bystanders, who rapidly congregated from all quarters, were in far too terrified a state to take any definite action. Happily, it occurred to someone to summon the local police-constable, P.C. Greedy, who was then off duty, but fortunately still at home, in mufti. Without wasting any time over changing his clothes, and merely taking a pair of handcuffs with him, P.C. Greedy made for the scene with all speed, and as he emerged into Parson's-street another report of a gun was heard, causing several people to hastily decamp. On reaching Pugsley's house, he came upon Mrs. Pugsley assisting her husband indoors, whereupon she turned to him and said, " Look what he (Quartly) has done for my husband."

**A COURAGEOUS ACT.**

As there was plenty of help at hand for the injured man, the constable determined to first solve the mystery connected with the report

Henry Quartly (above) and Henry Pugsley (below).

In June 1914, shocking news caused the *Free Press* to rush out a special Saturday edition of the paper; news had broken of an horrific murder in Porlock.

On the Friday evening, Henry Quartly, a mason, aged 55, had lain in wait in Parsons Street for his neighbour Henry Pugsley, a fruiterer and fishmonger who was returning from his rounds on Exmoor, and cold-bloodedly shot him in the back with a double-barrelled shotgun.

The two neighbours had been in dispute for some time, and that same day, Quartly had been due at Dunster Petty Sessions facing charges of abusive behaviour.

On hearing the shots, the village's off-duty policeman, PC Greedy was summoned

*'Without wasting time over changing his clothes, and merely taking a pair of handcuffs with him, PC Greedy made for the scene with all speed... On reaching Pugsley's house, he came upon Mrs Pugsley assisting her husband indoors whereupon she turned to him and said "Look what he (Quartly) has done for my husband."' June 6th 1914.*

PC Greedy then crept quietly into the house where Quartly lived with his sister, and

*'...undeterred by the danger which threatened him, found Quartly in the semi-darkness of a back room with a gun to his head. PC Greedy flung himself at the man, disarmed him and held him until two other villagers arrived to restrain the struggling man.'*

Quartly was taken to Dunster police station and after passing through the local Magistrates court was sent to Exeter Gaol. At his full trial at Shepton Mallet in October, Quartly refused all legal advice, admitted the murder, saying

*'It has all been through his wife; she has been the cause of all this trouble; and it was her that began it and left her husband to bear the burden of it. I shot him; I must expect to be killed. I can die only once; I fear no foe'. October 24th 1914.*

# THE INQUEST.

## VERDICT OF 'WILFUL MURDER' AGAINST QUARTLY.

———

## VICTIM'S TERRIBLE INJURIES.

———

## RIGHT LUNG RIDDLED WITH SHOT.

———

## P.C. GREEDY COMMENDED.

The Inquest was held at the Victoria Reading-room, at two o'clock, on Friday afternoon, before Mr. D. S. Watson, deputy-coroner for the district. In view of the gravity of the hearing a jury of 15 was empanelled, viz., Messrs. T. Rawle (who was chosen foreman), F. W. Cape, S. J. Conner, H. Perkins, J. Ridler, W. Rook, E. K. Brown, J. and S. Cooksley, H. Arnold, R. W. Cox, T. Pearce, L. Burgess, R. Brown, and F. Arnold. Quartly was given an opportunity of attending, but declined to accept it, and Messrs. C. P. Clarke and F. W. Willmott watched the proceedings on his behalf. P.S. Chant acted as coroner's officer. Previous to viewing the body, the members of the jury formally visited the scene of the crime, which was already well known to them, and the coroner also made a similar inspection.

Quartly was sentenced to death: the execution at Shepton Mallet was conducted by Thomas Pierrepoint, one of the notorious family which provided the nation's hangmen for the first half of the twentieth century.

❖

Interrupted only by this terrible murder in Porlock, the summer of 1914 now seems the last season of innocent delight and distraction. A political crisis was unfolding in the Balkans; Europe was stumbling towards the nightmare destruction of the First World War. On August 4th, Britain finally declared war on Germany after the Kaiser's forces had invaded Belgium.

The young men of the West Somerset Yeomanry were called up for service: their war was to be different from any previously experienced, but they were optimistic.

*'(The WSY) now has the reputation of one of the best in the service. The old sabres and carbines have been discarded, and both in shooting and drill, the men have proved highly efficient with the new weapons.' August 8th 1914.*

The annual Territorial Army manoeuvres underway on North Hill were instantly disbanded, and the Worcester and Gloucester brigades boarded trains home ready for deployment.

# GREAT EUROPEAN WAR.

## AMAZING GERMAN AGGRESSION.

## ENGLAND AND GERMANY OPPOSED.

## POSITION OF THE RIVAL FORCES.

## DEMONSTRATIONS OF PATRIOTISM.

Three months before the start of the war, the WSY were training at their summer camp near Allerford.

The WSY training camp near Dulverton.

Visitors to the district abandoned their holidays dealing 'a mortal blow' to local tourism, and the opening meet of the Devon & Somerset Staghounds was cancelled for the first time in fifty years.

Horse dealers toured the district buying up horses for military service. At the West Somerset Foxhounds annual Puppy Show at Bishop's Lydeard

> '…an agent of Government was looking over the Master's horses and knew that sterner duties lay before them than those of the hunting field. Instead of careering over the pleasant fields of West Somerset to the sound of the huntsman's horn, they will be galloping in the seried ranks of cavalry answering the trumpeter's call to "charge."' August 8th 1914.

The tourist charabancs that, for a few summer months had seemed to some an annoyance, were commandeered for the war: Messrs Staddons and Messrs Hardy & Co offered their three motor coaches for service. Their seats were removed and, converted into motor lorries, they were taken to Bulford Camp on Salisbury Plain.

Before the month was out, Lord Kitchener was making a nationwide call for 100,000 volunteers, and a big recruitment rally was held in Wellington Square in Minehead, addressed in front of the Queen Anne statue by one of Lord Kitchener's own emisseries, Major Archer-Shee, MP:

These Williton volunteers were told to assemble at Taunton, 'but their ultimate destination was unknown.'

> '…a bigger assembly was probably never seen in the Square, the proceedings, especially when recruits began to come forward, being of the most enthusiastic character.' August 29th 1914.

Twenty-two men stepped forward – from Dunster and Timberscombe, as well as from Minehead.

> 'The greatest enthusiasm prevailed throughout the vast meeting, and there was much cheering as the volunteers, one after another, stepped upon the platform. The band played Rule Britannia and the crowd took up the chorus and later, the National Anthem was sung.'

Similar recruiting rallies were held later around the district.

Within a month of the declaration of war, the *Free Press* carried the first account of the heroism of a local soldier.

A Williton man, Lieutenant Corporal Herbert Besley was sent with the Somerset Light Infantry straight to Mons to confront

## LORD KITCHENER'S APPEAL FOR 100,000 MEN FOR THE REGULAR ARMY.

## A PUBLIC MEETING

IN SUPPORT OF THIS APPEAL WILL BE HELD

IN MINEHEAD

## On SATURDAY Next, 29th inst.

Time and Place of Meeting will be announced by poster and handbills as soon as possible.

## MASS MEETING IN THE SQUARE.

### Appeal by Major Archer-Shee, M.P.

#### RECRUITS COME FORWARD.

On Monday evening a mass meeting was held in Wellington Square, the purpose being to ask for recruits for the Army, and a bigger assembly was probably never seen in the Square, the proceedings, especially when recruits began to come forward, being of the most enthusiastic character. A platform had been erected near the Queen Anne statue, and the services of the Brotherhood Orchestra were again secured to brighten up the occasion with music, though, as a matter of fact, no stimulant of that kind proved to be necessary. Major Archer-Shee, M.P. for Finsbury Central, and of the 14th Reserve Regiment, was the recruiting officer. Among those who came on to the platform were Col. S. Grant, Col. Barrett, Lieut.-Col. Page-Henderson, Col. Wilson, Mr. and Mrs. F. Clifford, Mr. and Mrs. Blofeld, and others.

## HEROIC CONDUCT OF A WILLITON MAN.

### Gallant Attempt to Save a Wounded Comrade.

A most thrilling experience befel the only member of the Somerset Light Infantry, Herbert Besley, who is among the wounded from the front in the Bristol Royal Infirmary. He is a native of Williton, and before going to the war was a reservist in the Glamorgan County Police, and was stationed at Penarth, near Cardiff. When the Reserves were called up he joined his regiment speedily, and was promoted to the post of lance-corporal, and was sent to Mons, where he and his comrades—a splendid lot of fellows—arrived in the early morning of August 24th. Fighting was going on, and the regiment was placed at the extreme end of the British left flank, and was in the thick of the fray as early as four o'clock. The onslaught was tremendous. The enemy numbered ten to one of the British, and, although the German rifle firing was poor, their shells, well directed, fell like a hailstorm, and did great damage. The conflict lasted all day, until 5.30, when it lessened. The men remained in the trenches all night, and were set upon again early the next day (Tuesday, the 25th). The numbers were again overwhelming, and as the French had not come up the order was given to re-tire, and the movement was carried out in

the German onslaught, where, outnumbered by ten to one, they were forced to retreat from the overwhelming barrage of German shell fire.

*'The ground was covered with the killed and wounded men. Whilst making his way down the hill, Lieut-Corp. Besley came across an artillery man with a bad shell wound to the head. Despite the torrent of projectiles, he picked him up, threw him across his shoulders and ran as fast as he could, with his burden, his arms and accoutrements across his back. He had not gone far when a shell exploded near him, blew his wounded comrade to pieces, carried away his own knapsack and hurt him severely in the back.' September 5th 1914.*

L/C Besley was returned to Britain, and to the King Edward VII Memorial Hospital in Bristol for treatment.

The report of his heroism was an example of the powerful coverage of the First World War in the *Free Press* and in many local newspapers. There appears to have been little censorship of letters home, which were, in fact, considered useful for gathering support back home for the troops.

Families came to Williton Station to see their loved ones off to war.

---

Count Hochberg on the right, with his personal servant.

The *Free Press* was concerned to stifle some of the local 'war hysteria' that followed the declaration of war on Germany. This centred on Count Conrad Hochberg, a German national who had lived at Croydon Hall, near Rodhuish, for several years and whose activities were now the centre of fevered speculation in the national press.

'According to one imagination word-artist, the count was arrested at Dover, as a spy, when about to fly the country, but before his arrest, he wired to a manservant at Croydon Hall ordering him to blow up the premises.

'The unfaithful servant metaphorically blinked the other eye and carried the telegram to the police, who searched the premises and found 300 rifles, 7,000 gallons of petrol and plans for the coast and defences around Minehead.

'Another story was that a complete Marconi wireless installation had been in operation in Croydon Hall for some time.' August 15th 1914.

The *Free Press*, for once, did not mince its words; 'Such piffle is hardly worth contradicting....'

The paper reports that Count Hochberg had indeed returned to Germany – before the declaration of war – and that the subsequent police examination of Croydon Hall involved nothing more than commandeering four horses from his stables for use by the West Somerset Yeomany.

'That he has gone back to Germany was no more than a German gentleman in his position was bound in honour to do and we have no quarrel with the German people as a whole, but with the German government.'

## WILD REPORTS AS TO COUNT HOCHBERG.

### POLICE IN POSSESSION AT CROYDON HALL.

What has happened to Count Conrad Hochberg and to his West Somerset residence, Croydon Hall, has been the subject of much speculation and space in the newspapers, and the twentieth century understudies of Ananias have had a fine innings this week. According to one imaginative word-artist, the Count was arrested at Dover as a spy when about to fly the country, but before his arrest he wired to a man-servant at Croydon Hall ordering him to blow up the premises. The unfaithful servant metaphorically blinked the other eye and carried the telegram to the police, who searched the house and found 300 rifles, 7,000 gallons of petrol, and plans of the coast and defences round Minehead. Another story was that a complete Marconi wireless installation had been in operation at the Hall for some time. Such piffle as the above is hardly worth contradicting, and yet this and similar nonsense has been circulated far and wide. As we reported last week, two of the Count's draught horses were brought to Williton on Thursday in last week, when Mr. C. L. Hancock was purchasing horses for the Army Remount Department. P.S. Woolley then intervened, and would not allow a sale to take place, the horses going back to the Hall.

On Saturday afternoon, Mr. Hancock again visited Williton, this time purchasing horses for chargers. He was, as before, accompanied by Mr. W. M. Scott, F.R.C.V.S., of Bridgwater, and P.S. Morgan, of Bishops Lydeard. Sir Prior Godney, C.V.O., C.B. was also present. During the parade of horses, at about two p.m., four horses in charge of two grooms passed along from the Minehead road going in the direction of Taunton. Two-thirds of the company present knew them at once as the Count's horses, and this was stated. Sir Prior Godney, who is a county magistrate, accompanied by P.C. Harris, got into his motor-car and went after the horses, which were overtaken on Tower Hill, the grooms being asked to return with them to the Egremont Hotel, which they did.

During the afternoon, the authorities took another step, and Sir Prior Godney, accompanied by Superintendent Perry and P.S. Woolley, paid a visit to Croydon Hall, which is near Roadwater, and in the parish of Old Cleeve. A warrant was produced, and these persons were informed that all the horses

## TOBACCO FOR THE SOMERSET LIGHT INFANTRY.

### SCHEME WHEREBY "FREE PRESS" READERS CAN HELP.

A Contribution of 6d. sends 2ozs. of Tobacco and 30 Cigarettes to gladden the heart of a Somerset Soldier at the Front.

We confidently ask for the help of West Somerset for this deserving object.

**APPRECIATION OF HEROISM.**

In submitting to our readers a scheme in which they can send some cheer into the hearts of the men of the SOMERSET LIGHT INFANTRY at the Front we do so with the confidence that the support will be considerable and worthy of the hospitable neighbourhood in which we live. While men are fighting our battles on the Continent the least those who cannot enter the ranks can do is to show some appreciation of their heroism. All our readers, therefore will, we feel sure, look on the scheme...

**ARRANGEMENTS FOR DELIVERY.**

We have arranged with Messrs. Martins, Ltd., the well-known tobacconists, of Piccadilly, London, for the supply of Compressed Tobacco and "Kitchener" Cigarettes, issued from their bonded duty-free warehouses at a nominal charge, and the military authorities have undertaken to forward all gift packages in bulk free. They will be shipped in large cases under the care of the War Office. In this way the problem of sending single packages to individual soldiers is overcome, and our readers are...

The *Free Press*, like every local paper in the land, did everything possible to rally support for the district's young men at war. No campaign was more vocal, nor so well supported, as the appeal to send cigarettes to the soldiers.

'Ever since our Army landed in France, the cry from the trenches has been "Send us something to smoke" and it is our solemn duty to answer that cry.

'Just picture to yourself the conditions of every day trench life. The nerve- shattering crash of heavy artillery and the death-dealing shells screaming overhead. In the midst of this inferno, our brave lads stand up to their wrists in mud and water and return shot for shot with the Kaiser's hordes, not knowing who will be the next one to be struck down.

'Do our heroic Tommies complain? Never! All they say is 'send something to smoke'. To us at home it seems a paltry thing to ask in return for risking their lives for our country. But to Tommy it is the very opposite of paltry...' January 23rd 1915.

❖

The local MP, Colonel Dennis Boles was among those to receive tragic news from the war. His elder son Hastings was among the brave pioneers involved in aerial reconnaissance over the battlefields of France, having volunteered as an observer with the Royal Flying Corps.

'Very early on the morning of May 24th, he was engaged in making a recce over the German lines and he was shot from an enemy anti-aircraft gun. The shot struck him in the side of the forehead, and passed out at the back of his head. When the machine returned to its base, he was at once attended to by surgical staff…but he died later that day.' May 29th 1915.

His commanding officer wrote to Col Boles;

'He was never in any pain. We buried him this afternoon at Bailleul. His grave is a quiet place, overlooking green fields. He had endeared himself to us all so much.'

Many families, of course, had several loved ones fighting in the war. But the record of one Luxborough family brought thanks from the King himself.

'The attention of His Majesty the King, having been drawn to the fact that Mr and Mrs T. Greenslade, of Tarr Water , Luxborough, had five sons serving in the Army… the Keeper of the Privy Purse wrote "His Majesty much appreciates the spirit of patriotism which prompted this example, in one family of devotion and loyalty to their Sovereign and Empire."' June 5th 1915.

And the *Free Press* reported that since the Greenslade family received the King's letter, another – a sixth – son had joined up, 'fighting to free Europe from the curse of Kaiserdom.'

———————— ❖ ————————

The war was the occasion of the first visit to West Somerset in recent history by a serving British Monarch. King George V and Queen Mary had visited wounded troops in Bristol and were journeying to inspect the Naval Dockyards at Devonport. They were travelling on a special train…

> '…the latest word in comfort… "a miniature Windsor Castle on wheels"…with sleeping saloons for the King and Queen, a magnificent dining car, a writing salon, bathrooms etc…all the fittings of the royal salons are of silver…electric light is used throughout.' September 11th 1915.

But the Royal train needed to overnight en route at a quiet and safe location; the royal aides considered the goods sidings at Bishop's Lydeard station to be the perfect place.

There had been local gossip for some days, after the unusual suspension of all activity in the goods yard.

> 'Stripped of all rolling stock, it formed a very suitable bay for the reception of the Royal train, and, for the convenience of their Majesties and their retinue, gravel walks were laid down on either side of the track…and to add to the general air of tidiness, anything which might be deemed unsightly was hidden beneath new tarpaulins.'

It is said that even the stocks of coal were painted a more pleasing shade of white.

Supt W. Perry of Dunster was made responsible for the personal safety of the Royal visitors, aided by another 33 sergeants and constables, in uniform and plain clothes, forming an impenetrable cordon to any unauthorised person.

Everyone wanted the ideal vantage point from the bridge carrying the road over the railway line, but the police were determined to ensure no-one parked or stood there for any length of time.

> 'Motor driven vehicles of all descriptions, from the smart landaulette to the popular motor bike and sidecar, as well as a legion of cyclists, plus horse drawn charabancs, breaks, dog-carts etc…were constantly moved on by the police… in consonance with His Majesty's desire for privacy and up to a point, the crowd raised little demur, hoping by a continuous parade to and fro to be on the bridge at the moment of His Majesty's arrival.'

The Royal train arrived promptly at 6pm, drawn by two engines bearing the Royal Coat of Arms: the King's carriage was detached and gingerly shunted into the sidings. Their Majesties retired early, apparently enjoying an excellent night's rest, but in the morning rumours circulated that the Royal visitors were astir.

> 'Shortly before nine , their Majesties, who looked extremely well, left their apartment for a short promenade on the side of the track nearest the village, a favourite terrier accompanying them, before returning to the carriage.'

Before the train departed, village schoolchildren, accompanied by vicar (Rev. G. P. Whatley) were marshalled on the up platform and sang three verses of the National Anthem.

———————— ❖ ————————

While letters home from the front regularly appear in the *Free Press*, there are no factual reports of the action involving West Somerset units. After the war, the paper published extracts from Everard Wyrall's *The Somerset Light Infantry 1914-19*, which give some flavour of the sacrifices they made.

In the summer of 1916 West Somerset units were in action in the Battle of the Somme.

> 'Less than two months passed since beginning of the Somme battles, but already the battlefield has been sprinkled freely with the blood of gallant West Countrymen and if blood be the price of victory, the men of Somerset have already spilt it freely.
>
> 'Four men were dug out of the mud who had been unable to move for three days. When the Somersets were finally relieved in the trenches, some of them only got out by leaving their thigh boots behind.'

**Their Majesties spend a Night at Bishop's Lydeard.**

———

A PRIVATE VISIT.

THE LOCAL STATIONMASTER HONOURED.

A restful break in an otherwise arduous week was afforded their Majesties the King and Queen on Tuesday, the night being spent in the Royal train at Bishop's Lydeard station. Among local folk as well as passengers on the Minehead branch the activities of a large staff of workmen in the goods yard at Bishop's Lydeard had been a subject of conjecture for several days previously, the result being that a host of rumours, all inaccurate, were circulated throughout the district. The story which generally found credence was that the King was paying an official visit to Sandhill Park to inspect certain units of the forces now quartered there, but, as events proved, the presence of troops in the vicinity was a mere coincidence and had nothing whatever to do with their Majesties' visit, which was of a strictly private character, in accordance with their expressed wish. They simply came to Bishop's Lydeard to secure a night's rest and quietude, and admirable arrangements were made to ensure the comfort and privacy of the Royal guests during their brief stay. The extensive goods yard had undergone a

Snatched periods of leave home from the trenches were precious indeed. One Exford man was so eager to get home, he had no thought to change, getting off the train at Williton still caked in Flanders mud.

*'Many curious and sympathetic glances were given to a stalwart khaki-clad character striding up Long Street in Williton on Saturday afternoon. Spruce Tommies in khaki are familiar figures everywhere now, but this was no visitor from home depot. It was Private Walter Hayes of the 1st Somerset Light Infantry, home for a week's leave and on his way to Exford.*

*'With rifle on shoulder, great-coat and trousers heavily caked with clay, and with full active service kit, including gas helmet and respirator, he had come straight from the trenches on Thursday night'. November 27th 1915.*

Private Hayes was a full-time solider before the war, had fought in the Boer War and had completed 12 years with the Somersets.

---

In June 1917, Lord St Audries, died at the aged of 63. Formerly Sir 'Alec' Acland-Hood, as the local MP he had risen through the ranks of Parliament to become Chief Whip in Balfour's Government. The *Free Press* had written much about Lord St Audries' contribution to the district. On his death, the paper carried a long and affectionate obituary;

*'He had many striking gifts, the power of organisation, of clear thought, forceful expression and, on occasions, a sparkling and mordaunt humour. Beneath a somewhat brusque exterior he had a heart of gold. Any case of hardship or suffering was sure of a patient and sympathetic hearing.*

*'On the outbreak of war, he said that all had to make sacrifices for the nation's effort. "Alas" he said " some of us are too old to be taken; at all events, I am waiting until the authorities raise the age to 61. But if we cannot fight, we can all do something to help our country." ' June 9th 1917.*

A huge crowd attended the funeral at St Audries Church, held in fine weather, including many tenants and schoolchildren from the estate. Lord St Audries was buried in a coffin made by estate workers from oak from the grounds of Fairfield House, Stogursey.

A memorial service was later held at St Margaret's, Westminster.

## Death of Lord St. Audries of St. Audries.

Everyone in West Somerset will feel the death of Lord St. Audries as a real personal loss. As to the cause of his untimely death —he was not 64—we may put it down quite certainly to his zealous work for his country. His life was as truly given for King and country as any lost in fighting at the front. When the war broke out Lord St. Audries in a public speech delivered in the autumn of 1914, said, speaking of the necessity of personal sacrifice. " It is not a call to one class; it is a call to all classes. We have all made sacrifices, and I am afraid we must all make greater sacrifices in the future. Alas! some of us are too old to be taken; at all events at present. I am waiting until the authorities raise the age to 61." His audience laughed. " If we cannot fight, we can all do something to help our country," said he. That something, in Lord St. Audries' case, was all that he could do and the best that he could do, and he literally gave his life in the doing of it. About six weeks ago he broke down. Overwork was the cause. Some slight improvement in his condition encouraged the hope that he might pull through. But a serious relapse occurred on Sunday night, from which he never rallied, and on Monday night the end came at eight o'clock.

Lord St. Audries was born at St. Audries in September, 1853, and came of families fam-

---

By October 1917, units of the Somerset Light Infantry were fighting Turkish troops in the Holy Land, pushing through Gaza towards Jerusalem. Again, Everard Wyrall's accounts published later in the *Free Press* give some idea of their heroism.

*'The Turkish trenches were stiff with machine guns. . .the only way to success for the attackers was to dash at the enemy's trenches and get on with the bayonet as quick as possible. . .'*

The Somerset's also played a crucial role in capturing a strategic ridge overlooking Jerusalem itself.

*'They spent a bitterly cold night in the open, 3,000ft above sea level, wearing nothing but khaki-drill shorts and tunics, with no blanket or greatcoats…… the leading wave pressed on, reaching the foot of a rocky hill, faced by steep and almost unscaleable terraces which they endeavoured to climb.*

*'Three Lewis-gun sections managed to scale the terrace and small parties of men actually reached the village — perhaps the most gallant feat of arms through the fighting — but none of these brave fellows was seen again.'*

Jerusalem fell to the Allied forces in December 1917, and many of the Somersets were then redeployed to France to face the final German offensive in the spring of 1918.

---

❖

---

It is not until the early summer of 1918 that reports in the paper suggest an expected end of the war. There is no sense of victory, no excitement nor celebration, just a terrible weary relief that it might all soon be over.

Even when news of the German capitulation finally arrived, the mood in West Somerset's villages was mixed. The words of one Williton parish councillor best summed it up: the parish's vice-chairman Mr J. Wedlake observed,

> *'…that it was the happiest and yet the saddest day of his life. They were all extremely grateful that the terrible war was over.' November 16th 1918.*

There were, of course, celebrations; as usual, Watchet seems to have been the first to hear news of the Armistice, this time thanks to W.G. Penny and his wireless set. News that the guns on the Western Front had finally fallen silent was received with….

> *'…a feeling first of mute satisfaction, which gave way to one of joyous expression.'*

But there was no repeat of the unrestrained celebration with which Watchet had greeted the last great day of national release, the relief of Mafeking in the Boer War.

> *'Remembrance of all those who had gone out, never to return, forbad any such display — but, as if touched by a magician's wand, every bit of bunting that has long lain folded up suddenly made its appearance.' November 16th 1918.*

At Minehead, rumours of the ceasefire were only confirmed

> *'…when a telegram from the Western Morning News arrived at Cox's Library and within half an hour a perfect transformation of the streets took place.*
> *'The Red Cross hospital (for wounded soldiers) was a blaze of colour, bunting of all kinds and colours being called into requisition by the hospital soldiers.'*

Youngsters of the town led the street celebrations…

> *'…decked in all sorts of bunting, and carrying flags and preceded by a wounded solider in a highly-decorated wheelchair, they paraded the town singing and cheering.'*

---

❖

---

## END OF THE GREAT WAR.

### SURRENDER OF GERMANY.

### DRASTIC ARMISTICE TERMS ACCEPTED.

#### Cession of Ships, Guns, Submarines, and Aircraft.

### ALLIED PRISONERS TO BE RELEASED IMMEDIATELY.

The war ended at 11 o'clock on Monday. At 5 in the morning Germany's representatives signed the Allies' Armistice conditions, and six hours later hostilities ceased.

**THE ARMISTICE IN BRIEF.**

In accepting our terms Germany practically surrendered unconditionally. She undertakes to evacuate not only Belgium, Alsace-Lorraine, and Luxemburg, but also all the countries on the left bank of the Rhine, including the great cities of Coblenz, Dusseldorf, Cologne, Aix-la-Chapelle, and Treves. Allied and United States Armies will occupy this territory, which has a population of 6½ millions, and comprises the most important industrial districts of Germany, but the work of administration will remain in the hands of the local German authorities.

Anthems of the Allies, followed by the Old Hundredth. The great concourse stood silent and uncovered while this and other hymns were played. After the rendering of "Now thank we all our God," the King, showing signs of deep emotion, stepped forward to the front of the balcony, and said:

With you I rejoice, and thank God for the victories which the Allied arms have won, and brought hostilities to an end and peace within sight.

Vociferous cheering greeted the speech, and with a final bow to the crowd their Majesties passed again into the Palace. Still the crowd remained, singing patriotic songs, cheering and shouting in unison, "We want King George."

KING AND QUEEN DRIVE THROUGH STREETS.

At 3.30 their Majesties accompanied by

With most soldiers still away from home, 1918 ended with an historic general election, the first in which some women were allowed to vote and the first for the newly-created Bridgwater constituency.

Colonel R.A. Saunders had been MP for the past nine years and stood again as the Coalition candidate, an alliance of the Conservatives and most of the Liberal party; opposing him, for the first time, was the candidate for recently-formed Labour party, J. Plummer.

While this was known as the 'khaki election', the main interest was, of course, the female vote.

The newly-enfranchised female determination to vote was nowhere better demonstrated than the three Labour-supporting women from Washford who, in the absence of any party transport to take them to the Williton polling station, found a novel solution.

*'A pair of handtrucks were borrowed, made as comfortable as possible with cushions and on these, the two miles to Williton was accomplished, the 'passengers' and the 'team'— about a dozen in all — recording their votes.' December 21st 1918.*

Counting was delayed until the arrival of the votes of soldiers still overseas; Colonel Saunders won with a handsome majority, but Labour were delighted with the 5,771 votes they won, given the late entry of their candidate into the political fray.

❖

The Cook family treasured this photo of their son Jim; five other sons also served in the ranks.

At the end of 1920, the *Free Press* reported a poignant footnote to the Great War. A wreath of flowers had been laid near to the Tomb of the Unknown Soldier, unveiled only a few days earlier, in Westminster Abbey.

The card attached to the wreath read;

*'In loving remembrance of our darling Jim Cook, who answered his country's call at the early age of 13 years 10 months and laid his life down at 17 years of age. Ever remembered by Dad and Mam, brothers and sisters, at home and abroad.'*

The Dean of Westminster initially refused to divulge the identity of the family who had laid the wreath, but eventually they were tracked down to Carhampton.

And if the dedication on the card was true, then Jim Cook had seriously misled the recruiting officers, given that he was two years below the minimum age for joining the ranks, and in so doing, made him one of the youngest to have fought in the war.

It turned out that Jim Cook was the son of Mr and Mrs T. Cook, of The Bridge, Carhampton.

*'Three times, unknown to parents, he had volunteered for the army, only to be sent back, but in 1915, he patriotically 'made a mistake' over his age, the deception being favoured by his inches, and enlisted as a trooper in the West Somerset Yeomanry.'* November 20th 1920.

Jim Cook's short life was to end early in 1918, after the German spring offensive had been rebuffed. Jim left the front, looking to meet a friend before joining him on leave.

*'He had not gone far when he came under observation of an enemy sniper and a second or so later the heroic lad fell, his brain pierced by a bullet. In vain, his friend awaited his coming.'*

# 1920s: The Kilve Oilfield, and exotic visitors

### Arrival of H.M.S. Fox at Watchet.

#### AN INTERESTING SIGHT FOR VISITORS.

In full view of hundreds of spectators, H.M.S. Fox entered the pier heads on Sunday morning at 9.40, and a minute later she picked up the ground in the western part of the harbour and her last voyage ended. It had been uneventful, save that she narrowly missed her tide here. She left Chatham the previous Wednesday evening in charge of Captain W. Organ, with a local crew, and in tow of two powerful tugs, the Roumania and Hibernia. Starting a day and a half later than was intended, it was impossible to reach Watchet by the following Saturday, although the town was thronged with people in anticipation of her appearance. The fine weather early on Sunday morning encouraged them to try again, and this time they were rewarded with a most interesting sight, though at one stage it rather looked as if the Fox would have to wait outside until the evening. The ebb tide had already set in when she reached the harbour mouth, but Captain Organ determined to have a try and was eminently successful. Detaching one of the tugs, he took a curve to the eastward, and at the right moment gave the order for the tug to go full speed ahead. His time was well chosen, for in spite of her great length and beam, the Fox glided into the harbour as gracefully as a yacht, without "smelling" either pier or creating any thought of mishap. For a craft of such dimensions it was a most creditable performance. The Fox pulled up about 100 feet from the pier, and in the hope of receiving the assistance of the tugs for berthing her close to the pier the harbour-master (Mr. G. Hunt) asked the skippers to remain until the evening's tide. This they did, but help was only given by one of them, the Hibernia, which, by jamming her stem against the port quarter of the Fox slewed her round a bit, but she was not shifted from the berth she had scored out. Then, to the surprise of the harbour-master, the Roumania put to sea, and the Hibernia quickly followed suit, and as there was no motive power in the Fox to

AFTER THE terrible losses of the First World War, and the huge drain on the nation's resources, normal life was slow to pick up.

The port of Watchet had by now recovered from its own near destruction in the devastating storms of 1900 and 1903, but the war had cut off all bulk trade, in particular the import of wood pulp from Scandinavia for the paper mills.

The trade resumed in March 1920, when the Swedish vessel *Forshult* docked, with 740 tons of wood pulp on board, it was a big boost to the town's morale.

*'After being unfamiliar for four years, the ring of the winches aboard, mingled with the hum of the steam cranes ashore make very merry music…' March 20th 1920.*

But soon, bigger things were on the horizon, much bigger. A Cardiff-based company, Cardiff Marine Stores, was buying up obsolete wartime vessels and wanted a base for a new ship-breaking business. They were impressed with Watchet's rebuilt facilities, with nine acres of enclosed water, and so, in late July, the biggest vessel ever seen at Watchet, the 4,360 ton cruiser HMS *Fox*, was inched gingerly towards the harbour entrance, having been towed from Chatham by two tugs.

The tide had just turned, but Capt. Organ was already a day behind his schedule, so he decided to risk it and ease the massive vessel in.

*'Detaching one of the tugs, he took a curve to the eastward, and at the right moment, gave the order for the tug to go full speed ahead. His time was well chosen, for in spite of her great length and beam, the Fox glided into harbour as gracefully as a yacht, without "smelling" either pier or creating any thought of mishap.' July 24th 1920.*

The *Fox* settled 100ft away from the pier and, embarrassingly, all attempts to push her alongside the dock on the next tide failed. The tugs had to leave for their next assignment, and so there the mighty HMS *Fox* lay for a couple of weeks, stranded in the middle of the harbour, until the next neap tide allowed her to be winched to the west pier.

She was then thrown open to the public, who had followed the saga with great excitement, and latterly, some amusement.

HMS *Fox* had seen service in the Gulf, intercepting German arms being smuggled on board local Arab dhows, and also off east Africa.

Gerald Lysaght had bought Chapel Cleeve at the turn of the century.

The national papers had for the past decade been fascinated by the one of the great heroes of Antarctic exploration, Ernest Shackleton. Early in 1923, the *Free Press* reported how a West Somerset resident had helped launch Shackleton's career of exploration.

Gerald Lysaght had bought Chapel Cleeve at Old Cleeve with money made from the family's steelmaking business. He had met Shackleton at the turn of the century, when the explorer was but a humble fourth officer on a Union Castle passenger liner and able only to dream of future Antarctic adventures.

Lysaght was immediately won over by Shackleton's 'unusual character-power and determination' and helped fund his Antarctic ambitions.

He even served as crew for part of Shackleton's last voyage in 1921, sailing with the explorer from Plymouth to Madeira on the ill-fated *Quest* expedition. Later in the voyage, while the *Quest* was moored at South Georgia, Shackleton suffered a fatal heart attack, and was subsequently buried on the island.

But in February 1923, a little over a year after the death of his friend, Gerald Lysaght presented to a gathering at Watchet's school hall unique film footage entrusted to him by Shackleton before the *Quest* expedition, which showed the fate of the historic 1914 *Endurance* expedition to the South Pole.

'Probably none of those present had ever witnessed a more graphic or realistic series of pictures than those presented to their view on this occasion.

'From the time the Endurance *entered the ice floes until she was crushed like an egg shell in the pack ice, every incident of note was faithfully depicted...the film of the ship being gradually broken up including the simultaneous toppling over of her main and mizzen masts was, the lecturer claimed, one of the finest pieces of photography ever known.'* February 23rd 1923.

Lysaght went on to describe the life of the ship's crew on the ice floes, and the epic voyage to South Georgia.

'For 16 days, the heroic boat's crew fought their way through the most tempestuous storm-swept area of water in the world, their course being laid on a scrappy little chart torn from a book and with an ordinary boat's compass which they were unable to illuminate at night.'

The man who made those vital compass-bearings, the captain of the *Endurance*, Frank Worsley, visited Old Cleeve in 1928; that night in Watchet in 1923, the film of the *Endurance* was shown by James Dell, who had been Shackleton's electrician on the *Discovery* and the *Quest* expeditions and who later worked for Gerald Lysaght at Chapel Cleeve.

❖

Early examination of the oil shales at Kilve.

In April 1921, a few short paragraphs had appeared in the paper that raised hopes of a financial bonanza for West Somerset.

Dr Forbes Leslie, MD – 'an eminent geologist, whose fame is a household word in the petroleum world' – had spent the summer of 1920 at Kilve, prospecting the shales around the Old Priory and the adjoining coast.

Further test borings in 1923 were encouraging, particularly as the oil in the shale was reportedly low in sulphur, which had proved problematic with the country's only other oil deposits, at Kimmeridge in Dorset.

And not only oil; there was also said to be commercial potential in the shale residue – the limestone in the area was already well-known for its hydraulic qualities, having in the past helped make water-resistant cement for marine constructions such as the original Eddystone lighthouse off Plymouth Hoe.

September 1923 saw the death of one of the most remarkable men of West Somerset, Colonel Aubrey Nigel Henry Molyneux Herbert, of Pixton Park, Dulverton who died, aged only 43, in a London nursing home. In that short span, Herbert had lived an extraordinarily exciting and varied life: in its obituary, The *Times* described him as 'traveller, diplomatist, soldier and politician.'

*Aubrey Herbert was the only serving MP fighting on the front in the first months of the war.*

Aubrey Herbert was half-brother to the fifth Earl of Carnarvon, who had funded the excavations in the Valley of the Kings in Egypt that led to the discovery of the tomb of King Tutankhamun the previous year.

The Earl had died in Cairo just five months before his half-brother Aubrey, giving rise to reports of the curse of Tutankhamun. Similar rumours attended the early death of Aubrey Herbert.

From childhood, he had suffered from poor eyesight; educated at Eton and Oxford, he overcame his physical disabilities to enjoy an exotic life of travel and adventure. He started as a diplomat, first in Japan, before moving to Constantinople in 1904. For the next ten years he came to know all the leading players in the turbulent decline of the Ottoman Empire, before its demise in the ashes of the First World War.

During this time, the *Free Press* reports,

'...he travelled in Macedonia and Arabia...and made many friends, especially among the Albanians, who are, as a rule, inhospitable to wandering and uninvited strangers...' September 26th 1923.

But this close relationship with Albania only developed after Aubrey Herbert had first fought for the Turks against Albanian nationalists. He was captured as a prisoner of war, but apparently soon made friends with his captors. He brought his love for Albania back from the Balkans to Exmoor, as the *Free Press* reported;

'*He had a faithful Albanian servant Kazim, whom he once took to Pixton in full gheg finery and who greatly astonished the Somerset people by his habit of cutting the throats of birds at pheasant shoots, in accord with Mahomedan custom.*'

Herbert was a driving force behind Albania's new-found independence after the collapse of the Ottoman Empire and the new nation invited Aubrey Herbert to become their first king, but he declined; the throne was then offered to the former English cricket captain C.B. Fry, among others, before Albania decided to become a republic instead.

During the First World War, Aubrey Herbert fought with the Irish Guards, being wounded at the Battle of Mons, and by 1915 he was back in the diplomatic service where, after working with T.E. Lawrence, he ended up using his impeccable Turkish connections in helping negotiate the armistice with the defeated Turkish army.

Since 1911, Aubrey Herbert had been an independent Conservative MP for Yeovil, but came close to resigning his seat, because of his now total blindness, in 1922.

On his death, the *Daily Telegraph* wrote:

*Herbert had first won the South Somerset constituency for the Conservatives in December 1911.*

'*Aubrey Herbert is dead. It is almost incredible, this bright, generous, chivalrous spirit cut off in comparative youth; this man of restlessness, this untiring and inexhaustible globe trotter is now at rest.*'

Huge crowds attended the funeral at the Church of St Nicholas at Brushford, the coffin being borne on a farm cart, drawn by a single horse.

'*The Albanian minister laid at the graveside as 'a token of grateful affection from the Government and people of Albania' a great wreath of laurel and aurum lilies tied with ribbons of red and black, the colours of Albania.*' October 6th 1923.

The bold claims being made for the potential of the 'West Somerset Oilfield' had yet to be proved, so early in 1924, the advocates rolled out 'men of eminence' in support of their cause.

The editor of *Petroleum Times*, no less, visited Kilve and declared the discovery 'a remarkable one, possessing enormous potentialities.'

*'Mining costs will scarcely enter into serious consideration, since the deposits are in the form of cliffs on the shore, and thus blasting will immediately render huge quantities available for transport either to the retorts or by water.' February 23rd 1924.*

By the week, the claims became more and more extravagant. One 'expert', a Mr G. B. Cavendish, wrote that he believed the West Somerset Oilfield was more important than the oil fields recently discovered in the Middle East:

*'Properly handled, here is at all events something which should enable us to forget Mesopotamia oil until the last ounce of that nine thousand million tons of Somerset shale has been freed of its precious contents…one cannot doubt the vastness of the proposition …Somerset has indeed struck oil.' March 15th 1924.*

It was perhaps not a coincidence that such claims were being published shortly before the promoters of the scheme invited investors to back the scheme with their cash.

*'Slowly, but with increasing confidence on the part of the promoters, steps are being taken for the development of the local oilfield. The Pioneers of the undertaking – the Williton Syndicate Ltd. – are in fact quite sanguine as to its ultimate success. Delays and difficulties, common in the creation of any large industry, have been encountered but these have already been largely overcome.*

*'Offers on a very large scale have been received from certain sources, but from the first, the object of the Syndicate has been to interest West Country people in what may be termed their own industry.' March 29th 1924.*

## THE WEST SOMERSET OILFIELD.

### ITS VALUE BEYOND QUESTION.

In the current issue of "The World To-day," Mr. G. B. Cavendish concludes an interesting article under the heading of "Somerset Strikes Oil," with the following :—" Properly handled, here is at all events something which should enable us to forget Mesopotamia oil until the last ounce of that nine thousand million tons of Somerset shale has been freed of its precious contents. . . . It is once more, let me say, all very incredible, but one cannot doubt the vastness of the proposition, and if its commercial or mechanical handling enjoys the ability devoted to its scientific treatment to date, Somerset has indeed struck oil—and cement."

With reference to the value of the deposits, the claims originally made by Dr. Forbes Leslie have been confirmed and re-confirmed by other experts, and on this point the promoters have satisfied themselves beyond any question. There remains the financial side of the undertaking and its development, to which attention is now being closely directed, and we understand that the underwriting of the issue will be commenced in the course of the next week or ten days.

The oil retort, showing the array of pipe-work for condensing the oil vapour.

By May, there was at last some evidence to support these claims. The new company – called Shalime Ltd – fired up an experimental retort, 30ft high, just inland of Kilve Pill, to burn the shales, and then to distil and condense the vapour into the actual oil.

But a few weeks later, all activity had come to a halt. Some said the project had collapsed; the promoters said they had to stop because of storage problems.

*'The production of oil has been so great that the promoters had no further storage room available, the shed adjoining the retort being now well stocked.' August 16th 1924.*

But the retort had gone cold; it was never to be fired up again. All the dreams of untold wealth came to nothing.

There's no immediate explanation in the *Free Press* but it's clear that sensible financial backers were more keen to put their money into the real 'gushers' of the Middle East and the United States, rather than the uncertainties of Somerset shale.

❖

The noble sport of polo had been played in West Somerset for several decades, starting on the beach at Minehead, before moving to its first real home in the Porlock Vale at Allerford.

In 1909, the West Somerset Polo Club moved to the lawns beneath Dunster Castle, closer to the homes of players and their stables at Minehead. There was now a real post-war revival: in May 1923, the lawns had witnessed Winston Churchill scoring for the visiting Oxfordshire Yeomanry team (they lost 9-1 to West Somerset) and now there was a real determination to establish Dunster as one of the top polo venues in the country.

So there was huge excitement when in 1925 one of the top teams in the world came to West Somerset, and what colour and exoticism they brought to the district. The Maharajah of Jodhpur brought his Indian champions to England for the season, and their first tournament was to be at Dunster.

*'A great deal of local interest has been stirred this week by the arrival of the Jodhpur polo team, with their many beautiful ponies and their retinue of dusky-skinned attendants. When the special train bringing the first thirty five ponies and nearly fifty men drew in at Minehead station on Monday evening, there was a large crowd gathered to see them detrain.' March 21st 1925.*

The players stayed at the Metropole Hotel on the sea front at Minehead and the 'native servants' were billeted in lodgings around the town.

After a couple of weeks of acclimatisation, and exercising the ponies on Minehead's beach, the Maharajah himself arrived. Dunster Lawns was packed with spectators and their cars.

*'In his magnificent Rolls Royce, his highness and members of staff entered the ground having motored down from London and amid the respectful salaams of the Indian players and the syces (Sikh grooms), he walked onto the ground where he was immediately the centre of interest.*

*'His highness showed himself very ready to oblige the snap-shotters, those who sought to photograph him receiving genial encouragement and during the intervals between the chukkas, he invariably took a part in helping to tread down the turf.' May 9th 1925.*

And Minehead put on its own colourful display of local exuberance for their visitors, after the polo had ended, outside the Metropole.

*'During Saturday evening, a Hobby Horse display outside the hotel afforded considerable interest and amusement to the Maharajah and the other Jodhpur guests.'*

(Left) Dunster had become one of the premier polo venues in the country.

(Right) The Jodhpur players were always happy to oblige the 'snap-shotters.'

## JODHPUR POLO TEAM ARRIVE AT MINEHEAD.

### FIFTEEN THOUSAND POUNDS' WORTH OF PONIES.

### PROBABLE AUTUMN VISIT OF MAHARAJAH OF JODHPUR.

A great deal of local interest has been stirred by the arrival this week of the Jodhpur polo team, with their many beautiful ponies and their retinue of dusky-skinned attendants. When the special train bringing the first thirty-five ponies and nearly fifty men drew in at Minehead station on Monday evening, a large crowd was gathered outside to see them detrain. The remainder of the ponies, sixteen, and natives, arrived on Tuesday, and on Wednesday came the members of the team themselves. The second lot of ponies had been in England, at Fleet, near Aldershot, for some while before coming to Minehead. The first lot of thirty-five with the native grooms, disembarked in London on Monday morning from the s.s. Mendala, and came direct to Minehead. The ponies are quartered in various stables in the town, the natives are "billetted" at the Pier Hotel, and the players are at the Hotel Metropole. The fact that the team has come to Minehead for the early stage of its stay in England is due to the action of Lieut.-Col. Hewlett, of Crowcombe, who made the arrange-

Daily exercise for the ponies on Minehead beach.

Doniford became an important centre for gunnery practice.

The summer of 1925 also saw the start of another regular summer attraction to the district, although for some the appeal was quickly to wear off.

Engineers and construction workers arrived at Doniford to lay down the  infrastructure for a large semi-permanent tented village, to house the gunners and sappers of the No 1 Anti-Aircraft and Signals Company.

The terrifying aerial bombardments of the First World War proved the need for improved anti-aircraft defences and Doniford was chosen as the ideal location for training the nations' gunners, with its flat sea frontage, uninterrupted skies north over the channel and being close to the railhead at Watchet, for transporting troops and equipment.

The folk of Watchet couldn't wait to hear the first of the big 20 cwt, 3-inch calibre guns thunder into action. The big attraction was the night-time exercises, from ten at night until one in the morning, when the huge searchlights swept the night sky for the planes towing their target sleeves, before the guns went into action.

Huge crowds gathered along the Watchet coastline from sunset.

> 'As daylight faded, long shafts of light growing in intensity every minute shot up into the heavens from a score of points.
>
> 'From the coastline they represented a fiery crescent, with the batteries in a central position between the horns, and the spectators watched with keen interest the play of the searchlights as those in charge endeavoured to spot the plane circling overhead.' May 23rd 1925.

But many in Watchet soon tired of the constant bombardment of their lives; fishermen and bathers complained they were endangered by shrapnel falling outside the designated firing zones. But everyone appreciated it was all in the nation's interest, and the visiting squaddies brought welcome business to the town's shops and pubs.

Doniford was to stage annual summer exercises right through until the start of the Second World War (during which it was rumoured to be staging top secret experiments in radar) and the gunnery was only finally abandoned in February 1957.

Jack White.

Since the end of the war, Stogumber cricketer Jack White had taken more than a hundred wickets each season for Somerset, captained the side for the past two years, and was now playing a crucial role in England's notable 4-1 Ashes victory in Australia under the captaincy of Percy Chapman.

While never a headline strike bowler, Jack White played a crucial support role that laid the foundations for victory. The *Free Press* quotes an assessment from the grand old man of English cricket Sir P.F. 'Plum' Warner

> 'White has taken only one wicket for something like 220 runs in his last three innings in the Test matches, but he has got through an amount of labour that even Hercules might envy and his stamina and determination have kept one end going, thereby enabling his captain to keep Tate, Larwood and Geary fresh for each spell of bowling.' January 5th 1929.

The cricketer's Bible, *Wisden*, named White as one of their five cricketers of the year;

'In addition to possessing much power in spinning the ball and great command of length, White uses his brains as much as any bowler today...a most unselfish bowler, White will give the "star" bowlers the end they prefer while he keeps the batsmen unhappy at the other end.' March 15th 1929.

# MR. JACK WHITE'S HOMECOMING

## A RAPTUROUS WEST-COUNTRY WELCOME.

## CIVIC RECEPTION AND BANQUET AT TAUNTON.

### PRESENTATION FROM THE WORKPEOPLE.

Amid the acclaim of a host of admirers, Mr. Jack White on Monday covered the last stages of his homeward journey to Yarde Farm, Combe Florey, after his memorable trip to Australia with the M.C.C. cricket team. It proved to him a day that will long live in memory, and in the honours of which his wife and his father (Mr. T. L. White) deservedly shared. Their hearty co-operation by carrying on the farm and matters incidental to it alone made it possible for "Mr. Jack" to make the trip "down under"—a sacrifice which the sporting public were delighted to acknowledge.

Gratifying as were the civic reception and banquet at Taunton, perhaps the welcome which Mr. White received from his own workpeople was the happiest feature of the day. The little presentation then made to him and the note of sincerity which characterised the informal proceedings spoke eloquently of the happy relations which exist between master and man.

So it was no surprise that after the victorious England side had finally docked after their long sea voyage home, there was a rapturous welcome for Jack White when he finally got off the train at Taunton.

After a civic celebration, he was joined by his wife and three daughters and drove the last few miles to Yarde Farm, Combe Florey where – still an amateur player – Jack White earned his living. He was greeted with a huge reception by the farm workers, who had kept the farm going in his absence and, in particular, by his father, Mr T.L. White.

Despite all the accolades, Jack White was his usual unassuming self; he told the crowds,

'Naturally, he was very pleased to be back among his friends in Somerset. They had had a wonderful trip and he supposed a fairly successful one. That, he thought, was due not to any one individual member of the team but to the team spirit shown by every member of the side.' April 27th 1929.

He was presented with a tobacco pouch, subscribed to by the farm workers.

'Mr Fred Worth said that he had not the slightest doubt when Mr Jack went over the books, he would find everything very satisfactory. "You ought to be very proud that to think you have such a father who has kept the wheels going all the time you have been away," he said.'

❖

For the last few hunting seasons, reports critical of some of the local hunts had been appearing in the national papers. Many of them had been written by a young freelance reporter Edward Hemingway who had come to the district in the early 1920s. He had also upset the polo fraternity during the visit of the Maharajah of Jodhpur in 1925, when he was caught sneaking into a hospitality tent to eavesdrop on private conversations.

Things finally came to a head in October 1928, to the fascinated delight of both Fleet Street and readers of the *Free Press* alike, in a two-day sitting of the Dunster Magistrates Court. The *Free Press* rushed out a Special Edition to report the full details.

Hemingway had been commissioned by the *Morning Post*, a London paper with particular interest in the activities of the great and the good, to report on a grand Polo Club Ball being held at the Metropole Hotel on Minehead's sea front.

# IMPORTANT NOTICE.

## The Recent Minehead Sea-front "Ragging" Incident.

Arising out of the above, Summonses have been issued and will be heard at the Dunster Police-court on Monday next.

## A Special Edition

OF THE

## Minehead Advertiser & Visitors' List

Will be published as soon after the close of the case as possible, and will contain a **FULL REPORT** of the Magisterial proceedings.

It will be on Sale (Price One Penny) at Cox's Libraries, Minehead and Williton, and by all our Agents in the District.

Two hundred attended the ball, many of them in fancy dress. Hemingway had been observing the celebrations; at around 10.30pm, he was leaving to write up his story, when he was confronted by three burly male revellers in a bizarre collection of *outfits*.

One was dressed as a Dutch waitress, with a red and white striped skirt, a blue blouse and apron, and wearing a Dutch cap; this was Capt. George Fanshawe, a regimental officer with the Dragoon Guards. With him, dressed in a sparkling shirt, chintz blouse and fawn stockings was Capt. A.W.M.S. Pilkington, of the 16th Lancers; and the trio was completed by William Bailey, of 127 Piccadilly, London, dressed as a cowboy, with a cowboy hat and hunting horn.

Bailey – the cowboy – grabbed hold of Hemingway, shouting "You are the b****** who keeps writing about hunting. You are coming with us."

The three dragged Hemingway out of the Metropole and frogmarched him onto the seafront, Bailey blowing his hunting horn, followed by 30 or 40 other revellers.

At the sea wall, the high tide was just on the turn. The three lifted Hemingway by his arms and legs and swung him over the wall, shouting "Let's drown the b*******." Hemingway fell six or seven feet into the sea, struggled for a time in the waves before scrambling out, only to be thrown back in for a second time.

Eventually he swam further along the sea front, got to a telephone box, and summoned the police. After returning to the ball, Hemingway identified the culprits, and Fanshawe, Pilkington and Bailey were duly charged with committing grievous bodily harm and with unlawful assault.

The Sunday tabloid, the *Sunday Graphic* had in particular splashed Hemingway's assault across its pages, so when the case came to court, the press and public benches at Dunster were packed.

# Saturday's Proceedings.

## CHARGE OF CAUSING GRIEVOUS BODILY HARM DISMISSED.

## A DRAMATIC SURPRISE AFTER LUNCH.

## An Amicable Settlement Arrived At.

After two days of colourful evidence and cross-examination, the case came to a sudden and surprising conclusion when the prosecution agreed to drop all charges, the defendants apologised to Hemingway for what they called their unjustified actions and agreed to pay for the cleaning and repair of his clothing.

*'The defendants then shook hands with the complainant and the court as one rose.'* October 20th 1928.

In May 1929, both Milverton and Minehead celebrated the centenary of the death of a local man who...

*'...ranks among the immortals of science, ...a man of extraordinary abilities, whom Somerset may well feel proud to claim as one of her sons...commemorated in Westminster Abbey with a memorial medallion which attests that he was "alike eminent in every department of human learning."' May 11th 1929.*

Thomas Young was born in Milverton in June 1773 but spent his early years in Minehead where his mother Sarah (nee Davis) had lived.

*'Long before he reached his teens, he showed himself to be a prodigy of learning...in his fourteenth year he wrote a biography of himself in Latin... in which he claimed to have read at two, and by four had read the Bible twice.'*

In his teens, Thomas Young left Minehead for further education in Herefordshire, after which he was sent to London to work with his uncle Dr Richard Brocklesby, a close friend of Samuel Johnson. On his death, Dr Brocklesby left young Thomas a considerable bequest to continue his scientific studies, and by the age of 20, he had been elected a fellow of The Royal Society.

Thus comfortably established, this young West Somerset prodigy made significant scientific discoveries, especially relating to colour vision and colour blindness, but Thomas Young really made his name by helping to crack the code of the Rosetta Stone and in so doing, open a window onto the civilisation of Ancient Egypt.

The Rosetta Stone, a black basalt fragment, lay in the British Museum, the spoils of war, having been seized from the French who had discovered it in Egypt during Napoleon's expedition of 1798.

Until this time, no-one had managed to interpret the hieroglyph symbols found on Egyptian tombs and statues. But tantalisingly, the Rosetta Stone was divided into three sections of script – the top third carried a script in hieroglyphics, the middle section was the everyday language of ancient middle Egypt, and the bottom third, the script in Greek.

The Greek had been translated but the hieroglyphics remained a mystery.

*'It was not even known whether the signs stood for sounds, letters, words or pictures..the most learned Egyptian scholar had not the faintest inkling of their meaning. It was the writing of a vanished civilisation.' May 11th 1929.*

But it was Young who succeeded in furnishing a clue to the meaning. By 1814, after four years poring over the scripts, Young had identified the meaning of 90 characters and in 1819, he published an article in *Encyclopaedia Britannica* giving a hieroglyphic vocabulary of up to 200 names or words.

A French linguist Francois Champollion was also working on the script at same time and there is some dispute over who really can claim to have actually cracked the code, but Thomas Young's work was clearly a major contribution and he remained widely honoured for his work in France.

He died in Farnborough in Kent in 1829, 'a conspicuous example of the prophet who is without honour in his own country.'

Thomas Young.

# 1930s: Deaths on the moor, voting against Hitler

Searchers on foot combed the woods, combes, ponds, and iron-workings around Mollie's home.

Hunt supporters, farmers and grooms set off on horse-back to search either side of the Barle, as far as Challacombe.

IN SEPTEMBER 1929, Exmoor had been transfixed by the disappearance of a 16-year-old domestic servant called Mollie Phillips, who worked at Rooks Farm near Exford.

Described as a 'comely girl, 5ft 3ins tall and thick set, with a dark complexion with dark hair brown eyes', she had last been seen leaving Rooks Farm for an afternoon off, saying 'Don't worry about the chickens; I shall be back before dark.' No-one had seen her since.

Weeks of extensive searching, on foot and on horseback, failed to reveal a single clue. Mollie had apparently vanished from the face of the earth; her fate had become national news.

*'Every possible theory had been examined. Every foot of land almost – woods, combes, ponds, iron-workings etc – within a mile or two of the girl's home has been scoured by searchers and an extensive area of Exmoor has been covered without any result.' September 21st 1929.*

Then 18 months later, in April 1931, came a shocking discovery.

*'A sensation was caused throughout West Somerset and apparently through the rest of England during last weekend by the revelation that remains, which have subsequently been found to be those of a human being, had been discovered on Exmoor. To those fully acquainted with the mystery of Exmoor of eighteen months ago… the question at once came "Have they anything to do with Mollie Phillips?"' April 4th 1931.*

The inquest at Minehead left little room for doubt that the bones and clothing found on Codsend moor were indeed the remains of the unfortunate girl.

But how had she come to be there, and more importantly, how did she die? The location was a long way from Mollie's usual route, and the body showed no evidence of assault.

The pathologist, Dr Carter from Taunton, said;

*'I am of the opinion that the girl caught her foot on a stone by a bog and pitched forward, throwing out her arm to break her fall and that the cause of death was exposure, with the possibility of final drowning.' April 4th 1931.*

The inquest jury added to the sense of intrigue: the foreman said they returned a verdict of death by misadventure, but added that

*'…the jury were of the opinion that she was hurrying away in fright from some person or persons, who were not necessarily near her, and that she fell into the bog.'*

If this was the case, who was she hurrying away from? The story was clearly not yet over and it was given a dramatic new twist by the words uttered a few days later at Mollie Phillips' funeral. The rector conducting the service, the Rev. Courtenay Jenoure of Cutcombe, spoke just prior to interment.

*'He had just finished reading the lesson when he mounted the pulpit and under stress of some emotion said:*

*"In a very few minutes, we shall be putting in their last resting-place the remains of Mollie Phillips and I am quite certain of this, that 90 per cent of the population of this district believe this girl to have been foully murdered.*

*"A great many of us knew her and we know the place where the remains were found and yet we are asked to believe this feeble story which might well have been culled from the pages of some nursery library that this powerful young woman, who knew the moor well, carelessly ran into a bog which in all probability at that time of year did not exist, and quietly laid there and died without a struggle.*

*"We of this neighbourhood consider the verdict of the jury on Thursday last would have been a disgrace to a jury of twelve-year-old schoolboys."' April 11th 1931.*

This was scandalous; the dead girl's rector, at her funeral, crying foul murder. Fleet Street loved it, and chased it for all it was worth.

The case was even raised in the House of Commons, where the Home Secretary, Joseph Clynes, said he would consider ordering a fresh inquest if there was new information, and if Mollie's family requested it.

Just such a request for a fresh inquest did arrive, but it was soon exposed as a ploy by an unscrupulous reporter, and Mollie's mother, Mrs Henrietta Ford, put the sad matter to rest when she issued a clear and heartfelt request.

*'I have not given my consent for an application to be made for a fresh inquest. I do not wish for the case to be re-opened. I am quite satisfied with what has been done.*

*'The newspaper reporters have worried us a great deal and we have had to threaten them to keep them away. They have offered me money to give them particulars of my life.*

*'I do not see that anything else can be done in the matter and certainly I do not wish for the case to be re-opened. I cannot stand it.' May 16th 1931.*

'One of the best known and most romantic figures of Exmoor' died in May 1931. John Gourdie had been born in Perthshire in 1849 and was one of the tough breed of Scottish shepherds brought to Exmoor in the 1860s and 1870s by Frederick Knight to help establish on the moors his flocks of imported Cheviot sheep.

And John Gourdie had been in charge of the last remarkable drive of sheep, apparently all the way from Bristol.

The *Free Press* quotes the account given in C.S.Orwin's *The Reclamation of Exmoor Forest*;

'*Most of the sheep came by boat to Lynmouth, but the last large purchase of Cheviot ewes, which arrived on the Forest in 1871, was trucked so far as Bristol, and then driven by its kilted shepherd (John Gourdie) over the eighty miles of road to Simonsbath.*' May 23rd 1931.

(There may be some doubt about this: the re-issued *Reclamation of Exmoor Forest*, published in 1970, revises this to read '...trucked by rail as far as Williton and then driven over the thirty miles of road to Simonsbath.' Whichever, it must have been quite a sight.)

John Gourdie took over Wintershead Farm, Simonsbath in 1898...

'...which he farmed successfully ever since and from nothing, he came to build up a reputation which credits him with becoming one of the wealthiest, if not the wealthiest, farmer on Exmoor.'

Allegations of hunt cruelty had been increasing over recent years, and the anti-hunt campaigners were getting more organised. They were now even challenging the hunts in their own backyard; the traditional opening meet of the Devon & Somerset Staghounds at Cloutsham Ball in August 1931 turned into a pitch battle between the opposing factions.

The League for the Prohibition of Cruel Sports had reportedly offered free rail tickets for their supporters to travel from London; coaches took them as far as Webber's Post and waving banners

The opening meet of the D & S in 1930; the event always attracted big crowds.

Cloutsham Farm, below Dunkery, the start of each season's opening meet.

('Abolish the shameful sport of staghunting', 'Staghunting is not cricket.') the anti-hunt campaigners – most of the women – marched towards Cloutsham Farm.

A dense fog had settled over the moors and hunting was out of the question but huge crowds nevertheless packed the lanes and hillsides, sparked by rumours of the demonstration. Visibility was down to 50 yards. Tension was high.

# ANTI-STAGHUNTERS ASSAIL CLOUTSHAM.

## LIVELY SCENES AT OPENING MEET OF DEVON AND SOMERSET STAGHOUNDS.

## DEMONSTRATORS MAKE A FORCED RETREAT.

### HUNTING IMPOSSIBLE OWING TO DENSE FOG.

*'A farmer follower of the hunt did not improve matters by riding to and fro along the line of demonstrators cracking his whip and jostling them about. And with the crowd getting angrier in mood, the demonstrators were soon in the midst of a rough and tumble, with many of the supporters of hunting, women as well as men, coming into conflict with them.*

*'A woman it was – an Exmoor farmer's wife – who captured the first banner. Grabbing it from one of the ladies of the party – there was a bit of a tussle for possession – she tore it fiercely to tatters and amid the cheers of the crowd trod the fragments into the road.*

*'Others strove to gain possession of banners and in the midst of an excited mass, the demonstrators struggled helplessly. Their banners were all destroyed, the womens' umbrellas wrecked, the League literature ripped to fragments.' August 8th 1931.*

The police stepped into the melee and shepherded the demonstrators back down from Cloutsham, back to their coaches at Webber's Post.

While all this going on, back at Cloutsham Farm, the newly-formed British Field Sports Association had set up in an outbuilding and was enrolling new members; 200 signed up in three hours.

❖

Early in 1931, the BBC announced that it planned to build a new radio transmitter at Washford Cross, completing one of the last links in a national network that would provide two radio channels to the entire country. The new transmitter would broadcast to a radius of seventy miles and would replace the transmitter near Cardiff which provided the first radio service to West Somerset.

*The BBC Washford station was one of the last links in a new national network.*

But in June 1932, construction on the site halted after one of the two masts, by now forty feet high, suddenly keeled over and collapsed, while three men were working on it at varying heights. One engineer, from Huddersfield, was killed instantly, while a second died later from his injuries.

The inquest into the deaths heard allegations that the masts had not been adequately tethered with steel ropes, but the jury recorded verdicts of accidental death and cleared the chief engineer on the site of any culpability.

When the BBC station opened in May 1933, the 500ft high twin masts were thirty times as powerful as the old Cardiff transmitters.

## DISASTROUS ACCIDENT AT THE B.B.C. STATION.

### Lower Section of a Steel Mast Heels Over.

#### ONE MAN FATALLY INJURED : TWO OTHERS IN HOSPITAL.

A most regrettable accident, resulting in the subsequent death of one workman and severe injuries to two others, occurred on the site of the B.B.C. West Regional Transmitting Station now in course of erection at Washford Cross, early on Friday afternoon. The equipment of the station will include two steel masts, some 500ft. high, which will rest upon concrete bases standing some 6ft. above the ground. The masts, which are triangular in shape, will rest upon ball sockets, thus allowing them a certain amount of "give," according to the direction of the wind, and to each when completed there will be attached 21 wire stays.

Memories of the pioneering days of aviation, with those rickety planes landing at Minehead in the 1910s, were revived twenty years later with the arrival of the first air Carnival in the district. Five Avro biplanes based themselves on Dunster Marshes for a day and a huge crowd was held spell-bound by their daring antics.

*'It was impossible not to be thrilled by the spluttering rumble of the planes as the propellers were swung and by that deepening roar as the silver-grey shapes taxied swiftly over the turf to wing away into the blue…' August 29th 1931.*

One daring airman even walked on the wings.

*'Clambering out of the cockpit as the plane piloted by Mr Kingwell thundered overhead at nearly 100mph, Mr Hearn, Great Britain's premier exponent of this daring feat, made his way leisurely up and back the length of the wing. Thrill followed thrill. Mr Hearn proceeded to climb on the top of the wing and stood poised there, arms outstretched even when the machine banked quite sharply.'*

Sir Alan Cobham staged air pageants at Dunster and at Dulverton.

Two years later, Sir Alan Cobham brought his De Havilland Moths to Dunster, part of his nationwide campaign to 'Make skyways Britain's highways.' Sir Alan said he hoped the air pageant…

*'was a step towards the realisation of an aerodrome at Minehead. He believed that every aerodrome should be a municipal development.' September 9th 1933.*

In 1935 Minehead UDC, encouraged by further visits by Alan Cobham's air circus, pursued the aerodrome idea with some determination for a few months – Minehead was thought a convenient midpoint between between the established airports at Cardiff and Exmouth on the 'west coast' route but it soon became clear that improved ranges of the modern aircraft would make redundant such a stopping-off point and the idea was dropped.

## MINEHEAD'S FIRST AIR CARNIVAL.

### Large Crowd Watch Thrilling Display.

The shattering roar from the engines of five Avro machines was awakening the echoes at Lower Marsh Field, Sea Lane, Dunster, on Wednesday afternoon. It was Minehead's first air pageant, and a large crowd were held spellbound by the flying feats they witnessed. It was impossible not to be thrilled by the spluttering mumble of the 'planes as the propellors were swung, and by that deepening roar as the silver-grey shapes taxied swiftly over the turf to wing away into the blue.
So the event was an enormous success.

Tragedy came to the quiet country railway station at Dulverton early in 1935, tragedy mixed with the heroism of a local tailor's assistant.

The *Free Press* headline ran: TRIPLE TRAGEDY AT DULVERTON STATION
HEROIC DEAF MUTE AMONG THE KILLED.

Albert Tarr, aged 54, had worked for a local tailor in the town for 20 years; he was both deaf and dumb from birth. Mr Tarr was seated on the mainline platform, waiting for the train to East Anstey, where his aged mother lived. The train from Tiverton had just arrived on the Exe Valley Line, and passengers were, as usual, ignoring the footbridge further down the platform and were taking the short cut, walking along the trolley path across the main Devon & Somerset line (see photo opposite).

Straggling at the end of this line of passengers crossing the double set of rails was Mrs Ivy Thomas, aged 39, and her four-year-old son Robert. Mrs Thomas was struggling with her son and

a load of parcels. Tragically she was unaware that bearing down the gradient into the station, her view perhaps obscured by a nearby road bridge, was the 4.10 train steaming in from Barnstaple.

Albert Tarr, although unable to hear the approaching train, certainly saw it and appreciated the danger quicker than anyone else; he leapt onto the tracks to try to sweep Mrs Thomas and her son out of the path of the oncoming train, but it was too late.

A railway porter later told an inquest that he, too, saw Mrs Thomas stranded in the middle of the line.

*'I shouted "stand clear". I saw her turn around to try to grab the child. She hesitated for a second on the crossing, as if the boy had something in his hand. Then I saw Tarr rushing to Mrs Thomas as the engine approached.' January 12th 1935.*

It was clearly too late for the train driver to avert the tragedy.

*'As he obtained a view of the unfortunate woman and her son on the track, the train driver at once blew a warning blast and applied his brakes but the distance was too short to enable him to pull up in time and the engine striking the unfortunate trio, they were killed outright.'*

The inquest returned a verdict of death by misadventure, absolved the train driver of any blame and recommended action be taken to stop passengers using the trolley crossing, adding a tribute to the bravery of Mr Tarr.

*'We commend the presence of mind and gallant action of Mr Albert Tarr in his great effort to save the child and his mother, which cost him his life'.*

A few weeks later, a brass plaque was erected in East Anstey Church to perpetuate the memory of his bravery. It read

*'Although deaf and dumb, and so unable to raise an alarm, he threw himself in front of an approaching train in a heroic effort to save a mother and her child.' April 16th 1935.*

Dulverton Station in the 1950s, showing in the foreground the Barnstaple train passing over the trolley crossing where the accident happened. The Exe Valley platform is on the right.

In April 1933, Watchet mourned the loss, at the age of 93, of one it its most renowned and best-known residents, one who 'had worthily maintained its traditions with the sea.'

John Short was born in Swain St in March 1839, the son of a local boatman. His early experiences in local waters only whetted an appetite to go to 'deep water' and by his mid-teens he crewed on a Bristol schooner to Malta and Sicily and the warm blue waters of the Mediterranean.

But this was just the start of voyages that took him to India and the Far East, to South America and the 'grey-beards' of Cape Horn, and, in the 1860s, on board vessels running the blockades in the American Civil War, earning him back home the affectionate epithet, 'Yankee Jack.'

But it was the sea shanties he learned on these voyages, the songs sung to ease the hard labour of rigging heavy sails and winding the huge anchor capstans, that were to give Yankee Jack not just a place in local history but also in the nation's musical history.

In 1914, the Rev. Dr Allen Brockington of Carhampton introduced Yankee Jack to Cecil Sharp, who since 1903 had made several visits to Somerset collecting folk songs and shanties that were to help revive the English folk music tradition.

In his obituary of Yankee Jack, in *The Times*, Rev Brockington recalled that over three days in 1914, Jack had sung them more than 60 shanties, 13 of which had not previously been recorded.

When Cecil Sharp published some of these shanties later that year, he recalled the power of Yankee Jack's singing:

'Yankee Jack' Short had been introduced to Cecil Sharp in 1914 by Rev. Dr Allen Brockington of Carhampton, seen here at Watchet habour.

'He has the folk singer's tenacious memory and, although I am sure he does not know it, a very great musical ability of the uncultivated, unconscious order. His voice is rich, powerful and resonant, and yet so flexible that he can execute trills, turns and graces with a delicacy and a finish that would excite the envy of many a professional vocalist...

'It would be difficult to find a more experienced exponent of the art of chantey-singing and I account myself peculiarly fortunate in having made his acquaintance and winning his generous assistance.'

Jack's vitality lasted to the end. Celebrating his 90th birthday in 1929, the *Free Press* had written:

'With a steady stride and a slight roll typical of those who have spent so much time afloat, his gait is suggestive of a man many years younger.

'His whole appearance and splendidly preserved faculties – he can read, if required, without glasses – strengthen such an impression.' March 23rd 1929.

The Regal Cinema in Minehead, built on the site of the town's old tannery, opened in 1934.

**REGAL** PHONE 439

**OFFICIAL OPENING**
MONDAY, 2nd JULY

At 5 p.m.   Doors open 2.30.   OPENING CEREMONY will be performed by
C. F. LUTTRELL, Esq., J.P.
Supported by   CLIFFORD MOLLISON
The Famous British Film Star.

FIRST TIME ON ANY SCREEN OUTSIDE LONDON
THE FILM SUPREME

**EVERGREEN**
With JESSIE MATTHEWS

ADMISSION:—Circle, 1/10; Stalls, 1/6 and 1/-.   BOOK YOUR SEATS
Box Office Plan open at Queen's Hall, Monday next, at 10 a.m.
EVENING PERFORMANCE, 8 p.m.   DOORS OPEN 7.30

Comencing Tuesday, 3rd July,
Continuous Performance.

DAILY, from 2.30—10.30.   Doors open 2 p.m.
BOOKING PLAN OPEN FOR MONDAY, JULY 2nd, ONLY   Throughout the Season.
NO BOOKING FOR CONTINUOUS PERFORMANCE

While still bowling his tight line and length for Somerset, Jack White's best cricket was now behind him. But it did not take long for West Somerset to produce another cricketing star for the county. And the difference in their styles could hardly have been more dramatic.

Harold Gimblett, another farmer's son, lived at Blake's Farm, Bicknoller, and had been taken onto the county staff after precocious batting displays for Watchet.

Aged 22, he was given his county debut against Essex at Frome, a debut that is now part of local legend. A last-minute selection to the team, Gimblett missed his lift to Frome and so had to hitch-hike to the match.

He had been selected as much for his steady medium-pace bowling and fielding, and batting at number seven, little was expected as he marched to the crease with Somerset struggling at 107-6.

What followed placed Gimblett firmly in the county record books, and made him headline news around the country.

*'A hurricane century by Gimblett, their young professional who was making his debut, probably set up a time record...he would have reached his 100 in an hour but for the fact that he lost the bowling on 99. As it was, he reached his century in 63 minutes and batted for 80 minutes before being dismissed for 123.*

*'Gimblett reached 50 in 28 minutes, hitting nine fours and two sixes. His second 50 included six more fours and at the end of his innings, he had hit seventeen fours and three sixes.*

*'He times the ball beautifully and the number of boundary strokes indicates the power with which he hit the ball.*

*'Only those who saw Gimblett's innings know that it was not a case of beginner's luck. His display stamped him as a born player and Somerset appear to have made one of their best discoveries for a very long time.'* May 25th 1934.

It was indeed the fastest century of the season, and the national papers gave Gimblett the full tabloid treatment. When he returned to Bicknoller on the Sunday morning, a posse of Fleet Street reporters and photographers were camped outside Blake's Farm (two had even flown down by airplane), ready to see the new hero get back to his farm duties.

*'He was at first rather reluctant to undergo the ordeal of being "shot"...but in order not to disappoint his visitors, he consented to do so and was for the most part photographed while busy feeding pigs.'* May 25th 1934.

The *Morning Post* summed it up best;

*'England needs another big-hitter. Let us hope the Somerset farmer's boy will at last fill the gap. His amazing 100 at Frome enables us to hope that a second Jessop has appeared...a variety of shots was shown, so he is not just a slogger.'*

The following year, Gimblett played the first of his three matches for England, in a low-scoring match against India at Lords. Opening the batting, he made only 11 in the first innings as the Indian bowlers dismissed England for 132 but in the second innings, Gimblett scored an unbeaten 67 and effectively won the match for England.

The *Daily Telegraph* said Gimblett was not flawless

*'...but is a player of natural genius and any attempt to curb his development with counsels of caution would be most unwise.'*

By August, Gimblett had been dropped and his form fell away. His last test for England was again at Lords against the West Indies, in June 1939, when he opened the batting with Len Hutton in 1939, scoring a couple of modest 20s.

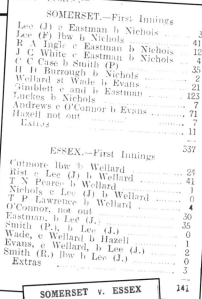

SOMERSET.—First Innings
Lee (J) c Eastman b Nichols ... 3
Lee (F) lbw b Nichols ... 41
R A Ingle c Eastman b Nichols ... 12
J C White c Eastman b Nichols ... 4
C C Case b Smith (P) ... 35
H D Burrough b Nichols ... 2
Wellard st Wade b Evans ... 21
Gimblett c and b Eastman ... 123
Luckes b Nichols ... 7
Andrews c O'Connor b Evans ... 71
Hazell not out ... 7
Extras ... 11
337

ESSEX.—First Innings
Cutmore lbw b Wellard ... 24
Rist c Lee (J) b Wellard ... 41
T N Pearce b Wellard ... 1
Nichols c Lee (J) b Wellard ... 0
T P Lawrence b Wellard ... 4
O'Connor, not out ... 30
Eastman, b Lee (J.) ... 35
Smith (P.), b Lee (J.) ... 0
Wade, c Wellard b Hazell ... 1
Evans, c Wellard, b Lee (J.) ... 2
Smith (R.) lbw b Lee (J.) ... 0
Extras ... 3
141

**SOMERSET v. ESSEX**

**Young Somerset Player's Remarkable Innings**

CENTURY ON FIRST APPEARANCE

HOME COUNTY'S FORTUNES RE-TRIEVED BY GIMBLETT AND ANDREWS

ESSEX COLLAPSE

DEFEATED BY AN INNINGS

Somerset had a great day at Frome on Saturday against Essex. A hurricane century by Gimblett, their young professional, who was making his debut; fireworks by Andrews, and then five cheap wickets by Wellard, assisted by Jack Lee, who made two grand slip catches.

CENTURY IN 63 MINUTES

Gimblett's amazing innings earned him the honour of being the second Somerset player to make a three-figure score on a first appearance, B. L. Bi good scored 116, not out, against Worcestershire, at Worcester in 1907. Gimblett is the first player to score a century for Somerset this season. His name was being discussed during the week-end by cricket enthusiasts in all parts of Somerset in particular, and in the cricket world in general. He is 22 years old and is the youngest son of Mr. and Mrs. Percy Gimblett, of Blakes Farm, Bicknoller.

Gimblett went in to bat against an acute attack which had brought about the downfall of six Somerset men for only 107 runs—an unenviable task for a youngster. He quickly dispelled any fears and showed himself to be a Hammond in the making.

*Harold Gimblett, towards the end of his career.*

# PREMIER'S RETURN FROM MUNICH

### "PEACE IN OUR TIME"

#### HISTORIC HOMECOMING

#### HUGE CROWDS GREET HIM WITH KING AND QUEEN ON BALCONY OF PALACE

A welcome home such as may never have greeted an English Premier before met Mr. Neville Chamberlain on arrival in London on Friday night from his mission of peace to the Dictators of Europe. Three great scenes without precedent in the history of statesmanship will live in London's memory :—

Mr. Chamberlain stepping from his 'plane at Heston and waving high above his head a type-written document. Plainly seen were the signatures " Neville Chamberlain," " Adolf Hitler."

Then the scene on the balcony of Buckingham Palace, when, in response to thunderous cheers, the Premier and Mrs. Chamberlain, with the King on one side of them and the Queen on the other, stepped out and waved to the throng.

And, finally, back home at No. 10. Downing-street, historic home of Britain's Premiers, when he leaned smiling and waving to an ecstatic multitude from a first-floor window. " I believe it is peace for our time. We thank you from the bottom of our hearts," said the Premier.

When the Premier arrived at Downing

Patrick Heathcoat-
Amory (top left)
and Vernon Bartlett
(top right).

In September 1938, Prime Minister Neville Chamberlain returned from his final meeting in Munich with Adolf Hitler, waving his infamous 'peace for our time' agreement. The following month, the voters of the Bridgwater constituency were called to the polls in a by-election, and in effect, to sit in judgement on Chamberlain's policy of appeasement.

This was to be the nation's only democratic vote on the Munich Agreement. For a brief moment, the whole country, the leaders of the European nations threatened by Germany, and even, it is said, Adolf Hitler himself in Berlin, awaited the result.

The Conservatives had chosen as their candidate a 26-year-old old Etonian barrister Mr Patrick Heathcoat-Amory, who loyally supported the stance taken by his party leader, Neville Chamberlain. The by-election was, he said,

> '…a great opportunity for the people to vindicate the Prime Minister and the great policy he had put forward…I would like to ask the constituency to support Neville Chamberlain in his efforts to preserve world peace.' October 29th 1938.

But both the Liberal and Labour parties opposed the Munich Agreement and they agreed to unite their efforts around an Independent Progressive candidate, Mr Vernon Bartlett, a veteran broadcaster and journalist, who had recently reported from Germany on Chamberlain's talks with Hitler for the *News Chronicle*.

Bartlett had long criticised the government's failure to address the German threat.

> 'If the government's foreign policy had been sound, there would have been no cause for Hitler to threaten war; and if the Government defence measures had been in an adequate state of preparedness, Hitler would not have dared the threaten war.' October 29th 1939.

# PROGRESSIVE CANDIDATE BEGINS HIS CAMPAIGN

#### FIRST MEETINGS HELD AT THIS END OF THE DIVISION

#### CONDEMNATION OF GOVERNMENT'S "WEAK AND VACILLATING FOREIGN POLICY"

#### "WE HAVE DRIFTED AWAY FROM PRINCIPLES"

SUPPORTERS of the Independent Progressive candidate, Mr. Vernon Bartlett, and others as well in the western corner of the division crowded to hear him when he opened his campaign last Saturday with meetings at Porlock and Minehead. " I am fighting this campaign exclusively on foreign affairs," he stated, and in the course of his speech—it was on similar lines at both meetings—he strongly condemned the foreign policy of the National Government as weak and vacillating. " Time after time," he said, " we give way and every time we give way war comes nearer home." Our present position was the consequence, he declared, of drifting away from the principles of international law and decency.

Vernon Bartlett launched his election campaign at the Village Hall in Porlock, before holding a big rally in Minehead. Later, at meetings in Bicknoller, Williton and Watchet, he repeated his message that the 'the eyes of this country are on this election' and that international papers were going to follow developments in West Somerset..

> '…because this election is a test of whether we are going to change our policy, to get more rigour into it or whether we are going to drift along in the same old way.' November 5th 1938.

For the Conservatives, Mr Heathcoat-Amory accused Vernon Bartlett of wanting to interfere in every part of the world,

*"I think you either have to negotiate or else you have to fight. While there was peace, there was still hope and however much they might dislike the internal government and foreign policy of another country, they should never on that account refuse to try to negotiate." November 5th 1938.*

Both candidates criss-crossed the constituency, broadcasting their messages from loud-speaker vans and encouraging the voters to have their say at the ballot box.

Come election day, November 17th 1938, the result was on a knife-edge; huge numbers had turned out to vote, parading their party colours – the traditional Tory blue, and yellow and mauve for Bartlett's Independent Progressives.

The following day, crowds gathered outside Bridgwater Town Hall for the declaration. At the last election, the Conservatives had won a massive 10,000 majority. But this was a by-election like no other. What did the voters of West Somerset really think about Chamberlain's policy of appeasing Hitler's Germany? Did they support this, or did they think the nation should confront Hitler head on?

Counting began at 9.30 in the morning; by 12.30 a tannoy announcement stated that no result was yet forthcoming. Finally at 2.55pm, the High Sheriff of Somerset, Sir Archibald Langman, made his declaration.

Vernon Bartlett had won by an astonishing majority of 2,332 votes, creating one of the greatest upsets in recent political history. Turnout had been more than 82 per cent – a record for the constituency – giving Bartlett and his anti-appeasement platform a convincing mandate.

Wearing his trademark bow-tie, Bartlett had to wait at the microphone for some time before he could speak 'owing to the cheering, interjected with some booing.' After thanking officials he said;

Vernon Bartlett.

*'I consider that the citizens of Bridgwater division have achieved something like a political miracle. The fact that over 82 per cent of the electorate voted shows how alive people are to the dangers of the present Government foreign policy.' November 26th 1938.*

He later told press reporters

*'I quite deliberately accepted the offer to fight in an agricultural constituency where, I was told, the chances were practically nil. I have been most encouraged by the way in which, even in the most remote villages, audiences have listened to and discussed questions of foreign policy.'*

Bartlett then embarked on a victory tour of the constituency in a convoy of 40 cars decked out in yellow and mauve, preceded by loud-speaker van.

Wellington Square in Minehead was packed with supporters surging forward to shake his hand. Later in Watchet he was carried shoulder-high to a platform on the Esplanade where he told a crowd of some 500 supporters..

*'...the whole of the world was interested in the way they were fighting for freedom of speech and for standing up to the dictators and he rather thought they might send a telegram to Hitler.'*

——————— ❖ ———————

For the first few months of 1939, it looked like Bartlett may have overstated the German threat, but any doubts were dispelled when in March 1939, German troops marched into the Czech capital Prague.

The country prepared for war. Locally, this meant continuing to recruit and train Air Raid Precaution teams, building air raid shelters, supplying gas masks and training the public how to use them, and most importantly, planning how to accommodate the thousands of evacuees that would flood into the district from London and the other urban centres in the south east most vulnerable to German air attack.

## A.R.P.

THE following are URGENTLY WANTED :—

12 LADIES as AMBULANCE DRIVERS for MINEHEAD.

16 MEN for FIRST-AID WORK at the MINEHEAD HOSPITAL.

16 MEN for FIRST-AID WORK at First-Aid Post, at SWIMMING POOL, MINEHEAD.

These men need not necessarily have training in First-aid.

Apply at once to

A.R.P. OFFICE, MINEHEAD.

## TELEVISION COMES TO MINEHEAD

### LOCAL RADIO FIRM'S ASTOUNDING SUCCESS

### GOOD PICTURES RECEIVED ON EXPERIMENTAL APPARATUS

A local firm of radio engineers, Messrs Wade and Steel, of Friday-street, have succeeded, after months of experiment, in bringing television to Minehead. Their first pictures were received a few days ago—in time, at any rate, for a part of the Cup Final at Wembley to be seen—and since then they had excellent reception of the outside broadcast given from Victoria Palace last Monday night, when " Me and My Girl," featuring Lupino Lane, was televised. Television has thus reached its farthest point west in the British Isles, for hitherto there has been no reception beyond Taunton.

At the invitation of Messrs. Wade and Steel a " Free Press " representative was this week privileged to view the first television received at Minehead. The experiments have been conducted in a bedroom at Mr. W. F. Steel's private residence in Lower King George-road—which probably explains to residents in the vicinity the meaning of the aerial, 38 feet high and of unusual design, which he has erected in his back garden. Here some very excellent and clear pictures, which, by the way, are built up by a spot of light no bigger than a pin's head, were received of Thursday morning's programme from Alexandra Palace, estimated to be over 150 miles distant. The distance is the circumstance which, in fact, emphasises the astounding success the experiment has attained, for it must be remembered that the few manufacturers of television sets do not guarantee reception outside the service area, which is at present limited to between 30 and 50 miles from the station at Alexandra Palace and, indeed, are loath to supply them outside this radius.

In the midst of reporting the preparations for war, the *Free Press* in May 1939 carried a short article, hidden away, reporting a significant technological miracle.

'A local firm of radio engineers Messrs Wade and Steel of Friday Street have succeeded, after months of experiment, in bringing television to Minehead. Their first pictures were received a few days ago – in time for part of the Cup Final at Wembley to be seen.

'The experiments have been conducted in a bedroom at Mr Steel's residence in Lower King George Road – which probably explains to residents in the vicinity the meaning of the aerial 38ft high and of unusual design which he has erected in his back garden.' May 6th 1939.

This was an extraordinary technical achievement, as the BBC, starting in 1936, was broadcasting a television service to only a few thousand receivers within a fifty-mile radius of the transmitter at Alexandra Palace.

The *Free Press* reporter was invited to witness the new wonder.

'Pictures, just over two inches by a little more than by three inches in size, are projected through a tube-like arrangement onto a screen at the other end. Once the apparatus is adjusted, it is possible to sit back comfortably and enjoy the programme.'

But poor signal strength meant Messrs Wade and Steel planned even an bigger 50ft high aerial;

'One result of this should be to eliminate interference caused by passing cars, which is indicated by smudginess of a temporary nature across the picture.

'As yet sound is not being received with the television but the partners anticipate no problem in arranging this item.'

❖

Over the summer, the anti-aircraft training at Doniford intensified. By now they were targeting not fabric sleeves towed behind Fairy Fawn planes but the radio-controlled 'Queen Bee' planes, launched from the gunnery by catapult mechanisms.

In August, the London Territorials were being put through their paces, observed by visiting London MPs and civic dignitaries, whose citizens would soon rely on the skill of these gunners during the Blitz.

Gunnery practice intensified in the summer of 1939.

The 'Queen Bee' targets were steered by radio operators on the ground.

## CRISIS EFFECTS IN WEST SOMERSET

### Many Visitors Cut their Holidays Short

#### HOUSE AGENTS OVERWHELMED WITH INQUIRIES FROM DANGER AREAS

A.R.P. AND NATIONAL SERVICE ACTIVITIES

ISSUE OF GAS RESP...

## GREAT BRITAIN AT WAR

### THE KING'S MESSAGE TO THE EMPIRE

#### FIGHTING TO SAVE WORLD FROM BONDAGE OF FEAR

PREMIER SETS UP WAR CABINET

Mr. Churchill First Lord: Post for Mr. Eden

Friday, September 1st was the date for the 101st Dunster Show; it should have been the best so far, the weather was glorious and the cattle entries were the best on record.

But it went down as the day that war became inevitable. The *Free Press* report of Dunster Show 1939 starts not with the usual highlights from the cattle or sheep classes, or the best of the show-jumping but with two sombre paragraphs.

> 'Held in Dunster Lawns, under the darkening shadows of the war clouds breaking over Europe...striking evidence of the anxiety that lay heavy on everyone's mind was afforded when, from a loud-speaker van on the ground, the one o'clock news bulletin announced that Poland was at grips with the German invaders.
>
> 'Judging was suspended, the band ceased to play, everything stopped temporarily, while all ears were intent on catching the fateful news.' September 9th 1939.

Friday September 1st was also the day the first wave of evacuees arrived in West Somerset. Despite months of meticulous planning, the huge task of moving one and a half million children and adults away from danger overwhelmed the authorities in London. In particular, mistakes made in arranging the destination of the trains led to huge headaches at the receiving end.

In West Somerset, these destinations were the railway stations at Minehead and Watchet, for evacuees staying in those towns, and at Williton and Dulverton, where local volunteers processed evacuees to be billeted in their respective rural areas.

Things went wrong from the very first train, which pulled into Watchet at a quarter to four that Friday afternoon. It carried some 800 children from London, packed into 12 carriages, which meant the train was too long for the platform.

It transpired that half of the 800 children were in fact, destined for Minehead, but in the rush to leave Paddington, no arrangements had been made for sorting out who was destined for which town, so the reception committee at Watchet had to select who was to stay and who was to move on to Minehead, there and then on the station platform.

> 'This proved a difficult and trying task for those in charge, who had to make selections here and there from the various compartments...many among the spectators could not refrain from shedding a tear at the pathetic sight of small children carrying their hand luggage, and, ready for instant use, their gas respirators.
>
> 'Many of the children were looking very tired after a journey which started at 8 o'clock that morning, while saddened faces told of the wrench occasioned by their having to leave home.' September 9th 1939.

Women and children headed to Minehead beach each day to fill sandbags for the defence of key buildings in the town.

Volunteers outside the Regal Cinema allocated the evacuees to their billets in homes around Minehead.

# MINEHEAD'S "SECOND SEASON"

## Nearly a Thousand Evacuees Billeted in the Town

### CHILDREN AND MOTHERS FROM THE EAST END

Nearly a thousand evacuees from London—unaccompanied children, mothers with babies and youngsters of tender years, expectant mothers, and blind people—are now billeted in Minehead and Alcombe. Between 800 and 900 of them are from the East End and another hundred or so consist of children from a big day-school at Streatham. Special trains brought the East End contingents last Friday and Sunday; the others came by road. The local organisation that had been set up to deal with the reception of the evacuees, to feed them after arrival, and to distribute them to their many billets —an organisation almost wholly voluntary—functioned splendidly, especially considering the brief notice given of the evacuation, and, though difficulties of one sort and another were encountered in distributing the arrivals to billets. " the town on the whole," was the view of the Chief Evacuation Reception Officer (Mr. A. G. Mansfield), "can congratulate itself on the way in which people rose to the occasion."

### FIRST DAY'S ARRIVALS

Local people and visitors gathered on Friday afternoon in large numbers in the G.W.R. station yard and the vicinity to witness the arrival of the first trainload, which was expected about 4 o'clock, with some 400 school-children from East and West Ham, accompanied only by teachers and helpers. There was one secondary school contingent from West Ham but otherwise

Williton Station received two trainloads in three days, stretching local volunteers to the full.

This well-known photo typifies the plight of the evacuees, with her gas mask and luggage label, detailing her name and destination.

By the time the 400 children reached Minehead, they were grateful for the warm reception that awaited them.

*'Drooping with fatigue of the journey and the heat — most had left their homes at 8.30 that morning — the little ones, whose ages ranged from just over five years to 14, were very glad of the tea which awaited them...and many of them were lively as they waited for their turn to come for allocation to their particular billets.*

*'But by the time they got to their billets, the novelty and excitement had worn off for a great number of children and many a homesick youngster wept himself or herself to sleep that night.'* September 9th 1939.

For months, the evacuation reception teams at Williton had laid meticulous plans to accommodate up to 2,000 schoolchildren and helpers among the families of the rural district.

So they were staggered to discover that when their first train pulled in at around 3.30pm on Saturday September 2nd, on board were not the schoolchildren they had planned for but around 700 mothers and toddlers and some expectant mothers.

A completely new billeting plan had to be hastily arranged through a series of frantic phone calls.

*'The detraining was speedily accomplished and the station yard was thronged... Most of the evacuated mothers and children were from the poorer districts of London and the majority had been about since the small hours. Travel-stained and weary, clutching their bags and the few things they had been able to bring with them, they huddled into their sections.*

*'Rain added to the discomfort. Mothers already overloaded with bags were issued with 48 hour iron rations and the bigger the families, the more there was to carry. There were mothers with seven or eight children. They toiled with their children, many of them wailing, but generally speaking there was a spirit of gratitude among the evacuees of what the local people were doing for them.'* September 9th 1939.

It was not until late into the evening that the station yard was cleared of the last evacuee. It later transpired that an official in London had been confused by the local Somerset place names; the evacuees who had arrived that afternoon had been intended for Wellington, not Williton.

There was similar confusion two days later, when another train arrived at Williton long after dark, packed with more than 700 exhausted mothers and toddlers from the Paddington and Putney areas.

That same day, Monday September 4th, the train carrying 750 evacuees destined for the Exmoor area finally arrived at Dulverton five hours late, again in pitch darkness, delayed because of air raid alerts in the capital.

*'Owing to an alarm in London, many of the women had had to leave with their aprons still on, and it seemed to be the case that, on their way to the station, they grabbed whatever children they could lay their hands on, in order to take them to safety...*

*'Rations for the ensuing 48 hours were issued on the platform — in many cases, it was found that these had disappeared by the following morning.*

*'Some of the evacuees appeared to be dissatisfied with their lot by Wednesday morning, and in spite of advice given to them that they should not return to the areas from which they had been evacuated, two or three parties returned to London.' September 9th 1939.*

It quickly became evident that it had been a mistake expecting Londoners to settle easily into the isolation of Exmoor towns and villages. This trickle of evacuees returning to their homes soon turned into a flood; by the third week, of the 691 mothers and toddlers received at Dulverton, 100 mothers had gone home, taking with them 144 children.

*'Our evacuees are going back fast. They are not used, as they say, to country life which they find too quiet for them and they have been really miserable here. With the cold snaps coming in, and the necessity for fires, some of them have indicated that they do not like coal and woodfires, but are used to gas.' September 23rd 1939.*

By the end of October, 400 evacuees had left the Dulverton district, and there was a similar exodus back home from other towns in the area.

## WILLITON TWICE "INVADED"

### Rural District Parishes take in 1,847 Mothers and Children

#### UNACCOMPANIED CHILDREN ONLY EXPECTED

#### LAST-MINUTE REVISION OF BILLETING PLANS

#### GREAT DIFFICULTIES SURMOUNTED

Williton, as the local Government centre for the large rural district to which it gives its name, was the "hub" of intricate reception arrangements over the week-end in connection with the Government Evacuation Scheme. Unparalleled scenes were witnessed at the railway station and the reception depots prior to the network of billeting, extending to nearly thirty parishes in the rural district. The stress of times of emergency fell with full force on the responsible body at Williton on Saturday and Monday, and the efforts of the local Reception Committee and their many helpers are beyond praise; they handled a great task with the utmost patience and understanding, labouring under many difficulties. They were harassing days, as those who saw anything at all of the conditions at the reception depots can testify. Apprised that in the Williton rural area 1,966 evacuees would be billeted, the Evacuation Committee appointed by the District Council have been at work for months on the arrangements, including the general survey, visits to householders, appointment of parish billeting officers, formation of reception committees, and the co-operation of a

Minehead and West Somerset Hospital was one of the key buildings protected against possible air attacks.

# 1940s: Junkers, Eisenhower and a gift to the nation

FIVE MONTHS into the war, and already the strain of housing so many evacuees was starting to tell; the families who had been the first to take in the Londoners now felt it was time other households did their bit.

There were also complaints that the allowances given for housing the evacuees were hopelessly inadequate.

There were few reports from the war itself. One of the first authentic accounts came from a survivor of the retreat from the beaches of Dunkirk. Sapper Ivor Dyer of Minehead described in a letter home how he had been stuck in an ambulance on the Normandy beaches, when they were attacked by a German fighter.

> 'Those of us who were badly hit managed to get to our naval units. I did about 50 yards with a gammy leg to a drifter and was then taken on board a destroyer. All the time Fritz was machine-gunning us in the water. When I come home, I will tell you a story that will make you feel proud to belong to a race which can take a licking against fearful odds.' June 8th 1940.

In July came news of the first local men held prisoners of war by the Germans.

> 'The announcement on German radio last week that Private Wilfred Beer of Channel View, Watchet, was a prisoner of war has since been confirmed by the receipt from him of a postcard from the camp at Stalag,

The *Glen Avon* was one of the White Funnel fleet rushed to Dunkirk to take the Expeditionary Force off the beaches. She didn't survive the war.

*where he is interned. Having mentioned that he is "all right," the writer adds that he would be glad of "some fags, chocolate and a cake", and steps to comply as far as possible with his request were at once taken.' July 27th 1940.*

Back home, the Ministry of Supply was asking local authorities to gather all possible supplies of metal for the war effort. Minehead UDC voted to remove railings from around Blenheim Gardens.

By September 1940, the *Free Press* carried its first reports of air raids on the South West, but all details were removed by the censors.

But the following month, the censor was quite happy for the paper to report full details of how a German Junkers 88 reconnaissance bomber, with a crew of four, had been shot down on the beach at West Porlock, after a dogfight over the Bristol Channel with a Spitfire.

*'The last few minutes of the raider, as it battled vainly with the British fighter, gave a spectacle that was witnessed by hundreds of people in West Somerset. Bursts of gunfire caused shoppers to look skywards, while others who were indoors just as incautiously rushed into the open to see what was happening.*

*'In one centre, it was observed that the fighter was hard on the heels of the bomber, while two other fighters, some distance in arrears, apparently leaving the 'quarry' to the leading machine.*

*'After two quick bursts of machine gun fire had been heard, the raider was seen to wobble and go into a shallow dive.*

*'The crash of the raider on moorland seemed to be imminent but, in fact, it travelled several more miles before coming to rest. Before it was given the coup de grace, it flew very low over a ploughed field in which a number of farm workers were engaged, with its rear gun still barking back at the fighter.*

*'The workmen had to duck or otherwise take cover; "bullets were flying down all around us" said one of them "and we were actually in danger of being shot." Three miles further on, it came to rest on the beach.' October 5th 1940.*

Three of the crew survived but the rear gunner had been killed. A resident of Porlock Weir told a *Free Press* reporter:

*'The Germans were very quiet and were not in the least arrogant... The pilot, a fine figure of a man and about 45 years old, was given the "Thumbs up" sign by one of those who came into contact with him, the sign being accompanied by the word "Spitfire."*

*"The German immediately turned his thumbs down and replied with a smile, "Spitfire too good."' October 5th 1940.*

The three German airmen were taken to Minehead police station for questioning. The fourth member of the crew was buried at Porlock the following day with military honours. The coffin carried a swastika.

It had been intended to give the wreckage of the Junkers to the Minehead County School, for the benefit of the Air Cadets, so there was dismay that everything useful was 'wantonly stripped' from the plane, as soon as the military guard was lifted.

(Left) The Minehead harbour gun emplacement; the old pier had to be demolished as it apparently obstructed the gun's line of fire down channel.

(Right) The Junkers J88 reconnaissance plane brought down in September 1940, while heading for Birkenhead.

The pilot, Herr Helmut Ackenhausen (centre), and his crew were held overnight at Dunster police station, after interrogation at Minehead.

A month later, there was a local disaster so huge that it could not be covered up by the censors; but the authorities were quick to rule out enemy action. Late at night, in total blackout, the driver of a Penzance-bound express train misread local signalling at Norton Fitzwarren and the train, packed with 900 civilians and military personnel returning from leave, plunged off the rails. Twenty-seven passengers were killed, and many more injured.

The landlord of the nearby Railway Inn helped to organise a human chain to guide the survivors, in pitch blackness, across the railway lines; the servicemen became stretcher bearers, ripping out carriage doors and broken woodwork for stretchers.

The passengers praised the servicemen:

*'The train did not seem to be travelling very fast but suddenly there was a terrific jolt which threw people from their seats. We could hear the sound of crumpling metal and the coach tilted over to its side with the corridor above us. For a time we could not open the door to the corridor but one or two tough fellows managed to open the window and we clambered out.' November 9th 1940.*

One of those servicemen was Jack Hurley, a reporter on the *Free Press*, who later became editor of the paper.

The winter of 1940-41 saw the devastating German aerial Blitz on British cities and industrial bases. Local fire crews regularly scrambled to help fight the destructive firestorms in Exeter and Bristol but nothing compared to the raid on Bristol on the night of November 17th 1940, a Sunday night when many were at church.

*'The raiders, flying singly, arrived almost continuously and were fiercely challenged by anti-aircraft batteries. They started to come over soon after dark and the first hint the city had that this was to be a night of trial came from the clean white light of the parachute flares drifting gently over the city.*

*'Before long, it was another kind of illumination that lit up the city. High explosive and incendiary bombs rained down and started fires in scores of places. Thudding bombs and the crash of anti-aircraft guns provided the accompaniment to the tortured scene.' November 23rd 1940.*

Fire crews from Williton, Watchet, Minehead and Dulverton all rushed into this nightmare world.

*'Police, firemen, ambulance parties and ARP wardens worked liked heroes and heroines while the bombs were falling and parts of shell cases were clanging and thudding all around them. Through the terrific crashes of the barrage, the throb of the fire pumps and the angry roar of the flames, there could be heard always the hum of the planes overhead and every now and then the whistle of a bomb as it fell. . .*

Minehead's main air shelters were erected in the centre of The Parade; here, the Home Guard and ARP crews are put through their paces.

The Minehead brigade set off in a breakdown lorry towing a heavy trailer pump but tragically, in the midst of this air-raid, driving through the blacked out streets of Bristol, they collided with stationary vehicle. One man, Mr Dovell, a married man who worked in Minehead's Lloyds Bank, died of his injuries. Others were injured, but the survivors joined the other crews, fighting the fires through the night and into the morning.

It was not until early afternoon that the West Somerset crews dragged themselves home, having been away for 19 hours.

## SPECIAL TRAIN FOR RABBITS ONLY

By the end of 1940, the Great Western Railway was operating a new service 'believed to be unique in railway circles.' Each weekday evening, a train left Barnstaple for Taunton, stopping at half a dozen stations on the way, to collect extra wagons or crates - filled with rabbits. Exmoor was doing its bit to help the nation's food supplies, and the arrival of the trains was quite an attraction. Dulverton and Wiveliscombe were particularly productive centres

*'Here some evenings there may be seen as much as three tons of "bunnies" crowded into a large covered van and packed together almost as tightly as the proverbial sardine...'* November 23rd 1940.

A full train pulling into Taunton might carry anything from 16 to 20 tons of rabbits on a single evening, to be taken to cities for sale next morning.

By early summer 1941, the war was entering a new phase. Hitler turned his attentions to Russia, the worst of the Blitz was passed and rumbling into West Somerset came the first tank divisions, for training manoeuvres on the hills and moorlands of Exmoor.

But, of course, we only read about this long after the war is over. The first units to arrive were the Home Counties Armoured Divisions, comprising regiments from Essex and Suffolk. The first tanks seen rumbling from Minehead railway station, up onto North Hill were the massive 38-ton Churchills and the lighter more manoeuvrable Valentines.

A light railway was laid out on North Hill between East Myne and Ennerscombe and the gunners blasted away at targets moving along these tracks.

*'While the North Hill was being used for this purpose, the greater part of it was of course "verboten" to civilians but occasionally, the local Home Guard companies were privileged to go up on the training ground and watch operations.'* November 15th 1958.

After the United States joined the war in December 1941, American and Canadian tank units started to arrive in the district for training, in preparation for the invasion of Europe in 1944.

One of Exmoor's most famous sons, Ernest Bevin, born in Winsford, was made Minister of Labour in 1940, called on by Churchill to mobilise the civilian wartime workforce. After the war, he was made Foreign Secretary, playing a crucial role in shaping post-war Europe.

———— ❖ ————

As Jack Hurley wrote, in his excellent *Exmoor in Wartime*, the middle years of the war, 1942 and 1943 were perhaps the most trying and the most tiring. At home, rationing – introduced in early 1940 – was even tighter; the government appealed for collections of anything that might be salvaged for the war effort – paper, metal, bones, rags; the farmers complained that there weren't enough workers left to bring in the harvest; and there was little good news from the war itself.

Since the start of the war, church bells had been silent, but in November 1942, the bells rang throughout the land in celebration of General Montgomery's victory at the Battle of El Alamein in Egypt.

## West Somerset Sportsman's Battle Honours

### M.C. FOR MAJOR E. W. WORRALL

### RALLIED HIS MEN WITH A HUNTING HORN

Mr. and Mrs. Harold Worrall, of Smokeham Farm, Bagborough, on the southern side of the Quantock Hills, had a message of good cheer on Christmas Eve. It was in the form of a cablegram from their elder son, Major Edward (Teddy) W. Worrall, Durham Light Infantry, to the effect that he was well and had been awarded the Military Cross. Of this gratifying award the world at large learnt through the B.B.C. on Wednesday night, and more particulars were available the following day in messages from war correspondents appearing in the Press.

### TALLY HO! CALL RALLIED TROOPS

One of the most graphic descriptions of the incident which led up to the award was that given by T. E. A. Healy, of the "Daily Mirror." Cabling from Cairo he stated :—

This is the story of a gallant gentleman who could only have been an Englishman. It is the story of a fox-hunting Major who, in the thick of a tank battle, rallied his men by

A few weeks later, the *Free Press* reprinted an article from the *Daily Mirror* celebrating the role of a Quantock man whose exploits at El Alamein had stirred the nation's imagination.

The report told of the heroic actions of Major Edward Worall, of Smokeham Farm, Bagborough, serving with the Durham Light Infantry, who before the war had hunted with the Quantock Staghounds (though doubtless he may have also hunted foxes, as the *Mirror* clearly preferred).

*'This is the story of a gallant gentleman who could only have been an Englishman. It is the story of a fox-hunting major who, in the thick of a tank battle, rallied his men by sounding "Tally Ho" on a hunting horn.*

*'The battle was raging fiercely. Across the desert swirled thick clouds of yellow dust. Enemy tanks were doing their best to make hell for the Durham Light Infantry. It was one of those tense moments that call for some inspired gesture.*

*'Major Worrall, blew his hunting horn…the weary men of the DLI pricked up their ears…there was a strange sound in the air, a musical note you could hear above the din of guns.*

*'They rallied, and like hounds on a hunt, they charged. With them went the Major, still blowing "Tally Ho!" The hunt was brief and ended with a kill. The enemy's positions were captured.*

*'After that Major Worrall, armed with a Tommy gun went hunting alone, clearing up machine gun nests. Despite intense enemy fire, he visited his dispersed men, giving them courage and cheer, and when casualties became heavy, he left his trench to organise the evacuation of the wounded.' January 2nd 1943.*

---

In November 1943, Wiveliscombe turned out en masse to mourn the loss of another respected member of the Hancock family – and the game of rugby mourned a man who had revolutionised the sport.

Frank Hancock, one of the nine sons of William Hancock, died at Ford House aged 83. Frank had joined the family brewing and banking business in 1882, but he was perhaps more widely known for his time on the rugby pitch.

Seven of the nine Hancock brothers played rugby for Somerset at one time or another, and his brother Froude played for England between 1886 and 1890.

But Frank, working at the family's new brewery in Cardiff in the 1880s, was selected to play for Wales on three occasions. And while playing for Cardiff RFC, Frank Hancock is generally credited with the idea of playing a fourth three-quarter behind the pack.

The game was still in its infancy; three three-quarters (hence their name) had only recently been introduced to provide a link between the two half-backs and the full back, as the rugby progressed into more of a running and less scrum-based game.

But Cardiff's selectors had a problem; Hancock had recently played brilliantly as a replacement for an injured three-quarter, scoring two tries, and Cardiff were reluctant to drop him, or any of the other backs, when that injured player was once more fit again.

So on February 23rd 1884, for

The Wales team of 1886, before their match against Scotland; Frank Hancock is seated on the front row, third player from the left, with the moustache.

their match against Gloucester, Cardiff decided to play four three-quarters, discarding a player from the scrum.

*'It was Mr Frank who suggested this daring experiment and being shortly afterwards elected to the captaincy of the club, he decided to adhere to this new formation.' November 6th 1943.*

Cardiff, under Hancock's captaincy stuck to this new combination, but it was not for another ten years that the four three-quarters system was universally adopted.

In February 1943, Sir Richard Acland had announced that he planned to present what was then, and still is today, the largest single donation of property to the National Trust, his estates at Holnicote and at Killerton, near Tiverton.

The Holnicote Estate embraced some of the most beautiful landscape and unspoilt villages in the West Country: 6,000 acres of moorland and 4,000 acres of arable land between Dunkery Beacon and North Hill that included the villages of Selworthy, Bossington, Allerford and Luccombe.

The Trust already owned 1,800 acres on Dunkery Hill and parts of the Holnicote Estate were already leased to the Trust, but this bequest would consolidate the land in public ownership.

And for Sir Richard, this issue of ownership was crucial. Sir Richard had been elected Liberal MP for Barnstaple in 1935, but he became more radical in his views, first opposing the Liberal Party's inclusion in the wartime coalition government and finally breaking from the party in 1942, forming the socialist Common Wealth party with the novelist and playwright J. B. Priestley.

True to his commitment to the public ownership of land, in February 1944, Sir Richard addressed a gathering of his estate farmers, tenants and workers at Allerford School, to formally hand over the estate to the National Trust.

Sir Richard said he had found himself in the impossible situation of advocating the public ownership of land, and yet being the owner of two large properties and able to enjoy 'their not altogether inconsiderable incomes'.

*'(This) imposed an ever and more heavy burden upon his conscience and therefore, he came to the conclusion that the right and proper thing was to find the means of ceasing to own these estates.' February 5th 1944.*

Sir Richard said he had observed how families such as his had been forced to break up and sell parts of their estates in order to pay death duties, taxes which he said were 'a right and proper instrument in promoting well-being in the country,' by redistributing wealth in society.

*'He thought that, of all estates which such a fate should not follow, the chief was the Holnicote estate. He spoke of the beauty of the countryside which it embraced...there was not an area of land south of the Peak District to compare with their valley, with the North Hill on one side and Dunkery on the other, for beauty.'*

Sir Richard joined the Labour Party after the war, winning the Gravesend by-election in November 1947, but later resigned from Labour in 1955 after its support for the Conservative government's decision to develop nuclear weapons. He became a founder member of the Campaign for Nuclear Disarmament in 1957.

*The Aclands had earlier leased large tracts around Dunkery to the Trust; in 1932 Dunkery Beacon itself had been given to the Trust by Col W. W. Wiggin and Mrs Allan Hughes.*

The summer of 1944 was quite the most momentous time, as the Allied forces gathered for the invasion of Europe, for D-Day. But where would the invasion force land?

One of the very few men who knew the details of D-Day was the Supreme Commander of the Allied Forces, the American General Dwight D. Eisenhower, and he was to spend some of the last few days before the invasion on Exmoor. By early spring, hundreds of thousands of his troops were in the camps in southern England, making final preparations for the invasion.

Many had come to Exmoor; several years later, the station master at Dulverton, Arthur Saunders, recalled how he had been told to get ready to receive up to 15 trains one day at his quiet country halt. The first train arrived at 7.15 in the morning, and the last one steamed in at seven at night, each one bringing up to a thousand American GIs, who then moved on to the great canvas encampments on Winsford Hill and on the Brendons.

And *Free Press* readers later learned a few tantalising details of General Eisenhower's visit to Exmoor in spring 1944, to rally his troops, and for some last brief moments of relaxation.

He, too, arrived at Dulverton Station by train, but this was no troop train; It had seven coaches including a dining car, two sleeping coaches, a drawing room car and even a cinema car.

Arthur Saunders was there to greet the General; he later told the *Free Press:*

*'I had no idea at all who was coming until his special train turned up. General Eisenhower got out and came and shook hands with me and said "I am very pleased to be here. Can I stay for two or three days?"'*

Word soon got around and youngsters gathered around the station, waiting for his autograph. 'He was very cool and collected.'

General Eisenhower visited his troops in their camps, and apparently even hired a horse for a ride across the moors. One report says that he…

*'…dropped into a cottage near Winsford and asked the good lady there if she would make him a cup of tea. She did so, though she had no idea who he was.'*

The General is also said to have sipped a beer at the Royal Oak at Withypool, before returning to his train at Dulverton and another last look at those invasion plans.

❖

At the same time, massing in the Bristol Channel ports was a huge armada of merchant shipping, ready to transport two divisions of the US Army, with their tanks, vehicles, stores and equipment to the beaches of Northern France. Almost half the merchant shipping destined for the D-Day beaches left from Bristol Channel ports.

*'Quite the greatest aggregation of shipping the Bristol Channel has ever known, though most of the people who lived along the coast never caught a glimpse of it, must have been that which sailed for France in 1944.*
*'Many of the ships were small coasters, carrying troops who were accommodated in tents erected on the hatches. By the evening of D-Day, the merchant ships which had left the Bristol Channel only 30 hours previously were anchored off the beaches of Normandy and had commenced to discharge troops, vehicles and equipment in support of the assault forces which had landed at dawn. The sailing of this Armada was, of course, shrouded in the utmost secrecy.' August 19th 1952.*

By September 1944, three months after D-Day, the Allies were slowly pushing back the German forces and for the first time, accounts appear in the *Free Press* of the actions of the local units at war.

*'A battalion of the Somerset Light Infantry, it is now revealed, took a leading part in the assault of Mt Pincon, a 1,200ft hill in the "Little Switzerland" of Normandy early last month. In one of the outstanding actions of the Normandy campaign, the men of the Somersets won this vital feature after a grim three-day struggle against the fiercest enemy resistance…' September 23rd 1944.*

Mt Pincon had dominated several key transport routes vital in the advance south, and reports of this success for the Somersets was to be the first of regular accounts from the front as they fought their way to the River Seine at Vernon and later, into Holland, fighting between Nijmegen and Arnhem.

❖

Back at home, with all threat of German invasion now removed, the Home Guard was stood down; each of the village companies making up the 1st Somerset (Minehead) Batallion staged their

## ALLIED INVASION OF FRANCE

### 10,000 TONS OF BOMBS BLASTED WAY

### Big Beachhead Gained

### AIRBORNE TROOPS IN CONVOY 200 MILES LONG

Allied Armies began the liberation of Europe early on Tuesday morning when the greatest invasion of all time was launched with landings from sea and air at several points on the coast of Normandy. Late on Tuesday night fighting was going on in the streets of Caen, an important road junction 10 miles inland at the base of the Cherbourg Peninsula.

Mr. Churchill, in a statement to the House of Commons on Tuesday evening, said that operations were continuing in a "thoroughly satisfactory manner," with effective landings on a wide front and with penetrations in some cases several miles inland. Losses were very much less than had been expected.

#### 4,000 SHIPS ENGAGED

It was revealed on Tuesday night that the invasion was postponed for 24 hours on the advice of the weather experts. The original date was the fourth anniversary of the last evacuation from Dunkirk.

The Home Guard's final march past in The Parade, Minehead.

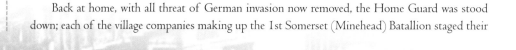

last proud parade. Many were inspected for the last time by their Commanding Officer, Lietenant-Colonel R.D. Alexander who told them:

*'The Home Guard came into being at a time of acute crisis for our country, and for over four years has stood prepared to repel any invader of our shores…you watched our coast, guarded the communications, and were ready to protect the war industries against sabotage or air attack…the work was often dull and monotonous. It was none the less important,' December 9th 1944*

The death in December 1944 of Alexander Fownes Lutrell, at the age of 89, marked the loss of a squire whose life was a tangible link with the past. When Alexander was born in 1855, the last Luttrell to stand as MP for old 'rotten borough' of Minehead, his great uncle John Fownes Luttrell, was still alive.

## DEATH OF MR. ALEXANDER FOWNES LUTTRELL

### GRAND OLD MAN OF WEST SOMERSET

#### 34 YEARS 'SQUIRE OF DUNSTER CASTLE ESTATE

Doyen of Local Government and Public Service in Somerset

VETERAN OF SOUDAN CAMPAIGN OF THE 'EIGHTIES

As a boy of nine, Alexander had in 1871 cut the first sod of the Minehead Railway for which his father George had worked so hard (and from whom he inherited the Dunster Castle Estate in 1910).

Alexander Luttrell had fought with the Grenadier Guards in Egypt and Sudan in the 1880s, before returning home for a lifetime of public service.

A lifetime Liberal, he campaigned for Sir Thomas Acland in his successful parliamentary campaign in 1885, and supported every Liberal campaign since.

*'Through his speeches on political and other occasions, there ran a quiet vein of humour and a statesmanlike quality always expressed itself in his remarks. On one occasion, long before the subject entered the realm of politics in this country, he advanced a system of national insurance for the nation, with pension of 5s a week at the age of 65 for everyone in it.' December 9th 1944.*

*Alexander Fownes Lutrell, seated in the centre, with Dunster estate tenants in 1933.*

He was a local magistrate for 58 years, served on Somerset County Council for 40 years and on the Williton RDC for 28 years. Perhaps his most permanent achievement was the establishment of the Luttrell Memorial Minehead and West Somerset Hospital, named in memory of his father George Luttrell, who had done so much to support the district's first hospital which had opened at Dunster in 1867.

Alexander Luttrell was buried in a coffin hewn from patriarch oak on his estate. He was succeeded by his son Geoffrey Fownes Luttrell who had some time earlier taken over many of his father's public responsibilities.

❖

News finally arrived back home of an important offensive by the Somersets; they had been the first Allied unit to cross into German territory and the first to capture a German village. One company of Somersets was led by a Minehead man, Major Norman Cox (who also worked for the *Free Press*).

The two companies of the SLI advanced over open ground on the village of Niederhelde:

*"'We engaged the German positions ahead of the wood with Bren and rifle fire…and German rifles came out with white flags waving. The going was pretty heavy with mud and shell-holes. Those Germans were waist deep in mud in their trenches. When our chaps went straight in at them, they soon gave up."*

*'The capture of Niederhelde was a brilliant opening to further British attacks to follow that afternoon. Surprise had contributed to the success of the operation.' December 9th 1944.*

❖

Friday Street in Minehead was festooned with flags on VE Day; the air raid shelters are still prominent in The Parade.

VE Day on Tuesday May 8th 1945, like previous days of national celebration, was colourful and boisterous, but also restrained by the experience of many years of hardship, of great loss of life, and of personal suffering.

*'West Somerset greeted VE Day in a sprit of tempered restraint but nonetheless expressive in its sense of relief and thankfulness at the termination of the long and dour struggle against Germany.*

*'On the previous evening and*

## UNCONDITIONAL SURRENDER

### All Enemy Forces in Holland, N.W. Germany, and Denmark

#### FIELD-MARSHAL MONTGOMERY'S TERMS

Field-Marshal Montgomery on Friday reported to General Eisenhower that all enemy forces in Holland, North-West Germany, and Denmark—including Heligoland and the Frisian Islands—had surrendered. The surrender was made to the 21st Army Group, to become effective at 8 a.m. on Saturday.

Negotiations had been in progress between Field-Marshal Montgomery and the German Command in Denmark since the previous Thursday, when the British 11th Armoured Division broke through the enemy's wrecked defences in the north and the Second Army took half a million prisoners.

The terms of surrender were signed in the caravan which Field-Marshal Montgomery uses as his headquarters in the field.

## WEST SOMERSET GREETS VE-DAY

### BUNTING DECKED STREETS AND BUILDINGS

#### CROWDED SERVICES OF THANKSGIVING

##### High Spots of Impromptu Celebrations

In a spirit of tempered restraint, but none the less expressive in its sense of relief and thankfulness at the termination of the long and dour struggle against Germany, West Somerset generally greeted VE-Day. On the previous evening and on the morning of VE-Day streets and buildings of town and village blossomed out into gay colour as flags of all kinds, festoons of streamers, and red, white, and blue bunting, brought out from attics where they had been stored since Coronation Day, or recently purchased, were put up, and there were few people who did not wear or dislay a rosette or some other device in the national or Allied colours. Services of thanksgiving and prayer held in practically all places of worship were largely attended, and among the chosen hymns one in particular, "Now thank we all our God," was fervently sung by all congregations.

heaped in the road and a bonfire made of it. While it burned, and from time to time it was replenished, an alleged "band," furnished with various instruments, including a big drum that had been unearthed from somewhere, filled the night air with weird sounds, with which alternated snatches of popular choruses from many of the large crowd that gathered round, or those who at intervals danced around the fire.

Elsewhere in the town Service men and some of the younger generation indulged their high spirits in song and bunch added to the merriment by riding up and down on a motor-car, propelled by push-power, and producing tortured sounds from sundry instruments.

Toc H. members, helped by Service men, were again responsible for a bonfire wind-up to V-Plus-1 Day. From

*on the morning of VE Day, streets and buildings of town and village blossomed out into gay colours as flags of all kinds, festoons of streamers and red white and blue bunting were put out.' May 12th 1945.*

Thanksgiving services were held in every church and one hymn in particular – 'Now thank we all our God' – was sung with special fervour.

*'There was little in the way of organised rejoicing, but by nightfall, at a number of places, including Minehead, bonfires and bangs, the latter produced mostly by troops stationed in the area, enlivened some localities.*

*'Most people, of course, went into "close session" with their radio sets at various periods of the day, especially in the afternoon when the Prime Minister made his historic announcement.'*

— ❖ —

No sooner had Victory in Europe been declared, and with thousands of men still fighting in the Far East, than the country was thrown into a General Election, the first for ten years, and one that was dramatically to change the face of the nation's industries and social welfare.

Vernon Bartlett, having won the dramatic by-election in November 1938, as an Independent, said he would stand again. But this time it would be very different. In 1938, Barlett had agreed with Winston Churchill's pre-war criticism of Britain's appeasement of Hitler; now he was standing against the party of the great war hero Churchill.

It was the problem facing any candidate opposing a Conservative candidate; if you voted against the Conservatives, you were voting against Winston Churchill and all he had done for the country.

The new Conservative candidate, Gerald Wills, spelt this out at his first rally at the Regal Cinema in Minehead:

*'A vote for either of his opponents would be a vote against Mr Churchill and a vote for the Socialist policy of the Labour party…a vote to change the very form and essence of the government of the country in very vital years, with a war not yet over.' June 2nd 1945.*

And Mr Wills warned voters not to let in Labour, with their radical proposals to nationalise key state industries and to create a tax-funded welfare state.

Labour's candidate, Norman Corkhill, said that returning the Conservatives to power, after the years of the wartime coalition would mean a return to…

*'…the terrible plight into which the nation was allowed to drift between the two wars, with its unemployment, deplorable health services and malnutrition in our schools and the great resources of the nation — mineral, material, and human — utterly wasted.'*

Polling day in West Somerset was on July 3rd, and despite the huge significance of the election, and the wide divide in the political argument, it was reported to be the quietest election within living memory. Many servicemen were, of course, still overseas, and the delay in collecting and counting their votes meant that it was more than three weeks before the result was announced.

When it came, it was a democratic bombshell; nationwide, a landslide victory for Labour, a rejection of Winston Churchill's Conservative party, and in line with this national trend, another personal victory for Vernon Bartlett, who was re-elected as Independent MP for Bridgwater with a majority of 2,313 votes over Gerald Wills.

— ❖ —

Life was still hard in the post-war years of austerity, so it seemed a cruel act of nature that the first few weeks of 1947 should bring the harshest winter weather in living memory. The first blizzards of snow blanketed the area in late January, but the Arctic weather, in particular the bitter cold, was not to relent until early March; West Somerset was in the grip of the freeze for more than six weeks.

The first blizzard struck on January 28th, the deep drifts cutting off villages, halting all transport and the intense cold, combined with strong winds kept, everyone in their homes. Everyone, that is apart from the emergency services who battled to reopen the main roads to get vital supplies through to the moorland villages in particular.

**CONSERVATIVES !**

**HELP MAJOR GERALD WILLS TO HELP WINSTON CHURCHILL TO FINISH THE JOB**

RALLY TO YOUR LOCAL CONSERVATIVE LEADERS AND ENSURE

**WILLS for BRIDGWATER**
**CHURCHILL for BRITAIN**

Gerald Wills, the new Conservative candidate.

No sooner were the Exmoor roads cleared than fresh blizzards blocked them again.

*'Possibly the most unenviable tasks occasioned by the snow have fallen upon the drivers of the snowploughs, and more especially those perched on tractor seats without an inch of protection...it was a severe battle between the speed of the ploughs and the force of the snow fall...' February 1st 1947.*

The thermometer in one Exmoor village fell to minus 20 degrees centigrade; even on the coast, at Minehead, it was down to minus 10. Simonsbath was cut off by 5ft drifts.

German prisoners of war were still being held in a camp on North Hill, Minehead, and they were now deployed to help dig a way through the blocked roads. Escorted by three local police constables and officers from the Royal Army Service Corp, about 20 German POWs left Porlock to dig a way through the drifts for an R.A.S.C. three-tonner loaded with bread and meat for the isolated villagers stranded in Oare.

The bitter cold was relentless; through February and into March there were 42 days and nights of frost. Fresh blizzards blanketed the frozen landscape on February 23rd and a third blizzard – the worst of all – fell on March 4th. This time, the snow fell for thirty six hours.

Early in 1949, the local councils were agonising over an unforeseen but very human consequence of hosting so many American GIs in the district during the war.

At issue was the future of the 'coloured war babies' now living in residential nurseries in Somerset, many of them at a nursery in Holnicote House. Many mothers of these mixed-race babies, fathered by African-American GIs, had abandoned their children, or given them up for adoption. But where should they go? There were about 45 children involved.

Somerset County Council was encouraging a scheme to send them to the United States, but some members of the county's children's committee strongly opposed sending these children to a country where the black population was subject to discrimination laws.

One councillor said nothing should be decided until the children were old enough to think for themselves. He said:

*'I think these children would have a much better chance in this country than in any other country in the world, a country where there is no colour bar. I think it would be a mistake to send them to a country where we hear so much about lynching, murder and the colour bar.' January 8th 1949.*

But the committee chairman said it would be better for them...

*'....to go back to their own country, where they would be welcome in the homes of coloured Americans. I have no doubt at all...that they will never be happy here.'*

The residential nursery at Holnicote House was home to the majority of the 'coloured babies' in Somerset.

But the county council's proposals to transfer the children, born in Britain and therefore British citizens, to persons who were not British citizens  contravened the Education of Children Act 1939: the county council pressed for a change in the law, saying that all the mothers of these mixed-race children supported this.

Finally, in April, the Home Secretary, Mr James Chuter Ede, refused to support such a change in the law adding that

*'...there is no unanimity of view that they would be better off in the United States than in this country. Further, any implication that there was no place in this country for coloured children who had not a normal home life would cause controversy and give offence in some quarters.' April 2nd 1949.*

———————— ❖ ————————

Before the end of the 1940s, two issues emerged that were to provide running controversies right up to the present day; hunting and the preservation of the natural landscape.

There had, of course, been attempts to ban hunting since the 1920s, but this time the politics had changed. The two anti-hunting Bills before parliament were indeed Private Member Bills, but now there was a Labour government in power, with a big mandate to change the country. And it was changing the country in so many ways.

To confront this challenge, hunt supporters from across the Devon & Somerset Staghounds territory, plus  supporters from adjacent hunts, packed into Dulverton Town Hall in February 1949 for one of the biggest rallies yet, in defence of hunting.

The meeting overflowed down the Town Hall stairs and into the street outside where loudspeakers had been set up to carry the speeches.

Victor Collins, who in 1945 became the only Labour MP ever to win the Taunton constituency, was greeted with cheers and blowing of hunting horns when he told the meeting that he would speak against the bills.

Dulverton Town Hall was the traditional venue for pro-hunting rallies; this gathering was held in 1925.

———————— ❖ ————————

In June, it was reported that the Forestry Commission was shortly to acquire, from Geoffrey Luttrell of Dunster Castle, a lease on 1,200 acres on the East Quantoxhead side of the Quantock Hills, on which they planned a plantation of conifers. This was to spark West Somerset's first conservation battle.

The campaign against the proposed conifer plantation was led by Lady Croom-Johnson of Dipford near Taunton, the wife of the former Conservative MP for Bridgwater. She said that all lovers of the Quantocks were...

*'...astounded to hear that one of the most beautiful and unspoilt combes is now being ravaged by extensive tree-felling.*

*'Either Quantockland will be for all time an area where people are free to roam, pick and market whortleberries, enjoy wild flowers, heather, wild life and listen to wonderful bird song, or it will become the raw material for the coal mines.' June 11th 1949.*

A Minehead company had already started to fell some of the natural scrub oak on the site in Hodders Combe and campaigners lobbied the Town and Country Planning Minister Lewis Silkin to impose a tree preservation order on the site, as requested by the county council and supported by the two local MPs Vernon Bartlett and Victor Collins.

Another local landowner, George Wyndham, of Orchard Wydham, Williton wrote to the *Free Press* to put Mr Luttrell's point of view. He wrote:

*'I am with the preservers in loving the Quantocks and in liking hardwoods where possible; but I do feel that this is a weak case on its merits.*

### CONIFER "BLANKET" ON QUANTOCK HILLS

#### Holford Residents' Petition Against a Possible Scheme

##### LETTER FROM LADY CROOM-JOHNSON

AMONG a great many residents in Quantock parishes and other lovers of this countryside, there is deep concern at the prospect, which they have cause to fear, of extensive "blanketing" of areas of the Quantock Hills, with conifer plantations. This concern has been aroused by the possibility, which appears imminent, of the Forestry Commission being given a lease of 1,200 acres on the East Quantoxhead side and, as indicated below, a petition, which a large number of people have signed, is being sent to the County Council's Planning Committee protesting against what it is felt may lead to the despoilation of a pleasant area of heath.

*'England is a poor country. Land is precious and we must have timber. We are all trying to keep the Commission off food-producing land; so some land we must lose. The oak above Hodders Combe is mostly poor scrub oak of about nine inches girth at 100 years — this means that it will grow no more, and die.' June 25th 1949.*

The Ministry eventually confirmed the county council's tree preservation order on the scrub oak, and the clearance of the site was halted. Round one to the conservationists.

❖

And the following month, there was shocking news which showed that Geoffrey Luttrell at Dunster Castle had had other, more pressing, issues on his mind.

After being in his family's hands for almost six hundred years, it was announced that Mr Luttrell had sold the Castle and much of the estates and, most shockingly, the new owners were a firm of property developers from Yorkshire. The report in the *Free Press* was blunt and to the point.

*'We understand from Mr Luttrell that, driven to it by the crippling taxation and death duties, followed by the confiscatory and hampering provision of the Town & Country Planning Act, and to the deep regret of himself and his family, he has sold Dunster Castle and the majority portion (about 8,000 acres) of his Estate — reserving Court House, East Quantoxhead, the Blue Anchor Camping Ground and also the Minehead portion (including the Golf Links) of the Dunster Castle Estate.' August 20th 1949.*

# SALE OF DUNSTER CASTLE
## AND ABOUT 8,000 ACRES OF THE ESTATE

### A Deeply Regretted But Unavoidable Decision

WE understand from Mr. Luttrell that, driven to it by the crippling taxation and death duties, followed by confiscatory and hampering provisions of the Town and Country Planning Act, and to the deep regret of himself and his family, he has sold Dunster Castle and the major portion (about 8,000 acres) of his Estate—reserving Court House, East Quantoxhead, and the Blue Anchor Camping Ground, and also the Minehead portion (including the Golf Links) of the Dunster Castle Estate.

in or having connections with West Somerset. The successive owners of Dunster Castle have not been "absentee landlords," but have lived on their Estate and looked after the interests of the Estate and their tenants and the relations between them as landlord and tenant have always been of the friendliest nature.

Since 1376

As is pretty generally known in the West Country Dunster Castle has been held continuously by the Luttrell family since it was purchased, in 1376, nearly 600 years ago, by Lady Elizabeth

### Gratitude to the Luttrell Family

The town of Minehead owes a big debt of gratitude to the Luttrell family for all these things, whilst, to come to more recent times, Mr. Geoffrey Luttrell, in addition to throwing open the Castle lawns for fetes, &c., has laid the town under great obligation to him by the construction of the magnificent Swimming Pool which was so badly needed and which has proved to be such an attraction to visitors and an

The *Free Press* clearly sympathised with the plight of the Luttrells and doubtless spoke for most in the district.

*'It will be with a deep feeling of personal regret that this news will be received by those living in or having connections with West Somerset.*

*'The successive owners of Dunster Castle have not been "absentee landlords," but have lived on their Estate and looked after the interests of the Estate and their tenants, and the relations between them as landlord and tenant have always been of the friendliest nature.*

*'Modern Minehead may be said to date from the time when Mr Luttrell's grandfather George Fownes Luttrell brought the railway to Minehead, the land and the whole cost of construction of the railway and the stations being provided by him.*

*'In addition to this, Mr George Luttrell and his successor Alexander Fownes Luttrell, spent very large sums on laying out and constructing the roads and sewers. They also spent large sums on the sea defences and making and maintaining the paths on North Hill and planting the shrubs and trees alongside the paths which have been a delight both to residents and visitors for many years past.'*

Mr Luttrell, apart from retaining Court House at East Quantoxhead, had also taken a five-year lease on Dunster Castle so the family would continue to live at the Castle for the time being.

The new owners of Dunster Castle and much of the estate was a Bradford-based property company, Ashdale Land and Property Ltd

They later reassured tenants and staff that they did not plan any great changes,

*'We are not intending to make any changes at the present time in the running of the estate. We have found a first class set of tenants, and with the present set of administrative staff, we are confident we shall be able to run the whole property as it has been run up to now.' August 20th 1949.*

# 1950s: Lynmouth Disaster, and Cold War spies

V ERNON BARTLETT – journalist, broadcaster and victor in the historic 1938 'appeasement' by-election – made his last speech as an Independent MP for Bridgwater at the Egremont Hotel in Williton on February 2nd 1950.

Just fourteen people turned out to listen to him, but apparently it was a dirty night. Bartlett paid tribute to the country's post-war achievements, in particular the creation of the welfare state. He told the faithful few at Williton:

> 'Britain is the only important country in the world today which has deliberately gone through a social revolution, without shedding a single drop of blood and without the loss of very much temper.' February 11th 1950.

The next day, parliament was dissolved and the Labour's achievements in a post-war Britain were tested in another general election. This time around, the Conservative candidate Gerald Wills, defeated by Bartlett in 1945, beat the Labour candidate with a comfortable majority of 5,679, as Labour nationally, hung on for another year in power.

Mr Wills said he was delighted to have returned Bridgwater to its true blue Conservative colours once again. He was to hold the seat for the next 20 years.

❖

The sale in 1949 of Dunster Castle and much of the estate to a Yorkshire-based property company had remained the cause of much speculation and unease. Seven months later, in March 1950, the *Free Press* reported that the Castle and 8,000 acres of land had been sold again, this time to the Commissioner of Crown Lands.

No clear explanation was offered for this sudden change of heart by the Ashdale property company, but everyone seemed happy with the new owners.

> 'This decision was taken as it was felt that no better fate could befall these historic lands than they should pass into the ultimate ownership of the Crown... and the benefits this brings.' March 18th 1950.

Geoffrey Luttrell was both relieved and surprised that the Crown now owned his family's estate;

Geoffrey Luttrell of Dunster Castle, seated centre, with Dunster's wartime Air Raid Wardens.

*'I am very pleased because it will mean that the property will continue as an estate whereas had it been sold to a private individual, it might at some time have been split into small units to pay for more death duties. Of course, had I any idea that the Crown Commissioners were interested, I should have approached them to begin with.' March 18th 1950.*

The Crown Commissioners said they paid £374,000 for the estate, not the £500,000 that had been reported.

❖

The following year, in February 1951, Mr Luttrell revealed that he was to hand over another historic asset developed by his family over successive generations – the harbour at Minehead.

Over recent years, a huge shingle bank had built up at the mouth of the harbour, and it had now been officially closed. The maintenance of the harbour had been a huge cost to the Luttrell family and after lengthy negotiations, the Luttrells sold the harbour to the Minehead UDC for £2, plus a £10 a year ground lease.

On a warm sunny day in June 1951, Mr Geoffrey Luttrell formally handed the 350-year-old harbour into public hands. The harbour and the approaches were festooned with flags and bunting and a huge crowd witnessed the event.

As soon as the handover was completed, the Campbells steamer, the *Glen Usk*, docked with 300 passengers from Cardiff; it then took the town's VIPs on a short return cruise to Porlock Bay.

(Above) It took a month to remove up to 6,000 cubic yards of shingle; much of it was dumped along the sea front near the old Red Lion pub.

(Left) Mr Luttrell handed the deeds of conveyance to the chairman of Minehead UDC, Mr William Webber.

(Right) The *Glen Usk*, arriving from Cardiff.

❖

Tony Collings, on the far left, at the Porlock Vale Riding School, training the British equestrian team for the 1952 Helsinki Olympics.

❖

The havoc and destruction that descended on Exmoor on the night of August 15th 1952 made headline news throughout the country and around the world.

The first two weeks of August 1952 had seen a relentless deluge; days of rain had drenched the upland moors and there seemed no end to it.

Worse was to come – the most destructive and deadly floods seen in the country for decades.

ANY LIVES LOST DURING NIGHT

Message of Sympathy from the Queen

NATIONAL RELIEF FUND OPENED—A TREMENDOUS RESPONSE

..MOOR rivers, swollen by a tremendous and sudden rainfall to torrents of unprecedented volume and violence, last Friday brought havoc and tragedy to North Devon and West Somerset.
Lynmouth and Barbrook suffered the most seriously when the flood waters, rushing down from the moorlands, wrought death and destruction in this part of " England's little Switzerland," with its population increased many fold by the hundreds of visitors ..ing there.   The catastrophe occurred during the height of the holiday season—Lynmouth's main industry with that of its twin ..ge, Lynton.
.he East and West Lyn rivers, overburdened by nine inches of rain in 24 hours, combined with the bursting of the banks of ..olhanger Lake, unleashed furious torrents of water which swept all before it and laid waste man's handiwork on either side.   Great ..s were uprooted and carried, with boulders of several tons weight, and debris of every kind, along the destructive course of the
.....any with such a variable population of visitors the authorities have been hard ..... were rendered homeless and the remainder of its

The real storm, torrential rain accompanied by shattering claps of thunder, started on the morning of Friday August 15th; by nightfall, it was as if a dam had burst, and in the terrifying hours of darkness, the flood waters came crashing down the narrow, steep gorges of the East and West Lyn Rivers, smashing with devastating force onto the homes and shops and hotels in the little harbour town of Lynmouth.

At daylight, the *Free Press* reporters were among the first on the scene; it was to be days before the true extent of the damage and death toll was known. Their first reports were sober but chilling;

*'The East and West Lyn Rivers, overburdened by nine inches of rain in 24 hours, combined with the bursting of the banks of the Woolhanger Lake, unleashed furious torrents of water which swept all before it and laid waste man's handiworks on either side.*

*'Great trees were uprooted and carried, with boulders several tons in weight and debris of every kind, along the destructive course of the waters to the sea.*

*'Many lives were lost in one night – exactly how many, with such a variable population of visitors, the authorities have been hard put to check. And such was the havoc caused at Lynmouth that a great number were rendered homeless and the remainder of its population had to be evacuated.'*
*August 23rd 1952.*

*Sappers laid temporary bridges in some Exmoor villages.*

Rescue services from all over the South West rushed to Lynmouth; by the time their work was done, it was known that 34 people had been drowned or crushed by the torrent, 89 houses either totally washed away or rendered uninhabitable, 72 more badly damaged and innumerable roads and bridges damaged or destroyed.

As soon as the scale of the disaster was known, a national appeal was launched for funds for the survivors; collections were made in all the main cities and resorts.

*'Her Majesty the Queen expressed the sentiments of the whole country in her message of sympathy, and she and the Duke of Edinburgh sent a handsome donation, the amount of which they requested should not be disclosed.'*

But the torrential rains also brought destruction to other parts of Exmoor. Dulverton, Exford and other Exmoor villages also had a harrowing time, though miraculously there was no loss of human life, as the torrents destroyed roads, bridges, property and stock.

Lives were undoubtedly saved at Dulverton thanks to the early warning given by the local constable, PC E.J. Hutchings; he had seen the River Barle upstream at Withypool rising dangerously high. Thanks to his warning, families in Dulverton living close to the banks of the Barle were evacuated from their homes but their property could not be saved:

## GALLANT ACTION AT EXFORD

### Incidents on the Night of "Black Friday"

A graphic account of the speed with which the floods rose at Exford, which suffered extensively in consequence was given to a "Free Press" representative by P.C. J.C. Hutchings, stationed in the village, in praise of whose work throughout Friday night and, indeed, the week-end, residents spoke warmly and with gratitude.

P.C. Hutchings, as it appears, had been on his way to inspect, on his motor-cycle, a road subsidence at Black Pitts, between Simonsbath and Brendon (which had been reported to him by Mr. C. J. Purchase), when, at a point near Gipsy-lane, and after getting through several accumulations of water hub-deep, he was engulfed by a rush of water coming off the common. He and

lost the tools of their trade. At Mr. P. E. H. Bawden's garage at the foot of Church Hill the floods forced the locked and padlocked doors of his garage, and burst the windows, so that four or five cars within were later found to have been immobilised. Worse still, electrical machinery used in the business of motor engineering was found to have been seriously affected, resulting in additional loss to the firm. Six cars in lock-ups on the banks of the river were found not to have been affected.

### BUSINESS PREMISES AND THE METHODIST CHAPEL

Mr. W. D. Batchelor's premises were flooded to a depth of some

moor Foxhounds, and Mrs. Jackson, whose home was among the properties to suffer from flooding.

P.C. Hutchings had made one attempt to release the trapped horses, but had been beaten back by the flood water, which was not surprising in view of the fact that it was later found to have reached a depth of eight feet in the stables themselves. Presumably the horses had held their heads above that level. At about half-past two Mr. Mullins, his stable assistant, Tony Garnshaw, and Sidney Bareley, the huntsman to the Devon and Somerset Staghounds, made another concerted effort and the remaining horses were released. Of the 22 all but two have so far been accounted for, and it is believed they have taken to the moors. They belong to Mrs. Holt, a visitor to the hotel. One is a dark grey gelding, standing 14.2 h.h., and the other a dark brown pony with a

*'...any preparations that might have been made were of little value in the face of the wall of water several feet high which eventually swept down the river, carrying huge trees and other debris with it...it swept away walls, hedges and other obstructions with roaring fury.' August 23rd 1952.*

Meanwhile PC Hutchings was soon caught up in the floods himself, as the River Exe burst its banks in Exford. He was using one of the few telephones in the village, in the White Horse Hotel, phoning warnings to other local police stations, as the water burst into the premises.

*"The water started gushing into the office and before I had completed calls to the fire brigade and ambulance — that is, within four minutes — the water was up to my chest."*

There were similar tales of destruction and rescue at Withypool and Simonsbath, as the Barle flooded homes, brought down bridges and ripped the surface off the roads.

By the following morning, the Regal Cinema at Minehead had been turned into an emergency evacuation centre; 400 evacuees from Lynmouth started to arrive around lunchtime, packed into army lorries, shocked and bedraggled and hungry.

*'The scenes at the reception centre recalled those early days of September 1939, when evacuees were arriving from London and the south coast; but these Lynmouth people, numbed by the disaster which had befallen their town and their own nightmare experiences through the previous twelve hours, excited in much deeper measure the sympathy of those who were dealing with their plight.'*

The whole town of Lynmouth was evacuated and the rescue operation turned into one of recovery and removal. Ten days later, the *Free Press* was again among the first party of reporters allowed back into the village; they were...

## MINEHEAD'S HELPING HAND

### IMMEDIATE ORGANISATION FOR COPING WITH EVACUEES

#### OVER 500 HOLIDAY-MAKERS AND INHABITANTS FROM LYNMOUTH DEALT WITH

Minehead's response to the emergency as soon as action to deal with evacuees from Lynmouth was requested on Saturday morning by the Chief Constable of Somerset. Mr. J. E. [Thor]ough. The Chief Constable came to Minehead about 10 a.m. on Saturday and, having in mind that the Regal Ballroom was turned to good account for the [re]ception of the evacuees at the [ou]tbreak of the last war, asked [Mr.] S. Jay, of Minehead Enter[tai]nments, Ltd., if it could be [ma]de available to receive during [the] day probably 400 or more [hol]iday-makers and inhabitants [of L]ynmouth who were homeless.

*'...deeply impressed by Herculean and ceaseless endeavour, widespread activity and cooperation. Individuals from all walks of life – civilians, firemen, soldiers, police and council workmen – are bending their efforts with a will to the task of cleaning Lynmouth of the masses of masonry, mountainous piles of debris, tree trunks and branches and even portions of houses, which – hurled pell mell down the Lyn valley – turned this little township into a scene of chaos.*

*'Lynmouth has become the spotlight of a nationwide effort at clearance, reconstruction and rebuilding.*

*'Residents grateful for the sunshine of a warm summer's day, had put out their furniture and furnishings to dry, spreading them on lines and strewing them on grass where they might catch the full extent of the sun's heat. Here and there, where the devastation had been more severe, smoking heaps in gardens and fields told their silent story of belongings which were no longer useable and had to be consigned to the flames.' August 30th 1952.*

Thirty days after the disaster, the first residents were allowed to return to their homes. As they started to rebuild their lives, they were visited by the Duke of Edinburgh, Prince Philip, who had arrived at Minehead by train, before driving through West Somerset to witness the recovery of the stricken village.

*'Hats waved, youngsters cheered, and flags fluttered at various points along the railway line, where groups had gathered to see his special train pass on its way to Minehead on Wednesday morning.*

*'At Minehead, he acknowledged the greetings of thousands of people mustered near the railway station and throughout the town. Almost everyone in Porlock turned out to cheer and flag him through their midst and along the high road over Exmoor, he heard the note of more than one hunting horn among the cheers that greeted him from little groups of mounted and foot-people who waited his passing.*

*'At Lynmouth, which was gaily decked with flags and bunting, the Duke saw the traces of the tremendous damage caused by the flooded rivers and he expressed admiration for what had been accomplished in way of restoration.' November 1st 1952.*

---

In the Queen's 1953 New Year Honours, the George Medal was awarded to Lynmouth's PC Derek Harper who, the citation read,

*'...on the night of the Lynmouth Flood Disaster rescued ten people from flooded homes, walked five miles to send the first S.O.S. and began the evacuation of the survivors.'* January 3rd 1953.

PC Harper, aged 24, was on his first posting in Lynmouth; he had found himself marooned on the Countisbury side of the Lyn, but crossed the torrent and for the next twenty-four hours, from the moment the first deluge crashed into Lynmouth, he worked tirelessly helping residents and holidaymakers to safety.

---

As early as July 1947, the government had suggested that Exmoor should become one of the first of the new National Parks. But it was to be another five years before there was any serious consideration of the plan, and initially, many in the district opposed the idea.

In December 1952, councillors on Dulverton RDC rejected the proposals, calling them 'the happy ideas of a lot of idealists' and 'fantasies of the urban mind.' Many feared that planning restrictions would wrap the moor in mothballs, that it...

*'...might stop progress and then we simply drift into stalemate and don't progress at all. There will be no building and no nothing, and the place will be depopulated.' December 13th 1952.*

Councillors on Williton RDC shared these concerns and rejected the idea. There was also the issue of whether the Quantocks should be included in a new National Park, as intended by the National Parks Commission. In July 1953, Somerset County Council also opposed the creation of

The Duke was Edinburgh was greeted at Minehead railway station.

Prince Philip spent several hours inspecting the destruction in Lynmouth.

the new National Park, fearing the extra costs of administering the Park with Devon CC.

But in the face of this united opposition to the plan, in January 1954, the chairman of the National Parks Commission, Sir Patrick Duff signed into existence the new Exmoor National Park, the nation's eighth national park – and excluded the Quantocks.

Sir Patrick said no list of national parks would be complete without Exmoor:

> 'We regard Exmoor with its lovely and majestic scenery, its renown, its romance, its fascinating wild landscape, as eminently falling in with the idea and terms prescribed by Parliament for National Parks.
>
> 'The designated area includes perhaps the finest stretch of wooded coastline in the British Isles, the whole of the heather-clad moorland of Exmoor (where the Exmoor pony and wild red deer still roam) the Brendon Hills and parts of the surrounding hills and wooded valleys.' January 30th 1954.

And why were the Quantocks omitted?

> 'The reason was that the Quantock area was separated from the main body of Exmoor by a tract of country that did not seem to be of sufficient scenic quality to be added in.
>
> 'Perhaps when the dust dies down, we may make a proposal that the Quantocks be added. You can rest assured that they will not be forgotten,' said Sir Patrick.'

---

Some stories in the *Free Press* seem beyond belief; one of the most incredible was the report in April 1954 that at a recent meeting of the United Nations General Assembly in New York, it had been alleged that the quiet market town of Wiveliscombe had been at the heart of an international Communist spy ring.

A former Foreign Under-Secretary of Czechoslovakia, a Mr Hadju, who had lived in Wiveliscombe during the war, had claimed that the British authorities had known that he had been a spy, and even that he had met the British in Paris to discuss his continued espionage.

At the UN in New York, the British representative, Sir Gladwyn Jebb, spoke to oppose a Czech motion critical of the west for its own alleged spying activities behind the Iron Curtain. Sir Gladwyn criticised the recent Soviet show trials in Czechoslovakia, but in challenging Mr Hadju's claims that Britain had known about his spying activities, then added insult to Wiveliscombe's sense of injury.

'Sir Gladwyn made caustic comments about the Prague trials and the fantastic claims of the Czech Communists... and added that he had never heard of Wiveliscombe.' April 11th 1954.

The British representative at the United Nations had never heard of Wiveliscombe? Fleet Street reporters descended on Wiveliscombe to find out more. The item was placed on the agenda of the next parish council meeting.

'There was a wave of amusement locally, but this has now given way to irritation and Wiveliscombe has had enough of the limelight... reporters had been practically sitting on the doorsteps since the spy story was first given prominence.

'Wiveliscombe people, while laughing off the Communist charge that their town was "a spy centre," appear to have been rather more concerned with Sir Gladwyn's remark that he had never heard of such a place. As a result, Sir Gladwyn has been sent a brief but salient description of the market town.'

It transpired that Mr Hadju had come to Wiveliscombe after the German invasion of Czechoslovakia in 1939 and later joined the Czech army in exile. His wife took a house in The Square, where Mr Hadju spent his leave and, as a matter of course, reported to local police as an alien person.

## WIVELISCOMBE AND THAT "SPY RING"

### Amusing Echoes of United Nations References

#### PARISH COUNCIL WRITE TO SIR GLADWYN JEBB

The monthly meeting of Wiveliscombe Parish Council on Monday evening was something of a historic occasion. It had attracted the notice of Fleet-street. Reporters from national daily newspapers had been sent to the West Somerset market town to gather any more information that might be going about the "international spy ring," which, according to Communists in the Iron Curtain countries, exists at Wiveliscombe!

Following the publicity the subject was given in the national Press a couple of weeks ago, after Sir Gladwyn Jebb, British representative at United Nations, had mentioned Wiveliscombe's name in the Assembly, and the wartime residence in the town of Mr. Hadju, former Czech foreign under-secretary, there was a wave of amusement locally, but this has now given way to irritation, and Wiveliscombe has had enough of the limelight. It was stated at Monday's meeting of the Parish Council that reporters had been practically sitting on the doorsteps since the spy story was first given prominence.

The apparent natural of order of things, that had been so dramatically tested in 1949 when the Luttrell family sold Dunster Castle, was happily restored in 1955 when the Crown sold the Castle, and part of the estate, back to the Luttrells.

*'There will be universal pleasure in West Somerset owing to the announcement by the Commissioner of Crown Lands that they have reached agreement with Mr Geoffrey Luttrell for the re-sale to him of Dunster Castle and grounds, amounting to 50 acres in all.*

*'Thus the second break in ownership of the castle – a period of some four and a half years – since the reversion of the property was purchased in 1376 by the Lady Elizabeth Luttrell, of East Quantoxhead, from the Lady Joan de Mohun, will now be happily restored.'* February 13th 1955.

---

# COMET DISASTER HITS PORLOCK

## Capt. Tony Collings Among Passengers on Ill-Fated Jet Air Liner

### PRINCIPAL OF PORLOCK VALE RIDING CENTRE AND TRAINER OF OLYMPIC EQUESTRIAN TEAM

#### A Horseman of International Repute

Fate dealt Porlock a tragic blow indeed when the Comet jet airliner G.ALYY, on which Capt. Tony Collings, (43), principal of the Porlock Vale Riding Centre, was flying to South Africa, met, last week-end, with total disaster over the Mediterranean which caused the loss of all her passengers and crew. When the B.B.C. announcement was made last Friday morning that the Comet was missing the anxiety felt among those who knew that Capt. Collings charger Vitamin, which had been just before the war placed third in the hack class at Olympia, rode for 39 hours " in full marching order," covering well over 70 miles.

During 1944, while he was in Italy, Capt. Collings was made an M.B.E. and shortly afterwards was mentioned in dispatches " for gallant and distinguished services " in that country. Before the war ended he saw further service in Belgium, Holland, and Germany.

In October 1953, Capt. Tony Collings of Porlock Vale Riding School had again been chosen to train Britain's equestrian team for the forthcoming 1956 Melbourne Olympics. But his career was tragically cut short; early in 1955, Capt Collings flew to South Africa to judge an international show jumping event, on board a Comet jet airliner.

*'When the BBC announcement was made last Friday that the Comet G.ALLY to South Africa was missing, there was intense anxiety among those who knew that Capt. Collings was among the passengers.*

*'The subsequent news that all on board had lost their lives further deepened the gloom that clouded Porlock and a sense of loss swept not only through West Somerset but, it might be said, the world of horses and horsemanship.'* April 17th 1955.

---

In August 1956, Britain's first commercial nuclear power plant came on stream at Calder Hall on the Cumbrian coastline; some months previously the Central Electricity Authority had secretly opened discussions with the Somerset County Council about a possible new site for the next generation of nuclear plants, on the coastline close to the Parrett Estuary, at a place called Hinkley Point.

In December 1956, these discussions became public for the first time; the CEA said the site had been chosen as it was close to the areas of demand, had firm sub-soil rock strata to bear the heavy load of the plant, was close to the sea and the large volumes of water necessary for cooling, and was located in an area with a low density of population.

The following March, the county's planning committee were assured that the plant would have nothing to do with nuclear weapons, nor was an atomic explosion at the plant possible:

*'Our approach to nuclear power is not that it is something to be afraid of, but that it is something to be treated with respect. But we feel that we must guard against even the million-to-one chance.' March 30th 1957.*

## CLIMAX OF POWER-STATION CONTROVERSY

### Two-Day Public Inquiry into Electricity Authority's Nuclear Project

### WILL STOGURSEY AREA HAVE A "MONSTER IN THE MIDST" OR AN "INDUSTRIAL GODMOTHER"?

#### Thrust and Parry Between "Scientists and Simple Folk"

THE mounting controversy over the Central Electricity Authority's proposal to build a giant nuclear power-station on shore land at Hinkley Point, in the parish of Stogursey, climaxed into a spate of words spilled in the course of the public inquiry at Bridgwater Town Hall on Tuesday and Wednesday.

The inquiry had been requested by Somerset County Council to give opportunity for a clear statement by the C.E.A. on every aspect of a proposal which has national importance, and opportunity for objectors, individual and collective, to have their say.

ing the activity, and with a site like this there would be ample time to warn everyone.

SAFETY ASPECTS

Mr. F. J. Farmer, chief safety officer of the Atomic Energy Authority, gave evidence of the safety aspects and said experiments had proved that the discharge of effluent from nuclear power-stations had no effect on fish life. They had advised the C.E.A. not to site such stations

Equally, there would be no threat from the waste water used to cool the plant;

> *'The element of radioactivity in water used for cooling purposes would be so slight that similar fresh water could be used as a sole source of drinking water for a normal lifetime.'*

But already several hundred people had opposed the plans, necessitating a two-day public inquiry held at Bridgwater Town Hall in May 1957.

Stogursey parish council welcomed the project: a labour force of 2,500 would be needed to build the plant, another 400 to operate it; the council thought Hinkley would bring back to life a dying village but Williton RDC's support for the scheme was criticised by one councillor;

> *'I cannot forgive a local authority like Williton RDC, charged with the preservation of a beautiful part of the country, thinking in terms of filthy lucre here.' May 18th 1957.*

Others opponents regretted its possible impact on the environment, calling the project 'a monstrous trespass;' one said

> *'You will bring utmost darkness to this lovely county of Somerset if this goes through.'*

But no local authority nor council opposed the scheme, and within six weeks, the Ministry of Power consented to the CEA's plans for the nuclear site. In September, the CEA gave more details of their plans; the Hinkley Point Magnox nuclear plant would cost around £60m to build and generate 500 megawatts of power; it would be by far the largest in the world.

———————— ❖ ————————

Nine years after local activists on the Quantocks had won the district's first conservation battle, with the preservation of Hodders Combe, the struggle now moved to Exmoor.

In June 1958, the Forestry Commission proposed a new plantation of conifers, this time on 1,200 acres of The Chains to the west of Simonsbath, land owned by the Fortescue Estate that included Chains Barrow, Pinkworthy Pond and Furzehill Common.

The Longstone up on The Chains.

Planning permission was not required for such tree-planting schemes but the Forestry Commission had to consult the new Exmoor National Park Authority before it could proceed. This was the first test of the park authority's powers to protect the environment. Their planning committee strongly opposed the plan saying,

> '...The Chains are in one of the wildest parts of Exmoor...the whole area is of considerable scientific interest, both from the physiological and ecological points of view, on account of the capture of the upper reaches of the River Exe by the Hoaroak Water and the West Lyn River.' June 7th 1958.

The proposed plantation on The Chains highlighted the conflict between the economic interests of the landowners, and the newly empowered environmental interests enshrined in the new Exmoor National Park.

The Devon Exmoor National Park committee also opposed the scheme;

> 'While we do not want to criticise any landowners, we do say that the National Parks Committees are set up to safeguard the amenities of the natural beauty spots. While owners have every right to do what they like with their land...the amenities of a place like Exmoor are the property of the public at large. We want to secure those amenities for the public.' June 7th 1958.

As a result of deadlock, the matter was referred to Ministry of Housing and Local Government (responsible for the National Parks) and Ministry of Agriculture (overseeing the Forestry Commission).

And there was one other notable outcome to the dispute over The Chains; in late November 1958, local conservationists who had petitioned against the afforestation formed the Exmoor Society, at a meeting at Simonsbath Lodge, the home of their first chairman, Major John Coleman Cooke. By co-incidence, on the same day, the Forestry Commission dropped their plans.

Looking back on this a year later, at the first AGM of the Exmoor Society, Major John Coleman Cooke said;

> 'I think that our action in trying to get The Chains was both wise and timely because experience has shown that when preservation societies take immediate steps to safeguard a thing of value, quite often they are successful and emerge far stronger than they were before.' October 3rd 1959.

———————— ❖ ————————

Wiveliscombe had always been known as the 'brewery town' so it was a terrible shock to the town when in August 1959, Messrs Arnold & Hancock - now owned by Ushers - confirmed recent rumours that they were closing their brewing and bottling plant at Golden Hill, and moving production to Rowbarton in Taunton.

*'It seems that an era of beer brewing and cider making in the town is at an end. It is believed that brewing has been carried on for nearly 200 years and that it was started in the eighteenth century by a member of the Hancock family, descendants of whom are still involved in it.*

Racking the casks in the old brewery, in the late 1950s.

*'The brewery has provided employment for successive generations of Wilscombe folk...It will be difficult to imagine Wiveliscombe without its brewing after so many years which brought the place the title of "the Somerset brewery town."' August 22nd 1959.*

# 1960s: Butlins, Beatles and the atom at work

TOWARDS THE end of summer 1960, Minehead received perhaps its most important post-war visitor; he was driven around the town, he visited the sea front and he took particular interest in the land to the east of the Esplanade, between the Lido outdoor swimming pool and the golf course at the Warren.

Construction of the camp was rapid; preparatory groundwork had started even before planning permission had been granted.

Mr Billy Butlin, the holiday camp 'king' was looking for a suitable site for another 'high class' holiday camp, following the success of his most recent venture at Bognor Regis.

After an encouraging first visit, further negotiations stalled for a time; Mr Butlin let it be known that he was considering five other sites in the region – including at Portishead and at Bude – and that Minehead risked losing an important new investment.

But Minehead was still thought to be Mr Butlin's favoured choice; in December 1960 he came back to the town to give the residents more details of his plans. More than a thousand packed into the Regal Cinema; the chairman of the Minehead UDC, Mrs F. Cameron, described it as 'one of the most momentous meetings in the history of the town.'

Mr Butlin said that his new camp would accommodate up to 500 guests and would cost £2m to build. He hoped to open for business at Whitsun 1962, and said the camp would employ up to 400 people throughout the year. He said:

*'It is very difficult to imagine any reason why the sort of thing I plan can hurt anyone in Minehead and it is equally difficult to imagine anyone who will not benefit in some way or other.' December 3rd 1960.*

An unofficial show of hands showed overwhelming support for the scheme, but Butlins still had to get planning permission. And because the plan contravened the county's development plan for the area, a public inquiry was held at the Regal Cinema which lasted for three days.

Billy Butlin himself appeared to present his case; he spoke of the benefits the camp would bring to the town – more jobs, increased income, greater publicity for the town.

*'There must inevitably be a change affecting holiday resorts as a whole and Minehead cannot possibly be exempt from this change. . .they should not only reconcile themselves to this but take a positive attitude. Unless the prosperity of the place grows, then it must recede.' May 13th 1961.*

The objectors had formed the Future of Minehead Association, boasting 900 members; their spokesman was forceful in his opposition.

> *'Minehead would become known as a holiday camp town, the camp would dominate the sea front and would be bound to be garish. It did not belong in an area adjoining a National Park; the whole district would suffer. He could understand the shop-keepers welcoming the holiday camp…but would not expect retired people to welcome a complete change in the nature of the town.'*

After an anxious ten-week wait, the inquiry inspector Mr E. L. Crawford approved the plan. Minehead would get its holiday camp, and all that this meant for the town. In his report, the inspector concluded:

> *'Although the camp will affect the visual appearance of the town and later its character, the advantages appear to outweigh the disadvantages.*
> *'Holiday habits have changed and Minehead needs services and amenities which can only be provided by increasing the town's prosperity as a holiday resort.' July 22nd 1961.*

The camp changed the panorama of Minehead's shoreline forever.

And just ten months later, at the end of May 1962, Butlins at Minehead opened its gates to its first holidaymakers. One or two had driven through the night to be first on site, but most came by rail or coach. The weather was grey and cheerless.

> *'Throughout the day, there was a constant stream of them, those who arrived by train being conveyed in Western National buses to the camp, with their luggage bringing up the rear in lorries, there to transfer them to the miniature trains which took them to their chalets.*
> *'There were all the comfortable facilities which the camp has to offer – theatres, dance halls, swimming pools, coffee bars, grill rooms, table tennis and billiard rooms, an indoor bowling green and if the youngsters were prepared to brave the cold, a fair ground, and quite soon many of these activities were in full swing.' June 2nd 1962.*

❖

January 1963 brought terrible blizzards to West Somerset. Huge snow drifts blocked the main roads to Taunton and to Bridgwater and for a time only the train could get through. Up on the moors, the

Helicopters from RAF Chivenor provided a lifeline to isolated Exmoor communities over a period of five weeks.

As the tide went out at Minehead, the foam froze on the beach; Watchet harbour froze over, unprecedented in living memory.

Dulverton highways department said conditions were worse than the great freeze in 1947. But this time, a new form of transport was on hand to help.

> 'On Monday, Exmoor residents telephoned an SOS for food from snowbound Simonsbath and at midday on Tuesday, a helicopter dropped 100 loaves of bread to be distributed around the village and nearby farms.
>
> 'Hedge-hopping helicopters from RAF Chivenor also dropped much-needed supplies of bread, milk, vegetables, and animal food to farms on top of Porlock Hill.
>
> 'At Oare, helicopters dropped supplies of insulin to Mr Bob Nancekivell of Cloud Farm who was ill in bed and had only two doses left. To help the helicopter find the farm, which is well up the Doone Valley, Mr Nancekivell's son Jim had marked out the word 'Cloud' on the snow with coal dust.' January 5th 1963.

Another blizzard, driven by an easterly gale, added to the chaos and this time even the trains were halted. A down train from Taunton with 20 passengers on board, hit a fresh snowdrift in a cutting between Williton and Watchet, and troops from Doniford camp helped to rescue the passengers.

After a brief thaw, temperatures plummeted again and for seven weeks, the district was locked in the grip of ice and frost. The Ministries of Defence and Agriculture co-ordinated the vital helicopter service to the isolated hill farms on Exmoor, the Brendon Hills, and now the Quantocks, too. Side roads were still blocked with drifts up to 12 feet deep.

And in early February, just as the worst seemed to have passed, a fresh blizzard blanketed the district. This snowstorm was said to be the worst of all, driven by an easterly gale, with fresh drifts blocking the roads and lanes that had only just been re-opened.

❖

## BEECHING PLAN SHOCK TO WEST SOMERSET

### Serious Effect on Holiday Trade Business

### MINEHEAD, DULVERTON & EXMOOR ISOLATED

#### CAN THE ROADS TAKE EXTRA LOAD?

WHEN details of Dr. Beeching's plan for the re-shaping of British Railways became known on Wednesday the slashing of the services in West Somerset and North Devon came as a great shock and caused no mean consternation in the district.

So far as the plan concerns the South-West, the suggestions are to do away with all branch lines, and that in our area means the Minehead branch. Taunton to Barnstaple branch, and the Exe Valley line will be closed, and consequently all the stations on the branches will be closed down. The nearest railhead for

For some months there had been fears for the future of the local branch railway lines. When in March 1963, British Rail finally published its plans for the future – the notorious Beeching Report – the news was worse than had been feared. In the South West, Beeching proposed closing ALL the branch lines; in West Somerset, this meant the Devon & Somerset line from Taunton to Barnstaple, the Exe Valley line from Tiverton to Dulverton – and the Taunton to Minehead branch line.

> 'The slashing of services in West Somerset and North Devon came as a great shock and caused no mean consternation in the district. If the Beeching plan goes through, Exmoor will be almost unbelievably remote from railways.
>
> 'The plan will be a heavy blow to the holiday industry and will result in greater congestion on roads which are not ready yet to take the loads which will be forced upon them.' March 20th 1963.

British Rail defended the proposals on simple economic grounds. If the line did not pay, it had to close. British Rail was a business, not a public service.

*'It is clear that the future of our railway system cannot lie in the continuance of a pattern in which 50 per cent of the lines are dealing with only five per cent of the total traffic.'*

It had been hoped that the arrival of Butlins might have saved the Minehead line but this was not to be:

*'The plain fact is that all-the-year-round traffic cannot hope to make the branch line pay. The summer season traffic involves the provision of expensive motive power and rolling stock which has to remain idle for the rest of the year.'*

Minehead traders described the proposals as a catastrophe; people would still want to come to the town but the inadequate roads would be terribly congested and the fact the nearest railhead was 24 miles away might put many off coming at all.

Watchet  UDC was worried about the impact the rail closure would have on the harbour trade while at Dulverton, councillors feared that if the Taunton-Barnstaple line closed, it would be hard for people to get in and out of Dulverton, which had only two daily buses to Minehead and to Exeter.

———————— ❖ ————————

For three days in March 1964, utter pandemonium descended on Minehead railway station and on stations up the line; the Beatles had arrived in West Somerset.

This was the very height of Beatlemania; the previous year, the band had staged their first four tours of the UK, and at each venue, the police – not used to such exuberance – were overwhelmed by the riotous adulation of the fans. What would happen at Minehead?

The Beatles were filming their first-ever movie *A Hard Day's Night.* They had started at Paddington Station and planned to use the Minehead branch line for three days to shoot further train-based sequences.

The 'special' bringing the Beatles was expected to arrive at Minehead Station around midday on Monday March 2nd. By nine in the morning, the station was besieged by fans, reporters and photographers, but the platform itself had been closed off.

Helmeted police strode six abreast along the railway line, as the crowds gathered in noisy anticipation. Cars were seen around the back of the swimming pool 'disgorging excited girls.'

Just before 1220, a train was seen approaching from Dunster...but it was a regular service.

*'Beatlemaniacs thronged barriers, squealed and screamed "We want the Beatles", but the bemused ordinary travellers were quickly ushered off the platform.*

*'The shrieking, chanting and singing continued until the great moment arrived . When the film unit's diesel approached, it could not be heard above the din.' March 7th 1964.*

The train drew in on the town side of the platform, with most of fans, now numbering around 1000, on the opposite side, crammed against the fence which bordered a stream.

(Left) Thousands of schoolchildren were given the day off for a glimpse of the Beatles.

(Right) The police struggled to maintain their cordon around the station.

There were concerted efforts to breach the station defences, with scores of screaming fans wading through muddy ditches; eventually a mass of fans stampeded across the stream, broke the police lines, and hundreds got to the Beatles' carriage before police cleared them off the platform.

Despite the tight security, there was a mad rush when the Beatles 'special' finally arrived.

*'Sitting calmly in the restaurant car, the immaculately dressed stars were munching their chicken lunch. Every now and again, one would grin, wave, smile or grimace at the frenzied mob outside, their expressions registered alternate surprise, bewilderment, boredom, pleasure or amusement. Paul and Ringo were sitting on opposite sides next to the window, with George and John at their sides.*

*'(They) grinned, cheered, clapped and bounced up and down in their seats, obviously moved by the loyalty shown by their fans...For the next hour, pandemonium reigned.'*

Two young fans were presented to the Beatles; the stationmaster had arranged for four-year-old Alison Clark of Williton, a 'hole-in-heart' patient, to meet the 'amiable mop-haired youths', and later, two-year-old Alison Atkins of Minehead presented them with a Teddy Bear embroidered by Minehead Secondary Modern School pupils.

These scenes at Minehead were repeated for the next two days. Unfortunately, for fans up the line, the Beatles 'special' whisked through most other stations without stopping. But word got around that the Beatles would be stopping at Blue Anchor for six minutes each day. And at Crowcombe, the Beatles even got off the train, to film Ringo and George peddling bikes along the station platform.

Four-year-old Alison Clark of Williton was one of only two lucky fans who met the Beatles.

The 'Fab Four' filmed a brief sequence on Crowcombe station platform.

For 200 years, the Plume of Feathers hotel on Wellington Square had been at the heart of life in Minehead. For generations, the stage coaches pulling in and out of Minehead used the Feathers as their base; the town's clubs and societies gathered there for meetings and dinners; in years gone by, when Minehead returned MPs to Parliament, the local voters were regularly 'entertained' there, in return for their support.

But now the present owners, the Watney Mann group, proposed demolishing the old coaching inn and replacing it with five shops and a pub. No objections were raised by the Minehead UDC; there was no campaign to save the historic hostelry.

The elegant coaching inn, photographed by Alfred Vowles in 1928.

Boarded up, and roof slates removed, the last sad days of the Feathers

But Jack Hurley, who was now writing *Notes By the Way*, wouldn't let the Feathers pass on unremarked.

*'Minehead without the Plume of Feathers? You might as well remove the nose from my face and expect to see no difference, as to take away the Feathers and think Minehead will be the same.*

*'I dare say some have raised an eyebrow on reading that Minehead Council offered no objection. It is true the hotel is not an historic monument in the accepted sense but it is old enough to be regarded with affection – a sturdy carry-over from Minehead past.'* May 30th 1964.

Demolition of the Feathers finally started in January 1966; within three weeks, it had been razed to the ground.

For some years now, especially since the creation of the Exmoor National Park, a storm had been brewing on the moors between conservationists, concerned to preserve the amenity value of the landscape, and the upland farmers, encouraged by the government to increase the productivity of their land.

The farmers felt they were being attacked by a vocal minority because of their efforts to bring more land under cultivation, to produce more food for the nation. The conservationists, led by the Exmoor Society, challenged the loss of open moorland, put freshly under plough or enclosed behind new fences.

By the end of 1964, the two sides met on a new battle-ground, on land alongside the A39 at the top of Porlock Hill. At the Exmoor Society's AGM, the society's president, Sir Gonne Pilcher, mourned the recent loss of the moorland on Porlock Common.

*'It is reclaimed, wired-in, ploughed and fertilised — with quite generous subsidies provided by the Ministry of Agriculture. One cannot blame the owner or tenant for taking up such subsidies but, on the other hand, the objectives of the National Trust, the Exmoor Society, and the National Park Commission are to preserve the natural beauty of the area.' October 10th 1964.*

The society's chairman, Mr John Goodland was even more vocal;

*'Unless public opinion can be roused to the danger, our generation will be the last to enjoy the landscape and the freedom of Exmoor.'*

For some time now, the National Farmers Union and the Country Landowners Association had argued that it was only thanks to their members, and their hard work, that Exmoor was a wonderful attraction.

*'Although much of Exmoor's beauty is natural, most of its charm is the result of man's reclamation, the banks and hedges, farmhouses and outbuildings. . .in fact, were it not for farming, Exmoor would be a depopulated and barren wasteland.' December 1st 1962.*

This struggle on Exmoor between production and preservation, and how to compensate one for the loss of the other, was to recur throughout the 1960s and 1970s until, after many thwarted efforts, government legislation achieved some sort of balance.

❖

It had been back in June 1957 that the Ministry of Power gave permission for Britain's largest nuclear power plant to be constructed at Hinkley Point. Almost nine years later, in April 1966, the *Free Press* reported the formal opening of the plant.

*'The West Country is in the vanguard of the movement into the nuclear age. On the coast of Hinkley Point, Stogursey, operating with little noise and no dust or smell, is the nuclear giant that was the first power station in the world to be built for an output of 500 megawatts.' April 30th 1966.*

## NUCLEAR GIANT ON OUR WEST SOMERSET SHORE

**Hinkley Point Power Station Shows Britain's World Leadership**

**HUNDREDS OF GUESTS AT OPENING CEREMONY PERFORMED BY MINISTER OF POWER**

AFTER A YEAR IN WHICH THE ATOM HAS BEEN AT WORK

THE West Country is in the vanguard of the movement into the nuclear age. On the coast at Hinkley Point, Stogursey, operating with little noise, and no dust or smell, is the nuclear giant that was the first power station in the world to be built for an output of 500 megawatts. Costing, as recently quoted in the House of Commons, £78¾ millions, Hinkley Point began to operate in February last year, when Reactor No. 1 started to supply power to the national grid, and Reac'or No. 2 followed in April. In December the design figure of 500 m.w. was reached, and in that month Hinkley supplied more power than the whole of the nuclear stations in the United States.

PRESENTATION

A vote of thanks to the Minister was moved by Mr. W. J. Prior, who presented him with a silver cigarette box bearing a picture of the station. Mr. Prior's daughter, 12 years old Gillian, who goes to St. Hilda's School, Otterhampton, presented a bouquet to the Minister's wife. Mr Prior said the occasion was the C.E.G.B.'s opportunity to show appreciation of those who helped to build the station, and those who were now operating it.

There was no little amusement when the Minister came to unveil a commemorative plaque, for this had been made in anticipation of that former Minister of Power, Mr Fred Lee, performing the opening ceremony. Then had come the General Election—and a change of Ministers. There had been insufficient time to have the name on the plaque amended to that of Mr. Marsh, and the comment that drew laughter was that it was apparent a simpler matter to change a Government than to change a plaque. The adjustment of the plaque will be made in due course.

TOUR AND LUNCHEON

The station superintendent then led the Minister and other guests

Construction at Hinkley had been rapid since work started in late 1957.

By 1962, the outline of Hinkley A's twin reactors was clear.

The first of Hinkley A's two reactors had in fact started operating in February 1965, and the second followed two months later. During the previous winter, the two carbon dioxide cooled reactors had generated more than 30 per cent of the electricity produced in the south west division of the Central Electricity Generating Board. In December, running at full power, Hinkley had generated more electricity than all the nuclear plants in the United States. Hinkley was indeed leading the world. The plant was formally opened by the new Minister of Power, Mr Richard Marsh;

*"'Let us remember that in the field of nuclear energy, we are leading the entire world and that they come to us to find out about such things. Here indeed, when electricity is being used, the chances are the atom is at work," said Mr Marsh.*

*'Even as he spoke, bulldozers were churning the adjoining area to the east of the station, in preparation for Hinkley Point B, designed for an output of 1,300 megawatts, more than twice the power of the present station.'*

❖

As the nuclear age dawned on the Somerset coast, six months later, on the southern slopes of Exmoor, the death knell sounded for a much-loved service that had thrived in the age of steam.

On October 1st 1966, the last train bound for Barnstaple left Taunton station, the last public journey on the old Devon & Somerset line.

Hinkley's main turbine hall.

*'It had been hoped to find a piper to play the train out (of Taunton) with a lament, but instead, there was a toot on a hunting horn, followed by the explosion of detonators.' October 8th 1966.*

En route, the scenes at Dulverton were somewhat subdued.

# HUNTING HORN "MORT" FOR A RAILWAY LINE

## Closure of Taunton—Barnstaple Branch

### MANY PASSENGERS FOR THE FAREWELL TRIP

*'A solemn greeting met the last few travellers when they arrived at the main entrance. On a notice board was the inscription, "Thank you for your patronage over the last 93 years. Goodbye from the staff."'*

It was a well-attended and representative "funeral." The mourners for the Taunton-Barnstaple railway turned up in force for the last run on Saturday, and it was by no means a doleful cortege, if one counts the sporting note provided by a hunting horn.

In recent years this 93 year old line has been carrying only a few passengers, and Saturday's scenes were reminiscent of the prosperous times. About 400 people were on the train for the last trip from Barnstaple to Taunton and back, and many had long memories of travel when the iron horse held sway. The passengers

ing met the last few travellers when they arrived in the main entrance. On a notice board was the inscription. "Thank you for your patronage over the last 93 years. Goodbye from the staff."

Yet there was a feeling among those gathered to bid the train farewell that it would not be many more weeks before the line would once again be in use! The merits of the bus service which is being provided as an alternative were under review. "What happens when they find sixty passengers waiting to get on one bus at Taunton?"

*'Only a few half-hearted cheers greeted the train's arrival, despite the desperate attempts of the bugle blower on board to raise the general spirits. About twenty people jammed onto the already crowded train and it left Dulverton, in the famous words of T.S. Eliot, "not with a bang but a whimper."'*

The last ever Devon & Somerset Railway service reached the end of the line at Barnstaple 45 minutes late, but nobody seemed to mind.

*'At each station and halt the Barnstaple British Legion band played tunes and (when) the train pulled in at Barnstaple...the passengers linked hands for "Auld Lang Syne" and danced the polka and the obsequies were not over until midnight.'*

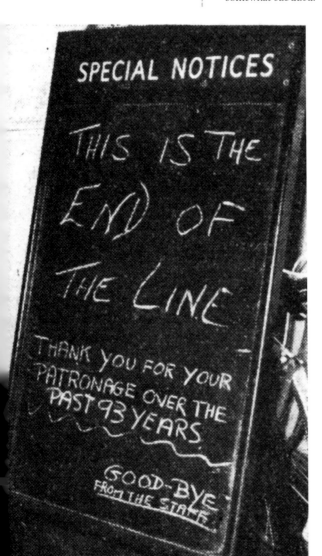

SPECIAL NOTICES

THIS IS THE END OF THE LINE

THANK YOU FOR YOUR PATRONAGE OVER THE PAST 93 YEARS

GOOD-BYE FROM THE STAFF

# 1970s: Thorpe in court, and the revival of rail

I T HAD long been clear that the Minehead branch rail line was doomed to closure. The final announcement came in a statement from the Minister of Transport Mr Fred Mulley in March 1970:

'The Taunton-Minehead railway is to close…subject to the provision of certain additional bus services for all the year round travellers.

'The Minister has reached the conclusion that the social and economic reasons for the continuance of the service are insufficient to warrant the grant of £141,000 a year to meet the loss the line is incurring.' March 28th 1970.

The size of the subsidy was challenged but there was general resignation that the battle had been lost; the last service would run on January 4th 1971.

But even before the last train departed, Somerset County Council said that they were investigating the possibility of running the branch line as a private railway, and asked British Rail to suspend removal of the track and property for at least six months.

## MINISTER AGREES TO MINEHEAD LINE CLOSURE

### Subject to Additional Bus Services

### BUT TRAINS WILL RUN UNTIL END OF SUMMER

The Taunton-Minehead railway is to close. On Wednesday the Minister of Transport announced that he has agreed to the proposal of the British Railways Board to withdraw the passenger service, subject to the provision of certain additional bus services in the area for all the year round travellers.

the year during which there might be some hardship as a result of closure is a relatively short one.

LINE'S LOSSES

Against the possibility of the occurrence of some hardship in this way the Minister has had to set the fact that the service is incurring a

One of the last scheduled British Rail trains prepares to leave Minehead Station.

130

Minehead's Town Band welcomed the arrival of the last train on the old BR line.

The last British Rail service on the Minehead branch line had been meticulously planned but unfortunately, it did not exactly go to plan; it seemed that BR failed to enter into the spirit of the occasion. Three hundred passengers, some from as far away as Glasgow, had packed onto the last return journey from Minehead to Taunton, a 'special' chartered by the Minehead Round Table.

But BR changed their minds about allowing a 30-minute farewell ceremony at Taunton, insisting that the train must depart back down the branch line as soon as possible.

> 'This came as something of a blow to many, who had looked to BR to allow a last bit of tradition but it was not to be…and so the last official train down to Minehead pulled out to cheers, waves and a volley of explosions from detonators placed on the rails.
>
> 'The bagpiper booked to play 'Auld Land Syne' was laid down by flu, and the Minehead Town Band, because of the rush to board the last train, found themselves stranded at the back of the nine-coach train and therefore unable to alight at the first few stations along the way, as planned, to play at each last stop on the line.' January 9th 1971.

After a noisy send off at Williton,

> '…it was not long before the siren of a ship in Watchet harbour was responding to the almost continuous hooting from the train as it rounded the last curve into Watchet Station.'

Finally, after noisy farewells at Washford, Blue Anchor and Dunster, at about 11.30pm the special finally rolled into Minehead…

> '… to the accompaniment of songs from inside and a roar of welcome from the waiting crowds. And some ten minutes later, again with blasts from detonators, the last service train pulled slowly and noisily out of a somewhat sad Minehead Station.'
>
> 'Far from ending with a whimper, the Minehead-Taunton line closed with a series of whistles, hoots, screams, bangs, shouts and cheers fit to raise the dead – but not unfortunately a dead railway.' January 9th 1971.

The following month, Somerset County Council established a rail feasibility group, chaired by a Taunton undertaker Mr Douglas Fear, to examine the prospects for preserving a rail service along the 21-mile branch line.

Three months later, the study group reported that while a purely commercial diesel service would not be economic, there was a viable business if this was combined with steam excursions and other summer holiday attractions.

The private railway would be longer than any other private line in the country and had the undoubted advantage of

> '…having a main line station at one end, and a thriving holiday resort at the other, the length of line between passing through some of the finest country in the West of England.' April 24th 1971.

**MINEHEAD RAIL LINE DEAL FOR £200,000**

British Rail have agreed to sell the Minehead branch line from Norton Fitzwarren for £200,000, says a statement issued by the West Somerset Railway Company Ltd, at Taunton.

The sale includes freehold property, station buildings, equipment, and the running rights into Taunton Station for the private company's trains.

British Rail offered the line for sale last October for £276,000, to which the company replied with an offer of £175,000. Further operation details will be published as soon as possible.

In May, the new company, the West Somerset Railway Company was duly created, suitably perpetuating the original company name, first used in 1856. In November, the new company paid £50,000 to British Rail as a down payment to buy the line and station properties for an expected final price of £276,000; an appeal was launched to raise the first £100,000.

---

The army had left Doniford Camp in the 1960s and the buildings were mothballed; but in the autumn of 1972, the premises were rushed into use once more – to house West Somerset's allocation of the 50,000 Asians expelled from Uganda by the dictator Idi Amin. It was a huge challenge for the local authorities and voluntary bodies.

*'A little more than a week ago, the camp was a bare shell, with no beds, no heating, no curtains and very little furniture... a vast army of volunteers had made preparations to turn the bare barracks into a warm and comfortable accommodation.' October 27th 1972.*

The first of the 200 Asian families who had been forced to leave their homes and livelihoods in Uganda finally arrived at Doniford exhausted, confused and distraught after travelling for 26 hours, first being flown from Entebbe to Stansted and then brought by coach to West Somerset.

## 260 ASIANS ARRIVE AT DONIFORD

By CILLA GOLDING

DONIFORD CAMP, Watchet, had its first intake of homeless Ugandan Asians on Monday evening, when more than 200 men, women and children arrived at their temporary billets in the former Army camp. By this morning the figure is expected to reach 260.

They still feared compromising the safety of those they left behind, so spoke only anonymously to the *Free Press* reporters.

*'We were allowed to bring only £50 out of Uganda, and whatever we could cram into a suitcase...we left our home, the contents, our car... Many Africans, particularly the soldiers, treat you like trash. A man can't stay in a country where there is no respect left for his people.'*

A collection centre was set up in Minehead and other local towns for blankets and supplies for the Asians, facing the harsh prospect of spending an English winter in a previously abandoned army barracks with few possessions of their own. Eventually, more than 1,200 Ugandan Asians were housed at Doniford. The camp closed six months later, in March 1973, when those who had not found homes in the country were resettled at other temporary camps.

---

Early in 1973, after more than a year of wrangling, the West Somerset Railway Company received the news they had feared: the County Council had apparently muscled in on the deal with British Rail, and agreed to pay BR £245,000 for the branch line and the station properties, in so doing, securing the prime sea front site at Minehead. The railway company's dream of independence was scuppered.

The County Council agreed to lease the line back to the WSRC, and to offer loans to the company, in return for a commitment to run all-the-year-round scheduled services. But local councillors attacked the County Council, alleging underhand tactics in their determination to get their hands on the Minehead site, at a time when property prices were rocketing.

The railway company said they hoped to run the first services by Easter 1975. In fact, it was not until December 1975, almost five years after the last BR train ran along the branch line, that their first train rolled over the now-privately run track.

The one-off journey was a private event: on board were the local MP Tom King, the WSRC directors and members of the railway supporters organisation.

### CHUFF! CHUFF! VICTOR COMES STEAMING IN
#### A seasonable fillip to West Somerset morale

*'West Somerset turned out in force to welcome back steam power and the first official private train on her very own line on Sunday. Many enthusiasts, who have waited five years to see the line re-opened, watched the first non-fare paying inspection train pull into Minehead Station.' December 12th 1975.*

For much of the 1970s, the local councils had been fighting plans by the government's Boundary Commission to absorb the Williton and Dulverton Rural District Councils, and the Minehead and Watchet Urban District Councils, into a 'super' council representing more than 100,000 people, merging the interests of West Somerset with those of Taunton and Wellington.

In November 1972, councillors heard with delight the news that while these old councils would indeed disappear, they had successfully fought off the new 'monster' council and that Somerset would now be divided into five district councils - including the new West Somerset District Council.

The new WSDC first met at the offices of the Williton RDC in June 1973, as a shadow authority before they took over from the old rural and urban councils in April 1974. The new council's first decision was to ban smoking for the first 60 minutes of future meetings.

The long-running saga over Dunster Castle was finally resolved in June 1975, when Col Walter Luttrell gave the Castle and the 50 acres he still owned to the National Trust. In 1949, his father Geoffrey Luttrell had sold the Dunster Estates, the castle and land ending in the hands of the Crown Commission; but in 1955, the Luttrells had bought back the castle and some surrounding acres.

But now, finally, the Luttrell family's 600-year connections with the castle were ended.

'Col Walter said it was extremely sad to break the family ties "but because of capital taxes, the only alternatives were a complete commercialisation, or a general decline of the castle and its grounds. Now at least the castle's future is assured."' June 6th 1975.

In October 1975, there was an incident late one evening up on Porlock Hill that was to have huge ramifications for the *Free Press*, for the fate of the leader of a national party in Parliament and which eventually led to what can truly be described as one of the Trials of the Century.

The story only reached the paper as the result of a chance conversation between a *Free Press* reporter, Bob Barron, with a local AA man in the Ship Inn at Porlock. Later that week, the *Free Press* splashed the story across its front page.

'All because of a book I'm writing'

# THE GREAT DANE DEATH MYSTERY

### Dog-in-a-fog-case baffles police

POLICE are believed still to be investigating at press time, a mystery a impenetrable as moorland fog, in which a self-described political writer i said to have claimed that an attempt was made on his life.

'Police are believed to be investigating, at press time, a mystery as impenetrable as moorland fog, in which a self described political writer is said to have claimed that an attempt was made on his life.

'The man was found on Friday on a lonely stretch of moorland road near County Gate, hugging the still warm body of his black Great Dane which had been shot through the head by a small-bore weapon.

'Police at Bridgwater refused to confirm or deny a story that had gained circulation — that the killer of the pet also tried to shoot the man but that the gun had jammed. Neither would they say that the owner of the dog is a Mr Norman Scott, of Park Lane, Combe Martin.

"All I can tell you is that we are investigating the shooting of a dog on Friday evening" said Chief Supt Rupert Ormerod on Tuesday.' October 31st 1975.

This was the start of the Jeremy Thorpe affair.

Mr Thorpe had been the Liberal MP for North Devon since 1959 and was well-known across the border in West Somerset, particularly for his support of campaigns to preserve the moorland of Exmoor. A flamboyant and extrovert MP, Mr Thorpe, more than any other politician of his time, had embraced the double-edged potential of the new television age and, on becoming leader of the Liberal Party in 1967, had raised both his own profile and his party's prospects in subsequent election campaigns.

In February 1974, Mr Thorpe had even been offered the post of Home Secretary by the Conservative leader Ted Heath as part of a proposed coalition deal, after an inconclusive general election.

So in October 1975, Mr Thorpe was one of the most significant politicians in the land. This meant the *Free Press's* 'scoop' was dynamite.

The paper's front page story continued;

*'The mystery started at 8.50 on Friday evening when AA patrolman Ted Lethaby of Heathcliffe, Countisbury was driving to Minehead with three friends.*

*"We got near the entrance to Yenworthy Lodge, when this chap jumped out in front of my car waving us down," he told a Free Press reporter.*

*"Lying against a bank nearby was a dead black dog, still warm and bleeding from what looked like a bullet hole through the head.*

*"(The man) told me his name was Scott and that...his fellow traveller had pulled a gun, shot the dog and tried to shoot him but the gun jammed and the man drove off."*

*'Mr Lethaby said the man told him "they" were trying to kill him because of a book he had written about Jeremy Thorpe, the Liberal party leader and MP for North Devon.'*

This allegation was, of course, enormously damaging to Mr Thorpe; the *Free Press* asked Mr Thorpe for his comments on Norman Scott's reported allegations. His agent in Barnstaple, Mrs Lilian Prowse, confirmed to the paper that Mr Scott's name was indeed known to Mr Thorpe.

*'"We are not aware that Mr Scott has written a biography or anything else about Mr Thorpe" she said.*

*"But about five years ago, he issued threats against Mr Thorpe, who took the case up with his lawyer, Lord Goodman."*

*'Asked about the nature of the threats, she said she could not elaborate, but commented that Mr Scott was just one of a certain kind of person encountered by well-known public figures.'*

The *Free Press* had for the first time made such allegations public: there had been persistent gossip around Westminster and Fleet St, but never before had it been published.

Fleet St followed up the *Free Press's* story over the weekend, but little new was learned. All went quiet for several weeks; in the House of Commons, a Home Office minister denied reports in the *Free Press* that it had issued a gagging order on information relating to the story.

The paper's front page photo, with an outline of Rinka.

Jeremy Thorpe, MP.

# COMMONS QUERY ON GREAT DANE CASE

THE outcome of a report in last week's 'Free Press'—questions were tabled in the House of Commons yesterday about police handling of information about the Great Dane shooting incident on Exmoor last month.

Mr. Robin Maxwell Hyslop, M.P. for the Tiverton constituency, put down a motion to ask the Secretary of State for the Home Department what restrictions on the publication of information by the Press concerning the case due to be heard before Minehead Magistrates the Government had imposed or requested—and the reasons for such restrictions on reporting.

A second question from Mr. Maxwell Hyslop was whether the Home Department or, with ministerial agreement, any other Government department had requested the Somerset Police Force, or instructed them, not to inform the Press concerning proceedings against any individual charged with shooting a dog unlawfully; or to restrict in any way the giving of such information; and the reason for any such action.

But the legal process had started, and soon the press was to be free to report details revealed in court. The first news again came from the *Free Press*, which had learned that a so far un-named man was to appear before Minehead magistrates on December 19th after his arrest at London airport. He was to answer

*'...a firearms charge following the unexplained death of a Great Dane bitch called Rinka found shot in the head on an Exmoor road last month.' November 28th 1975.*

This was Andrew 'Gino' Newton, a former airline pilot, the alleged hit-man. He made a brief appearance at Minehead, charged with being in possession of a Mauser pistol and ammunition

# SHOT DOG —AIRPORT ARREST

A man will appear before West Somerset magistrates at Minehead on December 19th on a firearms charge following the unexplained death of a Great Dane bitch called Rinka found shot in the head on an Exmoor road last month.

Police arrested the man at London Airport last Friday and he was questioned at Bridgwater before being released on bail.

The dog was owned by Mr. Norman Scott, a 35-year-old writer of Combe Martin, North Devon, whom an Automobile Association patrolman found weeping by the dead Rinka on the road between Porlock and Lynmouth.

Information about the puzzling incident has since been restricted on Home Office orders.

Andrew 'Gino' Newton.

Norman Scott.

with intent to endanger life, and the case was adjourned. After two further brief appearances at Minehead, the case against Newton was ordered to be heard at Exeter Crown Court in March 1976.

Fleet St could barely wait; Norman Scott had been called to give evidence against his alleged would-be assassin. The *Free Press* could not refrain from a brief comment on its own role in this growing national scandal;

> 'Thus, the ramifications of a case originally brought to public notice in as humble a country newspaper as the Free Press *have built up into national news.' February 6th 1976.*

But the *Free Press* itself was under attack; before Newton had his day in court, the Insight investigation team on the *Sunday Times* suggested that the *Free Press* and *Private Eye* were involved in a conspiracy against Mr Thorpe.

In his evidence before the court in Exeter, Newton maintained that he simply wanted to frighten Scott who, he alleged, was blackmailing him over nude photographs of him that Scott possessed. But he did admit to shooting the Great Dane, Rinka.

Perspiring heavily, Norman Scott then gave his first public account of that dark night up on Porlock Hill,

> '...how Newton twisted his arm behind his back and held the gun to the side of his head.
> 'Moments later, Mr Newton threatened him again with the gun. Mr Scott showed the hushed court room how he alleged Mr Newton held out his arms pointing the gun at him "He put his hand up like that and fired, but there was no bang," said Mr Scott.
> 'Mr Newton then screamed, shouting "I'll get you" and drove off.' March 19th 1976.

Norman Scott denied trying to blackmail Mr Newton over the nude photographs.

> 'I am no blackmailer. I have lived a life of being morally blackmailed by Mr Thorpe.'

Newton was eventually sentenced to two years imprisonment for illegal possession of a firearm and intent to endanger life.

Again the Thorpe Affair went quiet; it was not until Newton emerged from prison in 1977 that the real action started. And again, West Somerset, and the *Free Press,* was at the heart of it.

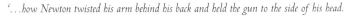

Lord Montague of Beaulieu waves off the first public fare-paying service on the revived West Somerset Railway.

West Somerset Railway staff and volunteers had spent thousands of hours getting the track and stations ready for the first public train service which finally pulled out of Minehead Station at the end of March 1976 on a short return journey to Blue Anchor.

*'For more than 250 passengers on the first train, it was an expensive trip to Blue Anchor and back at £3.00 a head — more per mile than flying supersonic on Concorde. But judging by the fur coats and champagne treats enjoyed by some of the lucky few, they could afford it.' April 2nd 1976.*

Thereafter, until May, there would be a daily steam excursion to Blue Anchor and back for 50p return, with plans to extend the service to Watchet and Williton by Whitsun and a full diesel commuter service to Taunton by the autumn.

And for the first eight days, 5,000 passengers piled onto the train, and there was a good response to the appeal for £65,000 working capital.

But then came the hammer-blow, the news that was forever to restrict the operation of the branch line. The Taunton branch of the National Union of Railwaymen — who also represented the bus drivers working on the Taunton-Minehead route — were angry that while the Somerset County Council was prepared to loan public money to a private railway company to run commuter rail services, they would not similarly subsidise the bus services, which would compete with the railway. The *Free Press* reported:

> *'If their attitude continues, the company's diesel commuter service, due to start in the autumn, would get no further than Norton Fitzwarren, the junction for the WSRC leased line with main BR line …the NUR men have told the bus drivers they will refuse to operate signalling and points for the trains destined to reach Taunton Station.' July 2nd 1976.*

The NUR said they did not intend to be dictatorial but…

> *'…when Minehead and Bridgwater bus stations are threatened, why should the county step in and help the private railway company?'*

# RAILWAY COULD END AT NORTON

A boycott threat to the West Somerset Railway Company chugging into Taunton station was described this week as "an internal British Rail matter."

The Taunton branch of the National Union of Railwaymen are angry because they say Somerset County Council has provided money for the private company but cannot find extra cash to subsidise bus services in the area.

This NUR blockade on the rail company's plans to run commuter services to Taunton meant the company had to abandon their scheduled winter services; the company's operations were mothballed, 14 staff were laid off, and the loss of the winter income was estimated at £26,000.

Even more worryingly, the County Council said their loan to the WSR was dependant on the company running commuter services all the way into Taunton; if these services were frozen, then so too was their loan to the railway company. The crisis led to a massive trading loss for the railway, resignations from the board and eventually, in November 1976, to the acrimonious departure of the company's first chairman Douglas Fear. The two sides later settled out of court.

The accounts for 1977 showed a better performance, but the railway was still losing money and the County Council was not happy.

This was the start of years of struggle between the County Council, who were expecting index-linked increases in the rent under the 20-year lease, and the WSRC, doing everything possible to maximise its income but, with few tangible assets, unable to raise finance elsewhere — except in regular appeals to its supporters locally and around the country.

———————— ❖ ————————

The intractable 'amenity versus agriculture' row continued to be a national issue but it was most fiercely fought on Exmoor. The Exmoor Society and other conservation bodies had for the past decade lobbied for government action to protect the moor, and the Labour government finally responded in April 1977, by announcing an independent inquiry under Lord Porchester.

Lord Porchester reported before the end of the year. Central to his proposals were the issuing of moorland conservation orders, backed by legislation, to protect for all time 12,800 acres of Exmoor. In return, farmers and landowners would be eligible for compensation.

The proposals were immediately attacked by the NFU as unworkable;

> *'…the absolute presumption against improved methods of agricultural husbandry could be extremely serious …and the suggestions for compensation fall far short of meeting the losses farmers would suffer.' December 2nd 1977.*

But for the conservationists, Guy Somerset, chairman of the Exmoor Society described Lord Porchester's ideas as…

> *'…a great victory for the preservation of the National Park. They are very much in line with the views which conservation societies have been putting forward for some time.'*

But Porchester's proposals just gathered dust; no action was taken and by Spring 1978, the National Parks were lobbying government to put the plans into law.

❖

The Thorpe Affair had for some months dropped away from the headlines; Norman Scott's allegations had been denied but they had not gone away. Jeremy Thorpe had by now resigned as leader of the Liberal Party, but the full drama was still to come.

It started when the alleged 'hitman' Andrew Newton was released from jail in October 1977, having served his sentence for endangering Scott's life with a firearm. On his release, Newton told the *London Evening News* that the incident on Porlock Hill had not just been an attempt to frighten Scott. He alleged that

> *'…he was paid about £5,000 to kill the man who says he had a homosexual relationship with Mr Thorpe, in a plot involving a member of the Liberal party. "It was a contract to murder" Newton was reported to have said.' October 21st 1977.*

Newton's allegation that, in fact, this was a murder plot caused the police at Bristol's Central Division to start a fresh investigation; finally, the full allegations were becoming public.

Ten months later, on August 4th 1978, the Right Honourable Jeremy Thorpe MP, appeared before Minehead magistrates, with three others, accused of conspiracy to murder, the most serious charge ever made against a senior British politician in recent times. All four denied all charges.

# THORPE: the drama returns to where it first hit the headlines

West Somerset has been thrust into the centre of 'the Norman Scott affair' with the appearance at Minehead magistrates court on Friday of Jeremy Thorpe, M.P. for North Devon, and former Liberal party leader.

He appeared with three others, charged that 'on divers dates between October 1st, 1968 and November 1st, 1977, in the county of Devon and elsewhere, they conspired together, and with others, to murder Mr. Norman Scott.

Rumours that charges would be made had been current last week but it was not until 1 p.m. on Friday that police confirmed that the four would appear at 2.15 p.m. before West Somerset magistrates.

hearing as it was here that police enquiries started into the shooting of Mr. Scott's Great Dane, Rinka, first reported by the "Free Press", at a lonely Exmoor spot near Yenworthy, on the A39 between Porlock and Lynmouth in October, 1975. Security is also good at Minehead, with the courtroom being within the police station premises.

By lunchtime, the police station was besieged by more than 30 national newspaper reporters, photographers, and television crews, and a large crowd of holidaymakers gathered, some with balloons and ice-creams.

The four accused arrived separately in private cars, Mr. Thorpe travelling with his legal adviser Sir David Napley, and Lord Avebury, formerly Eric Lubbock, MP, who was to stand bail for Mr. Thorpe.

Inside the closely-guarded police station, all four were charged by Detective Chief Superintendent Michael Challes, of Avon and Somerset Police, who has

Edward Donati, Mrs. Anne Crawford and Mr. Ronald How. Also in court were the Chief Constable of Avon and Somerset police, Mr. Kenneth Steele, Detective Superintendent Davey Greenough, who has helped in the investigations ordered by the Director of Public Prosecutions, and Chief Superintendent Clifford Searle,

Thorpe was also separately charged with inciting Mr David Holmes, the Liberal Party's deputy Treasurer, to murder Norman Scott. Again, Mr Thorpe denied the charge.

The date for the full committal hearing at Minehead was set for November 20th. Needless to say, West Somerset had never seen anything like this.

Newspapers from Fleet St and beyond despatched their top reporting teams to Minehead; the BBC and ITV set up television gantries along Townsend Road outside the court for their broadcasts, and the hotels and guest houses took on extra staff to handle this out-of-season bonanza.

There was fierce competition for seats inside the small court room: measuring 30 feet by 36 feet, Minehead Magistrates Court was not designed to accommodate a trial of this magnitude.

Eventually, room was found for 31 reporters and 16 members of the public, many of whom had queued for hours for their chance to witness history in the making, in their own rural courthouse.

But this was no circus; the court was to hear Mr Thorpe and his three co-accused face a most serious charge — that they were involved in a conspiracy to murder.

There was enormous pressure on the three local magistrates to handle events in their court with proper dignity and professionalism. The usual weekly fare of pub licence applications and motoring offences was not the best preparation for a case of such importance, where, quite literally, the eyes of the country were upon them.

The chairman of the magistrates was Mr Edward Donati, recently retired from his Minehead-based architecture practice; to his left sat a local farmer, Mr James Henderson, grey-haired and bespectacled, and on his right was Mrs Margaret Griffiths, well-known for her voluntary work in the district.

These three rural JPs had to decide if there was sufficient evidence to support referring the case to a higher court.

Before them sat Jeremy Thorpe, David Holmes, and the two others accused of the conspiracy, John Le Mesurier, a South Wales businessman and George Deakin, a gaming machine operator from Port Talbot.

Deakin's QC, Mr Gareth Williams, caused an immediate sensation when he asked for the usual reporting restrictions imposed on such a committal proceeding to be lifted. The Press, who had thought that they would be able to report little more than the details of the charges, the defendants and a few anodyne descriptions from court, suddenly knew that they'd be reporting for the first time the full details of the alleged conspiracy. Back in Fleet Street, the front pages were cleared in readiness.

So started three weeks of gripping courtroom drama, as the prosecution counsel, Peter Taylor QC, laid before the Minehead magistrates their case against Mr Thorpe and his alleged co-conspirators:  the key points, all denied by the defendants were

that Mr Thorpe started a homosexual relationship with Norman Scott in 1961,
that Mr Thorpe became concerned that public knowledge of such a relationship would damage
   him politically and so discussed with a fellow MP Peter Bessell the need to kill Scott,
that Mr Thorpe incited David Holmes to kill Scott,
that Mr Thorpe discussed killing Scott with John le Mesurier and George Deakin,
that Mr Thorpe hired Andrew Newton to kill Scott and
that Mr Thorpe diverted Liberal Party funds to pay Newton

Each week the *Free Press* carried detailed day-by-day reports of the proceedings; it also reported the favourable observations of the proceedings in the national press;

> *'Comment and observation from the national press has touched on the efficient handling of the court by Mr Edward Donati, the presiding magistrate and his two colleagues Mr James Henderson and Mrs Margaret Griffiths…..*
>
> *'The* Sunday Times *has given special mention to the Free Press staff reporter Bob Barron, who, in the course of making his routine inquiries three years ago came upon the shooting of Mr Scott's dog and whose  duty it was to report in this newspaper the original story that we titled "Dog in a Fog" case.' December 1st 1978.*

The defendants arriving at Minehead. George Deakin (top) and Jeremy Thorpe (bottom).

At the end of the third Tuesday of the proceedings, the chairman of the magistrates, Mr Donati, told the packed courtroom that he and his two colleagues would retire to consider if the prosecution had presented evidence suffcient to support the charges, and that they would return with their verdict the following morning. The sense of drama was intense.

> *'A few minutes before 10am, Jeremy Thorpe and his three co-defendants were directed to stand in line below the Magistrates Bench.*
>
> *'The long proceedings in the case that has attracted worldwide attention were in their last minutes. The magistrates had reached their decision.*
>
> *'Mr Edward Donati (chairman) told the defendants "On the charges of conspiracy to murder, we find there is a prima facie case in respect of each of you."*
>
> *'To Mr Thorpe, Mr Donati said "We also find there is a prima facie case against you, on the charge of inciting David Holmes to commit murder."*
>
> *'The four defendants appeared to take the announcements calmly. They were asked if they wished to say anything.*
>
> *'Mr Thorpe said "I plead not guilty and will vigorously defend this matter."' December 15th 1978.*

This was to be Mr Thorpe's one and only public statement about the allegations.

Both the Crown and the defence counsel agreed that the interests of justice would be better served if the trial was held on 'neutral ground' and that the London Central Criminal Court – the Old Bailey – would be most suitable.

*'Thus was concluded a hearing that began on November 20th and continued in the glare of publicity probably unparalleled in British court history.*

*'Its background, though few saw it as such at the time, was the October 1975 incident, first reported by the* Free Press, *when self-styled "hit man" Andrew Newton, travelling in a car with Norman Scott on the coast road between Lynmouth and Porlock, shot Scott's Great Dane dog.'*

The trial at the Old Bailey started in May 1979, just after Thorpe had lost his North Devon seat in the General Election. Thorpe did not give evidence but his defence counsel George Carman QC argued that although Thorpe and others had discussed frightening Scott, they had never conspired to kill him. Nor did Mr Carman accept that Thorpe and Scott had had a homosexual relationship. After 31 days in court, all four men were cleared of all charges. Some parishioners in Mr Thorpe's old constituency held a church service of thanksgiving.

❖

The 'winter of discontent' of 1978-79 that marked the last months of Jim Callaghan's Labour government was made even more miserable by the heavy snowfalls that blanketed the area. Once the drifts were cleared, West Somerset's farmers had problems getting feed to their stock because of strikes by transport workers. Watchet harbour and the paper mill were picketed by members of the Transport and General Workers Union as part of the lorry drivers' dispute.

So it was no surprise in the General Election in May 1979, that the sitting Conservative MP for Bridgwater, Mr Tom King, should win his largest ever majority – 14,450 – and in Mrs Thatcher's new Conservative government, his ten years on the back benches were rewarded with a ministerial post at the Department of Environment, where among other issues, he would be responsible for the controversial Moorland Conservation policy.

(Another new minister, as Chief Secretary to the Treasury, was John Biffen, whose parents lived on Tower Hill in Williton.)

Mr King had first won the Bridgwater seat in 1970, on the death of Sir Gerald Wills, and had safely held the seat in the two elections in 1974.

# 1980s: Nuclear fears, and the Beast

T HE EARLY 1980s saw the British economy in deep recession, with the Conservative government under Margaret Thatcher forced to make financial cuts across all areas of public spending, including local government; among other things, this only complicated relations between the Somerset County Council and the West Somerset Railway Company.

And it didn't help that the railway was still making considerable losses, while still depending on loans from the council to keep afloat. In September 1981, the new chairman Derek Portman announced that all weekday winter diesel services would be stopped, and the following month, most of the salaried staff on the railway were sacked, leaving just four permanent members of staff, and an army of committed volunteers, to run the longest private railway in Britain.

The WSRC had a new survival plan:

> '. . . a heavy reliance on voluntary workers, the scrapping of loss-making services including commuter trains and more emphasis on steam and special excursions.' November 20th 1981.

For the next few years, the railway concentrated on running just the most profitable services, with costs pared to the bone; gradually, the West Somerset Railway Company seemed to haul itself back on track.

## Beast spotted chasing deer

THE beast of Exmoor killed at least two sheep in the Dulverton area at the weekend—but the latest eye-witness accounts suggest that it may now be turning its attention to deer.

Police now believe that the beast, which has claimed over 100 sheep along southern Exmoor, is a lurcher dog.

After the weekend killings, Avon and Somerset police held urgent talks on Monday with the Devon and Cornwall Constabu-

"It was a scruffy-looking thi about the size of an alsatian said Mr. Floyd, "It reminded n of a lurcher.

"But it made a funny noise like a bear. I have never heard an ordinary dog do that. It was about 50 yards behind the deer."

Mr. Floyd was working on the Hollam Estate, near Barlynch Abbey. Directly opposite is the League Against Cruel Sports' Barlynch Woods sanctuary where hundreds of deer roam.

Despite the killings, Winsford Hill farmers are not yet organising themselves in the way that South Molton farmers did, with

---

In late spring 1983, the *Free Press* carried the first report of what quickly became dubbed 'The Beast of Exmoor'.

'A phantom sheep-killer, which eye-witnesses say is like a wild cat and the size of a large dog, has foiled all attempts to flush it out of its hiding place near South Molton. The animal is believed to be responsible for the killing of 60 sheep and lambs in the area.

'Organised hunts, helicopter patrols and night-time vigils by police using infra-red binoculars have so far failed to corner the beast.' April 29th 1983.

By June, after more brutal killings over the summer, Marines from 42 Commando based at Plymouth had been deployed; they claimed to have made a positive identification. It was definitely a dog.

'"Our men have scotched the suggestion that it is a puma or panther" said a spokesman.' June 17th 1983.

The Marines had camped out on the moors, equipped with night sights and high-powered rifles, and said they had spotted the animal on several occasions.

'But is has either been unsafe to shoot, because of proximity of houses, or the thing had moved so fast and exposed itself so little. It is completely wild and very cunning. It uses cover very well and rarely moves out into the open.'

Then the trail goes cold. The Beast appears to have gone to ground.

Jack Hurley, the former editor of the *Free Press*, received his MBE at Buckingham Palace in June 1981. Jack had joined the reporting staff of the *Free Press* in 1930, aged 17, and apart from his war service years, worked for the paper all his life. He was a gentle and knowledgeable editor from 1970-80, perhaps best known for his inimitable *Notes by the Way*, and his wonderful accounts of the wit and wisdom of Will Widden. Jack died in 1983.

By 1984, there's a new focus for those concerned to conserve the natural landscape; and this time, it's a force more powerful than the farmer's plough.

In March 1984, the *Free Press* reported the first rumbles of discontent at Porlock, where villagers were concerned at the damage done repeatedly by storm seas to the shingle ridge stretching from Bossington westwards to Porlock Weir.

The mile-and-a-half long ridge was acknowledged as among the ten most significant such features in the United Kingdom, and protected valuable arable fields just inland. Its fate was to be the subject of heated debate, long into the 1990s: was it possible to defend the shingle ridge and if so, at what cost?

Further east, at Blue Anchor, the County Council had spent tens of thousands of pounds over the decades trying to shore up the coastline, and the defences, while deflecting the incoming waves, seemed also to cause the sand to be stripped from the beach; sand two feet in depth had disappeared in the past ten years.

Hydraulics engineers were now modelling new defences, using seven-ton boulders to absorb the energy of the waves. The county surveyor, Fred Johnson, agreed that a solution was urgently needed.

*'A continuation of the present rate of erosion will mean an almost complete disappearance of sand from Blue Anchor with the next five or ten years. Already there is very little sand left.' March 30th 1984.*

New defences were finally agreed and by March 1987, 25,000 tons of rock had been laid along the sea wall.

---

In February 1985, the *Free Press* reported ambitious plans to run a new hovercraft service from Minehead to Barry, initially twice a day, landing on the beach close to the railway station. Hover West company boss Clive Griffiths told the paper

*'People will find this is a new gateway to Exmoor and the West Country and could herald a new era for Minehead.' February 1st 1985.*

But the local fishermen were worried about the damage the hovercraft might do to the fishing grounds and the threat to visitors using the beach. Their spokesman was John Martin:

*'It will destroy the peace and quiet the resort is famous for...swimming will become dangerous and it will interfere with surfers, water-skiers, sailing boats and motor boats.'*

The champagne corks popped on May 23rd when the first 38-seater SRN6 hovercraft roared onto Minehead's beach. But within two weeks, the new service was running at a loss.

Hover West went into liquidation in July, citing the impact of poor weather on passenger bookings.

*The 14 mile 'flight' from Barry had taken 25 minutes, costing £16 return.*

Hinkley Point B, the new generation Advanced Gas-Cooled Reactor, had come on stream in 1976 and, after early teething problems, had enjoyed a good safety record. But late in 1985, a leak of radioactive gas at the plant forced the immediate evacuation of the 400 workers on the site, and – for the first time in the history of Britain's nuclear industry – the issuing to staff of potassium iodate tablets to counter the effects of possible nuclear contamination.

The leak had been sealed within five hours and the CEGB said that at no time were staff at any real risk, as the reactor was depressurised at the time for regular maintenance. The issuing of the radiation tablets was simply a sensible precaution.

But fears for the safety of the Hinkley reactors escalated when only a few months later, in April 1986, the world woke to the news of the nuclear reactor disaster at Chernobyl in Ukraine.

The CEGB insisted there could never be such an incident at Hinkley; the reactor designs were totally different and the safety plans at Hinkley were robust.

But the timing of the Chernobyl could not have been worse for the CEGB plans for Hinkley: three weeks earlier, the *Free Press* had reported CEGB plans to build a third reactor at Hinkley, Hinkley C. This would be a Pressurised Water Reactor, cheaper than the gas-cooled design, and it would have a longer operating life. Another 3,500 construction jobs would be created. But the political fall-out of Chernobyl had changed everything: Somerset County Council, now controlled by a Social Democrat-Liberal Alliance coalition, called on the CEGB to abandon its plans for Hinkley C.

The council's leader, Mr John Gillham told the *Free Press*

> *'The attitude of the people of Somerset has been dramatically changed by the Chernobyl disaster. . .the scale of Chernobyl showed that authorities were faced with mass evacuation of large areas of populations. . .Somerset, Avon, Devon and Dorset, and not just a few houses nearby.'*

The CEGB formally presented their plans for Hinkley C in August 1987, starting a year-long public consultation that culminated a year later with a full public inquiry, which opened at Cannington College in October 1988.

The public inquiry lasted a year, cost about £2m to run, and despite sustained local opposition, in 1990 Hinkley C was eventually granted planning permission. But by then, the financial climate had changed.

In 1989, the Conservative government announced plans to privatise the non-nuclear power industries, and insisted that it had no plans to build new nuclear plants.

By the end of the 1980s, the West Somerset Railway, after years of struggle, has stabilised its business but needed to move on. From 1985, the company turned in small operating profits, but it was still paying annual rent to the County Council for the use of the track and stations. In September 1988, the County Council agree to sell the rail company a 99-year lease on the line, for £210,000.

By April 1989, the WSRC had raised an extraordinary £265,000. There was a spirit of optimism; the WSRC's commercial manager, James Hatch said,

> *'Our membership is now worldwide and we have a lot of people from around the country who spend their holidays working on the railway; we really are a success story at last.' April 21st 1989.*

Sir Richard Acland – who in 1944 had donated the Holnicote Estate to the National Trust – returned to Horner Wood in 1985 to plant an oak tree in recognition of his 80th birthday.

# 1990s: Hunts at bay, but the ponies are saved

THE SEA storms of the 1980s had battered mainly the less populated stretches of the West Somerset coastline. Early in spring 1990, it was made painfully clear that unless urgent action was taken, the homes and lives of many of the district's residents were imperilled by inadequate sea defences.

Householders in West Street in Watchet were especially badly hit – only a four-foot high wall stood between them and the crashing storm waves; but residents in Minehead, Blue Anchor, Doniford and Kilve were also mopping up after the storm. The council launched an urgent assessment of their sea defence needs along the 33 miles of coastline and two harbours they were responsible for – and wondered where the money might come from.

Huge chunks of
Minehead's old sea wall
were washed onto the
Promenade.

By the end of following year, the repairs at Watchet, including a new sea wall, had been completed, and attention turned to Minehead. The sea defence survey, led by the National Rivers Authority, had highlighted the vulnerability of Minehead's mile-long 70-year-old sea wall. Together with the District and County Council, in September 1993 the NRA presented a £7m seafront defence scheme designed

> '...to protect the town from flooding for the next 100 years and open the way for developments to restore it as a major British seaside resort.' September 23rd 1993.

The scheme proposed building a new sea wall from the harbour to the golf course, to raise the level of the beach along Warren Road by up to six feet by bringing in fresh sand, and to build five stone groynes to retain the sand.

Once the Bossington shingle ridge had been abandoned, the sea regularly inundated the Porlock marshes. This photograph was taken in 2002.

———— ❖ ————

As it was being agreed to shore up Minehead's sea defences, further west at Porlock, the villagers were angry that no-one was prepared to protect their shingle ridge.

In October 1992, independent consultants concluded that it was too expensive to try to maintain the ridge. The National Trust suggested a policy of 'managed retreat', to allow the natural function of coastal erosion and to manage the amounts of sea water mixing with the fresh water in the marshes inland. A Trust statement read;

> 'We wouldn't try to "do a Canute" and hold it back. There is something to be said for letting that land become marshy because the sea marsh has its own environment. People's homes are not threatened in Porlock Bay. But it is acknowledged that agricultural production may be further limited by adopting such an option.' October 23rd 1992.

The District Council supported this approach, but Porlock villagers felt they'd been betrayed. When the policy of 'managed retreat' was confirmed early in 1993, the chairman of Porlock Parish Council, John Sharpe said

> 'This policy doesn't mean a damned thing except abandonment. It is an absolute outrage that after many centuries of maintenance by the people of Porlock Vale, the shingle bank will be allowed to disappear completely into the sea within two years.
> 
> 'World championship barley is grown on this land, which is going to vanish under salt water, to say nothing of the wildlife that will be destroyed.' January 15th 1993.

❖

Late on the night of January 17th 1991, British warplanes joined the first Coalition attacks on Iraqi forces occupying Kuwait; the final details of the land war were still being worked on.

Opening time — Mr King unveils the new sign above the villagers' shop.

# Celebrations as MP opens saved shop

And yet in the midst of this, the Defence Secretary, the local MP Tom King, one of the few at the heart of Prime Minister John Major's 'war cabinet', broke away from the Gulf crisis to drive to West Somerset to open a small local shop, at Wootton Courtenay.

The villagers had clubbed together to raise more than £120,000 to buy the local store which was threatened with closure; in doing so, they had created what was believed to be the first community co-operative shop in the country.

The narrow streets of the village were crammed with well-wishers, television camera crews and reporters, as Mr King's ministerial Daimler drew up.

*'Villagers clad in their waxed jackets and mittened against the cold beamed with excitement as they gathered amongst the media hardware and drank hot cider supplied by the newly-named Wootton Courtenay Villagers' Store.' January 18th 1991.*

One particular reason for Mr King's presence was that his mother once lived in the village. He told the crowd;

*'The reason I have come such a long way to be here today is because I think you have done something very remarkable. . .you have shown you are determined as a community to keep your shop.'*

And with that, he returned to the developing conflict in the Gulf.

❖

In March 1991, the West Somerset Railway celebrated the arrival at Minehead of the first through-train from Paddington since the old BR line closed 20 years previously. A BR diesel brought the passengers to Bishops Lydeard, where two WSR steam engines took over to pull the 13 coaches to their destination.

But a few days later, the railway escaped what could have been a disastrous accident. A 'works' diesel train parked at the highest point of the line, at Crowcombe Station, rolled out of control, unattended, for five miles down the line towards Taunton, rolling right through Bishops Lydeard Station and only coming to a halt at Norton Fitzwarren. The *Free Press* gave more details:

*'The driver of the engine had left the hand-brake only partially engaged and while he was out of the cab, the train began to roll down the gradient. From a high point of 400ft at Crowcombe, the class 14 diesel rolled along at an estimated 25mph until it came to a halt at the Taunton Cider freight yard.'*

Railway staff had jumped into their cars to try to catch up with the runaway train, hoping to stop it at Bishops Lydeard, but they were too late.

The driver was immediately suspended; a later inquiry emphasised that this could happen only on a 'works' train and assured the public that WSR passenger trains were all equipped with a fail-safe vacuum braking system.

Up on Exmoor, the emphasis had changed from protecting the moorland to finding new and creative ways to boost farm incomes, without damaging the environment. At the 1990 annual meeting of the Exmoor Society, chairman Guy Somerset had said:

*'A start has been made on turning around the agricultural engine of destruction into one which favours conservation.' September 28th 1990.*

The following year, the Exmoor National Park Authority reported that they had been swamped with applications from farmers to join their new farm conservation scheme, the first of its kind in the country.

Farmers would be paid for conserving the environment: higher rates would be paid for higher 'conservation value' land, such as moor, heath, broadleaved woodland, wetland and flower-rich grassland. Payments would also be made for footpaths, bridleways and a flat rate of £50 for caring for archeological sites.

More than 110 farmers registered interest in the scheme but only 12 were accepted for the first pilot project.

Supporting the scheme, the NFU's senior policy adviser, Anthony Gibson said;

*'The days are gone when farmers were regarded simply as food producers. Now they are expected to "produce" a certain type of countryside as well, and it is only right and proper that they should be rewarded for that.' May 3rd 1991.*

And by November 1991, there was finally help from Westminster. Exmoor was only one of six areas in the country to be granted Environmentally Sensitive Area status – something for which the district had lobbied for the past four years; this meant that farmers were now eligible for grants for preserving and improving moorland landscape.

———————— ❖ ————————

For many years, the residents of Washford, Bilbrook and Carhampton – all bottlenecks on the busy A39 to the coast – had lobbied for village by-passes. Every year, they had to battle for priority with other road projects in Somerset, and every year the A39 villages missed out and the traffic just got worse.

In November 1988, Somerset County Council's surveyors outlined an ambitious plan to solve these bottlenecks in one imaginative project – a Super Highway which would leave the A39 to the Quantock side of Williton and sweep westward by-passing Williton, Washford, Bilbrook and Carhampton, rejoining the existing A39 at the Dunster end of the village.

It took another two and a half years – until May 1991- before the county published three possible routes. By now all three proposed routes rejoined the A39 at the Withycombe straight and included a separate by-pass for Carhampton; and the budget had risen from the original estimate of £11m to £20m.

Two of the proposed routes went north of Washford and bisected Old Cleeve and Chapel Cleeve, while the third went south of Washford; this last route was judged an immediate non-runner because of its impact on the ancient monument of Cleeve Abbey.

A public consultation meeting was held and the proposals immediately divided the district; critics of the northerly route, complained of the environmental damage to the landscape:

*'If we cover it with roads, traffic fumes and petrol then we will be going against everything most of us are fighting for. . .we will be losing 100 acres of valuable farmland and our beautiful countryside forever.' May 24th 1991.*

But others spoke of the daily misery caused by the traffic snaking daily though Washford and Bilbrook.

*'Everybody seems very concerned about the countryside, and so they should be. But who cares for the villagers who walk up that road (A39) and are brushed by traffic and their shopping baskets are knocked out of their hands? They are rudely told to move their prams out of the way by speeding motorists.'*

## Staghounds tried to beat ex-Beatle to Exmoor land

DEVON and Somerset Staghounds and anti-hunt campaigners are embroiled in new controversy after the purchase of Exmoor land as a deer sanctuary by rock superstar Paul McCartney and wife Linda.

The ex-Beatle and his wife announced at the weekend that they were handing over 80 acres at St John's Wood, Skilgate, near Dulverton, for the League Against Cruel Sports to manage.

He said: "We don't regard it as of tremendous significance because it is only a small area added on to another little site owned by the League. They have about 2,000 acres, which leaves us with around 600,000 acres.

"We knew about the purchase but did not make determined efforts to buy because they have paid three times the market value."

But the McCartneys are already thought to be showing growing interest in the anti-hunt cause, which could result in more backing for it in the future.

Somerset County Council said they would consider an approved route for the 1993-94 road programme, if the money could be found.

The Super Highway figured on successive county plans throughout the 1990s and into the new millennium, but other Somerset road projects were always judged more necessary; it remained on the drawing board.

———————— ❖ ————————

Paul McCartney last made the pages of the *Free Press* in 1964 when, along with the other members of the Beatles, he was mobbed by excited teenagers at Minehead railway station during their breaks from filming *A Hard Day's Night*.

In August 1991, McCartney was back in the local news when the *Free Press* revealed that he and his wife Linda had bought 80 acres of land at St John's Wood, Skilgate and given it as a deer sanctuary to the League Against Cruel Sports, in a practical demonstration of their opposition to hunting. The D & S chairman, Dick Lloyd, denied the hunt had competed with McCartney over the purchase and said they were relaxed at the news.

*'It's only a little area, added on to another little site owned by the League. They have about 2,000 acres, which leaves us with around 600,000 acres.' August 2nd 1991.*

The following week, the *Free Press* carried 'a personal statement' to the paper and its readers from the former Beatle and his wife, explaining the reasons behind their land purchase.

*'Like many people, we think that hunting is an outdated practice, like so many other so-called sports practiced through the ages. I don't think it is necessary to live in an area to understand what goes on there but, unfortunately for hunt supporters, my wife and I are against hunting.' August 9th 1991.*

The McCartneys apparently paid £100,000 for the 80 acres.

In March 2003, Exford welcomed home Sir Ranulph Fiennes after his record-breaking unaided crossing of Antarctica. Fiennes and Dr Michael Stroud pulled their sledges 1,350 miles, stopping at the South Pole only briefly for a cup of tea.

In March 1992, the skittlers of the Wyndham Arms in Williton smashed the world record for the most pins felled in 24 hours. Helped by an army of supporters, stickers-up, first aid attendants and tea-makers, the relay of eight skittlers knocked over 82,500 pins, easily beating the previous record of 78,223 held by a Portishead pub team and far surpassing their own 1990 record of 73,453 pins.

In the Spring of 1992, it became clear that new measures designed to conserve Exmoor's natural landscape in fact endangered the survival of one of the moorland's most loved and iconic species – the Exmoor pony.

To qualify for the new Environmentally Sensitive Area grants, farmers had to agree to keep all their livestock off the moorland in winter. And it became clear that this requirement included the Exmoor ponies.

The Exmoor Pony Society insisted that if the ponies were overwintered on less rigorous lowland pastures, that this would in time weaken the distinctive upland character of the herd. The Society's secretary, David Mansell, was clearly worried about this;

*'(These plans) would seriously weaken, if not wipe out, what is already a critically rare breed. The free-living Exmoor Ponies are not domesticated animals; they are as wild as the red deer and have been part of the moorland ecology for thousands of years, arriving long before the first farmers.' April 24th 1992.*

But if the farmers kept the ponies on the moor over the winter, they would lose these ESA grants; the Exmoor Pony Society feared that some ponies may even be slaughtered.

And the EPS emphasised the rarity of the herd – 'more rare than the Panda' was a regular description. Only about 150 ponies still roamed the moor and there were fewer than 800 worldwide, and only about four distinct bloodlines.

After nine months of pressure, the Ministry of Agriculture, Fisheries and Food relaxed the ESA rules and allowed farmers to overwinter the ponies on the moor without losing their grants.

❖

In 1993, the whole future of hunting on the Quantocks was thrown into the balance when the Liberal Democrat-run County Council in Taunton voted for an immediate ban on hunting over land they owned on Over Stowey Common – a strategic 140 acres at the heart of hunting country.

Because the League Against Cruel Sports also owned land close by, this ban, if imposed, would mean hunting would be impossible on the eastern end of the Quantocks. The leader of the County Council, Chris Clarke, said;

> 'In a few years time, people will look back and wonder, why, so late in the twentieth century, this activity was allowed to continue.' July 9th 1993.

The Quantock Staghounds vowed to challenge the ban in court, and in February 1994, the High Court quashed the ban, saying that the County Council…

> '…had no right to base its decision on members' moral and political views.' February 11th 1994.

Hunting was a national issue and Parliament did not intend to give local authorities powers for 'piecemeal' bans. The judge concluded;

> 'Whether hunting should be banned or limited seems to me to be pre-eminently a matter for the national legislature'.

❖

Science fiction writer and visionary Arthur C. Clarke – often referred to as Minehead's most famous son – was awarded NASA's highest possible civilian accolade in August 1995, when he received their Distinguished Public Service Medal, joining an elite band of astronauts, cosmonauts and space pioneers.

Arthur C. Clarke had been born in Minehead in 1917, and educated at Huish's Grammar School in Taunton; after working on radar with the RAF in the Second World War, Clarke embarked on a series of books on rocketry and space flight, both fiction and non-fiction, and is credited with first suggesting and then developing the idea of using geostationary satellites for global communications.

The NASA director in Pasadena, Daniel Goldin, paid tribute to Clarke's achievements;

Snowy, a famous white hind, had roamed the Quantocks for some 20 years before being shot by poachers in 1993.

A reward of £1000 was offered for any information; her remains were finally found in Yeovil, but no police action was taken.

> 'We need dreamers because dreamers are able to communicate to the people of the planet. You are the fuel that helped us to go, you have helped us to visualise it. No writer, living or dead, has done more to demonstrate to the public the practical value and future potential of continued space exploration.' August 25th 1995.

In Minehead, they were already wondering how to mark the year 2001, in recognition of Clarke's epic collaboration with film director Stanley Kubrick in the movie *2001; A Space Odyssey.*

Various projects were put forward, ranging from an ambitious £20m planetarium on Minehead's seafront, complete with a 100ft viewing tower, to the conversion of Elgin Towers on North Hill into an Arthur C. Clarke Museum, but they all came to nothing.

In 2001, a blue plaque was placed on the exterior of 13 Blenheim Gardens to mark his first home in Minehead.

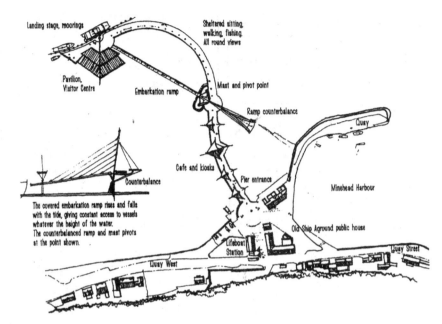

Arthur C. Clarke was later to lend his support to another imaginative project in Minehead designed to usher in the New Millennium – a new £5m town pier.

Ever since the old pier was demolished as a wartime measure in 1940, there had been talk of building a replacement. The Minehead Pier Association was formed in 1996 to make a bid for Millennium Lottery money to realise that dream.

In January 1997, the promoters presented plans for a space age, state-of-the-art, sweeping curved pier, designed to mirror the sweep of Minehead Bay. At the end would be a small pavilion with a roof suggesting the sails of boats in the channel.

The Millennium Commission liked the proposal and in February 1997 placed it among the last 119 projects short-listed for funding from an initial long-list of 2,000 applications; it was the only project in Somerset deemed worthy of funding.

But the pier project fell at the last hurdle, mainly because of a failure to attract matching funding from an EU regional development scheme.

———————— ❖ ————————

Several times in the past, the National Trust had considered banning hunting on its property, and each time the ban had been dismissed.  But in 1995, the Trust commissioned Professor Patrick Bateson, of Kings College, Cambridge, an acknowledged expert in animal behaviour, to study the physiological effects of hunting on deer.

At the beginning of April 1997, the Trust had received his report – and, on a unanimous vote, the Trust finally banned the hunting of deer with hounds on its property, on Exmoor and the Quantocks, to take effect from the end of that month; this was without doubt the most serious threat yet faced by the local packs of staghounds.  The ban did not apply to the hunting of foxes.

Prof. Bateson said there was clear scientific evidence of the cruelty suffered by the deer during a hunt and he concluded that deer hunting with hounds could no longer be justified on welfare grounds.

The *Free Press* highlighted some of the key evidence presented by Prof. Bateson, who had compared the experience of hunted wild red deer, farmed deer and red deer stalked and shot by marksmen.

> 'The average hunt lasted three hours and the exertion of the chase resulted in more extreme changes to muscles and blood than anything a red deer would experience in normal life.
> 'It also found contributory factors to stress during a chase, including biting by hounds, whipping by people, close proximity of humans and their noise, and chasing with vehicles.'

Prof. Bateson concluded

*'We approached this study with an open mind, expecting to find some middle ground. Instead, our inescapable
conclusion is that the level of total suffering would be markedly reduced if hunting with hounds was ended.'
April 11th 1997.*

The Devon & Somerset Staghounds and the Quantocks Staghounds had co-operated with Prof.
Bateson's study, allowing his researchers full access to their hunts. They were, of course, appalled at
his conclusions.

The Joint Master of the D & S, Mrs Diana Scott told a meet at Whitstones on Porlock Hill:

*'I am an animal lover and I care passionately about the deer – I would not be here today if I thought it
was cruel. I do think that local people have a better understanding of hunting that any professor who was
only down here on two or three visits.' April 11th 1997.*

The hunts challenged the science, and called for fresh studies. In particular, while saying they
respected Prof. Bateson's sincerity, they pointed out that he was an expert in animal behaviour, and
not in the biology of animals under stress.

The D & S chairman Tom Yandle issued a statement on behalf of the Master of Deerhounds
Association.

*'In our opinion, and that of most people on Exmoor, such a ban without a mutually agreed deer management
scheme would cause immense suffering and large scale reductions in the number of the wild red deer.'
April 11th 1997.*

Over the close season, the hunts considered their options. For the first peacetime year since
1869, the D & S were unable to hold their traditional opening meet at Cloutsham Farm – land now
owned by the National Trust – and so met at Honeymead, near Simonsbath.

But there was further bad news for the hunts later in November, when the Forestry Commission,
basing their judgment on the Bateson report, followed the National Trust, and banned any hunting
of deer with hounds on their property.

The hunts later commissioned a fresh independent study by an expert in animal biology,
Prof. Roger Harris: the Joint Universities Study challenged the conclusions of the Bateson
report, but the bans remained.

In 1996, the former
Prime Minister, now
Baroness Thatcher, and
husband Denis came to
Minehead to celebrate
Tom King's 25 years as
local MP.

# 2000s: Barricades and moorland revolts

WEST SOMERSET joined in the nation's celebrations of the New Millennium with hilltop beacon blazes, fireworks and candle-lit processions; thankfully the night was clear and dry.

More than two thousand gathered at Minehead's harbour after a procession through the town; Watchet's Esplanade fireworks were gloriously reflected by the full tide filling the harbour. Many walked to Selworthy Beacon, just one of the hilltop bonfires ushering in the year 2000.

The police reported few disturbances – for them, it was 'quieter than the usual Friday night.'

Then it was back to business as usual. Many of the early headlines of the New Millennium reflected a hangover from a big housing deal secured in 1998 by the West Somerset District Council.

In March 1998, the council sold all its housing stock to the Dorchester-based Magna West Somerset Housing Association for £23.5m; the council was delighted, they said they had negotiated the highest per unit price achieved by any local authority in such a deal – around £13,000 per property. The *Free Press* reported the deal had made the fourth smallest local authority in the land one of the richest, per head of population.

But the deal had been dogged by allegations of excessive hospitality offered to certain senior council officials. Despite months of investigation nothing was found to justify charging anyone with any offence.

In April 2000, Tom King announced that he was standing down after 30 years as MP for Bridgwater; he had first won the seat in the by-election of 1970 – when West Somerset's youngsters became the first in the country to vote at the age of 18.

He told the Free Press

> '*I think it is time for a new and younger face to take over from me. I am sure it is the right decision both for myself and for the constituency, but that does not make it any easier giving up representing a constituency of which I am so fond.' April 7th 2000.*

Tom King had held a succession of high offices in Margaret Thatcher's Governments between 1983 and 1992. He had short tenures as Environment Secretary and Transport Secretary before more substantial challenges, first as Employment Secretary during the miners' strike, and Northern Ireland Secretary during the negotiations with Dublin over the Anglo-Irish Agreement.

Later, as Defence Secretary, Mr King was at the heart of international events, first with the end of Communism in Eastern Europe following the collapse of the Berlin Wall, and then in the 'war cabinet' during the first Gulf War.

The leader of West Somerset District Council, Steven Pugsley said;

*'We have been extremely lucky to have an MP who has held such high office and at the same time has been ready, willing and able to put that experience and the contacts he naturally has, at the disposal of the authority, to the benefit of its residents.' April 7th 2000.*

After the 2001 general election, Tom King was given a life peerage, taking the title Baron King of Bridgwater.

❖

British Nuclear Fuels Ltd announced in May 2000 that Hinkley Point A station was to close. The Magnox plant was one of the first generation of gas-cooled nuclear reactors opened in the 1960s and the plant's two reactors had produced electricity for the past 35 years.

It had been mothballed for the past twelve months and the costs of another refit were deemed to be uneconomic. The closure came as a surprise to the 345 workers, but there was no immediate threat of large scale job losses as many would be needed for the decommissioning of the plant. Removing the uranium fuel alone would take ten years; it would be another 100 years until decommissioning was complete.

The BNFL chief engineer Norman Agnew said;

*'These stations were pioneers in the nuclear industry and have made a huge carbon-free contribution to the energy generation industry.' May 26th 2000.*

❖

During the weeks of February 2001, farmers throughout West Somerset were anxiously hoping that they would be spared from the disastrous outbreak of foot and mouth that had hit other parts of the country.

By the end of the month, five cases had been reported in Devon; the virulent disease was moving closer. West Somerset's farmers put up the barricades; disinfected straw was spread across all lanes onto farm property, all movement of stock was reduced to a minimum, most public footpaths were closed. The countryside was locked down; every aspect of life was affected.

**Stay away from the no-go areas**

EXMOOR and West Somerset are set to be effectively closed off from the outside world, with the national park, North Hill and numerous public footpaths all labelled as out of bounds.

People will be committing a criminal offence if they walk, ride or cycle across any tracts of land covered by the emergency legislation.

MAFF gave statutory powers this week to all local authorities to legally ban people from vast swathes of the countryside in a bid to prevent foot and mouth

rural West Somerset.

In the national park, the legislation affects all open areas, moorland, woodland, all footpaths and rights of way.

National park staff have also curtailed their activities, postponing farm visits, cutting down on travel, cancelling all activities at Pinkers outdoor education centre and putting the stop to training days.

Chief national park officer Dr Nigel Stone said the authority had taken action last week, even before it became clear just how serious the outbreak was.

The farmers were virtual captives on their own land; licences had to be obtained to move stock to the local markets and abattoirs. All exports of British meat had been banned. Tourism was another immediate victim; hotels saw a flood of cancellations from visitors now unable to walk or ride on the moors and the sudden drop in visitors hit the income of many other businesses in the district.

All hunting stopped and there were fears for the deer which, unlike horses, could catch the disease. All sporting events were cancelled, including the point-to-points. In the third week of the outbreak, fears of a case at Dulverton proved unfounded and Somerset was still free of the disease. Further south, in Devon and on Dartmoor, farmers watched in desperation as the pyres of their dead cattle burned in the fields.

By the end of March, local businesses were really struggling to keep afloat. Two hundred attended a crisis meeting called by the Porlock Tourist Association. People arriving at the meeting were greeted by the sight of a dozen horses with 'For Sale' signs around their necks. Kim Youd of the Porlock Vale Riding Centre, said he had lost £17,000 this year already, compared with 2000.

Cathy Powell, of the Exmoor Falconry and Animal Farm at Bossington, spoke for many;

*'The economy is collapsing. . .if nothing is done, then we are just going to go under.' March 23rd 2001.*

Guy Thomas-Everard
mounted a public and
ultimately successful
defence of his herd.

Others reported business down by 60 or 65 per cent. Humphrey Temperley, chairman both of Exmoor National Park Authority and the Somerset County Council said;

*'If we allow the infection to happen, we will be in the same situation as Dartmoor and Devon and we will have lost the image of Exmoor in the eyes of potential visitors and that would be a disaster.'*

But after weeks of anxious precautions, some dared to believe that the disease had been kept at bay. Footpaths along the coastal belt and away from farmland were being re-opened; the government was concerned to let visitors know it was 'business as usual' in the unaffected areas.

In the third week of April, Somerset was declared officially free of the disease after restrictions were lifted around one confirmed case near Axbridge. Then, in the first week of May, the *Free Press* reported some terrible news.

*'A nightmare scenario hit the Wiveliscombe area this week with two cases of the foot and mouth disease confirmed in animals belonging to a roving farm relief worker.*
*'A third case is suspected and it is feared that up to 15 farms in the Wiveliscombe, West Somerset and Exmoor areas could have come into contact with Pitsford Hill farmer Rob Norman.' May 4th 2001.*

It could not have been worse; this was not just a confirmed case in the heart of the district, but the source was apparently a travelling relief milker, Mr Norman, who had visited many farms in the area; it was believed at the time he may well have brought the disease into the area after attending a foot and mouth vaccination course at Hatherleigh in Devon, a hotspot of the outbreak.

MAFF vets shot his ten beef cattle at Styles Lane, and another three cows and a calf two miles away. The third suspected case was in a herd of 400 goats which were overwintered with the cattle. They, too, were all culled, and later it appeared that these goats may well have been the cause of the local outbreak, and not Mr Norman.

But for now much of West Somerset was deemed an infected zone, centred on Wiveliscombe and ranging as far as Williton, Bishops Lydeard and Skilgate. And of course, the search was now on for all the farms recently visited by Mr Norman.

This search led to one of the most publicised events of the entire national outbreak that seemed to symbolise the agonising plight of the farmers.   MAFF vets discovered that Mr Norman had visited Broford Farm, near Dulverton, run by the Thomas-Everard family. MAFF ordered the immediate slaughter of the family's entire herd of 986 Aberdeen Angus cattle.

But Guy Thomas-Everard was convinced the herd was not infected; the cattle displayed no symptoms of foot and mouth, which they should have done by now, if they were indeed infected, given the dates of Mr Norman's last contact with the herd. Not only that, but a second local herd visited by Mr Norman also showed no signs of the disease.

Guy Thomas-Everard barricaded the entrance to Broford Farm with a cattle truck, to keep the MAFF vets off his land, and his determination to save the family herd was widely reported across

the TV news bulletins and the national papers. And it paid off; after blood tests on the second suspect local herd proved negative, MAFF lifted their slaughter order. Mr Thomas–Everard's defence of his herd was vindicated. He said:

*'It's fantastic. The vets have just finished their inspection and we're delighted. This past week has been absolutely hectic and it's a huge relief that the whole thing is finally over.' May 11th 2001.*

But by now, animals at twenty other farms in the Wiveliscombe and West Somerset area had been slaughtered, as part of the two-mile contiguous zone culling policy. A total of 5,451 cattle were killed in Somerset as a result of the outbreak

Thankfully, there were no more confirmed cases in the area. The nightmare of contagion spread through the district by an unsuspecting relief milker proved unfounded. In late May, the Exmoor National Park Authority was able to announce the re-opening of a large number of footpaths in time for the Whitsun Bank Holiday, but it was not until October that the government finally declared that the epidemic was over.

---

Early in 1993, the last commercial vessel had docked in Watchet's harbour. Shipping had been at the heart of Watchet, but the recession of the early 1990s meant that the small port always struggled to make money.

It was clear the town had to re-invent itself and a consultants' report in 1994 recommended that the harbour should be redeveloped as a yachting marina.

After years of uncertainty, in May 2000 the Environment Secretary, John Prescott, approved the closure of Watchet harbour and for its change of use into a leisure facility. The harbour's commercial shipping days finally over and the regeneration of Watchet as a tourist and yachting attraction was about to start.

Construction of a barrier sea wall and berths progressed so rapidly that in a little over a year, the town was ready for a grand opening. In the summer of 2001, in blazing sunshine and bobbing on an inflatable dinghy, the round-the-world yachtsman Sir Robin Knox-Johnston cut the ribbon across the harbour entrance and declared open the new £5.1m marina. A flare shot into the clear blue sky and the foghorns sounded.

Three thousand people thronged the harbourside and the marina was packed with vessels of all sizes – fishing boats, yachts, motor cruisers, small dinghies. Sir Robin had entered the harbour in a flotilla headed by a replica of Watchet's old 'flatties', the small double-ended boat, with no keel, that had been used by generations of the town's fishermen.

Sir Robin told the crowds he believed the marina would be a big success.

*'July 28th 2001 will be the day when something dramatic changed in Watchet. People don't realise that yachting is the second biggest participation sport in the country...the Bristol Channel has not been very hospitable to boatmen because there has been nowhere to leave their craft.*

*'Everywhere a marina has been developed in this country we have seen regeneration of the local economy.' August 3rd 2001.*

Round-the world sailor Sir Robin Knox-Johnston launched Watchet's new future as a tourist and sailing attraction.

West Somerset went to the polls in June 2001 in the General Election that returned Tony Blair's Labour government for a second term. Tom King's Conservative successor for the Bridgwater constituency was Ian Liddell-Grainger, who increased the Tory majority to almost 5,000.

And in the Taunton constituency, the controversial LibDem MP Jackie Ballard, an outspoken critic of hunting, was ousted by just 235 votes by the young Tory candidate Adrian Flook. She was certain that hunting had lost her the seat.

*'Primary I lost because the people who are pro-hunting, in West Somerset particularly, were much more motivated to go out and vote than were people in the urban part of the constituency. I know my stance angered a lot of people who were determined to get rid of me.' June 15th 2001.*

Within a few weeks of the election, the Boundary Commission published plans to redesignate Dulverton, Brushford and several Exmoor parishes as part of a new Bridgwater and West Somerset constituency but most likely not until the election after next. The Taunton constituency would be redrawn as Taunton Deane.

At the end of 2001, Williton was in uproar. In November, the West Somerset District Council had announced that it planned to vacate its old premises in the village and move west to Minehead, to the Clanville car park site. Consultants had recommended the move, as a step towards greater efficiency and to allow the regeneration of the heart of Williton.

> *'Given the distribution of population, a centralised facility at Minehead will offer greater benefits than the site at Williton; a new purpose-built facility will offer greater scope for operational improvements than an enlargement of the existing facility at Williton.'* November 2nd 2001.

But Williton parish councillors were outraged; they claimed they had no prior consultation over the proposals and said the plan had been rushed through. Chairman of the Parish Council, and a district councillor, Ian Aldridge said;

> *'The council is the largest employer in Williton: if at Port Talbot you said you were going to take away the steel works, what would the opinion be?'* December 7th 2001.

Five months later, the council drew back from the Clanville site; this saga was to run for another four years during which the council proposed three alternative sites in Minehead – on the Vulcan Road car park, alongside the railway station and then on its existing Blenheim Road site. The council's chief executive Tim Howes argued that the council needed to get closer to more of its ratepayers:

> *'Within a mile of Minehead there are 10,000 people, within a mile of Williton there are 2,500…at this point you begin to say what is best for sustainability.'* November 7th 2002.

But now many in Minehead had joined Williton in opposing the move, fearing the loss of valuable amenity land to the project. Six thousand objectors signed a protest petition and 500 marched on the old council offices. In October 2005, the council finally voted to stay in Williton and to redevelop its existing site, at a cost of £4m.

———— ❖ ————

*Time Team presenter Tony Robinson examines some of the pottery unearthed in Celia Hardy's garden in Stogumber.*

Channel Four's popular archaeology programme, the Time Team, spent several days in 2003 excavating the back garden of Celia Hardy's fifteenth-century home in Stogumber.

The dig was televised live to the nation, and the archaeologists were pleased with the results, removing from the garden's flower beds pottery that showed the village was developing as far back as the eleventh century.

Villagers in Stogumber, and in particular the landlord of the White Horse, were delighted with all the attention. The bar manager, John Hawes said

*'We haven't had anything like this since Van Morrison sang at the church at a wedding here a few years ago.'* July 11th 2003.

For months now, those who followed the district's hunts scented trouble. Hunting deer with hounds was already banned on National Trust and Forestry Commission property; finally, after decades of thwarted attempts, it now looked certain that Parliament itself would finally pass legislation banning all hunting with hounds.

In West Somerset, the local authorities commissioned the most authoritative report yet on the economic and social impact of banning the hunting of deer on Exmoor and the Quantocks.

In November 2003, the Promar report estimated that staghunting alone contributed £9.5m a year in direct and indirect business, and supported 584 jobs, many of them in the winter season when there was little prospect of alternative employment.

But fifteen months later, in February 2005, the Hunting Act, banning the hunting of all mammals with hounds, came into effect. It was a sad day for all hunt followers, as the *Free Press* reported;

The Quantock Staghounds held their final meet before the new restrictions under the Hunting Act came into force.

*'Hunt supporters across West Somerset were both defiant and despondent today as their centuries-old sport was finally outlawed and hunting with dogs became a wildlife crime.*

*'After an emotional mass turnout of packs across the district on the last legal day of hunting yesterday (Thursday 17th) many are planning to demonstrate their faith in the future of their activities by riding out again tomorrow.*

*'But although a significant number of supporters had previously signed a declaration to flout the new Act, most hunts were now preparing to keep within the letter of the law, by billing their meets as hound exercising or using artificial scents.' February 18th 2005.*

Many questioned if the police would have the resources to enforce the new law. Avon & Somerset Police had 21 hunts in their area: Superintendent Adrian Coombs said;

*'If people hunt, and break the law, then the full circumstances will be investigated and the law upheld in the same way as any other breach.'*

Most hunts, while being determined to overturn the ban, accepted that it would take time. Speaking for one of the smallest hunts, the Minehead Harriers, hunt secretary Tim Holt said;

*'We believe we are in for a long haul and are pinning our hopes on a change in government at some stage. But the enthusiasm is there to keep going.'*

They believed it was quite possible to control the hounds and keep within law, in particular to use pairs of hounds to flush out foxes before humane killing.

The League Against Cruel Sports said they would closely monitor all hunt activities; the League said this was the culmination of decades of campaigning, but not a day for gloating.

*'Of course we are delighted, but we welcome the decision by hunts to hunt without cruelty – that is what we have been pressing for decades to achieve. We take no joy from the dislocation of communities but we are very happy that sentient animals will no longer be chased around the countryside.'*

❖

The first prosecution in the country for illegal hunting came in August 2006, for an offence allegedly committed within two months of the new law coming into effect. The huntsman of the Exmoor Foxhounds, Tony Wright was convicted by Barnstaple Magistrates for allowing hounds to chase a fox on April 29th 2005. He was fined £500, plus £250 costs.

The prosecution had been brought by the League Against Cruel Sports, at a cost of £100,000, after the police declined to press the case. During the week-long hearing, Mr Wright, from

In 2006, lifeboats
rescued contestants in
the annual Blue
Anchor-Minehead Raft
Race; scores were
struggling in the heavy,
choppy swell and
strong westerly winds.

Police told the pro-
hunting rally at Exford
the new law had to be
upheld, no matter how
emotive and sensitive
the issue was in the
area.

### 'Hunting Act has failed'

THE Crown Prosecution
Service (CPS) has lost an
appeal against the acquittal
of the first huntsman to be
prosecuted for breaching the
Hunting Act.
The High Court found in
favour of Tony Wright of
the Exmoor Foxhounds and
rejected the CPS's claims
that "hunting" a mammal
included "searching" for it.
The CPS had also
claimed it was up to Mr
Wright to prove he had been
hunting legally.
On Wednesday, Mr
Wright said he hoped the
High Court's ruling would
prevent other people from
suffering a similar ordeal to
his.
"This prosecution has
now dragged on for over
three years and during that
time I have been living
under the threat of a criminal conviction," he said.
"If this judgement,
though, makes it less likely
that other people will face
the sort of vindictive prosecution that I have been
through then it has all been
worth it."
Mr Wright was originally
fined £5,000 for breaching
the act when he was con-
victed by Barnstaple magistrates in August 2006.
● Continued on Page 2

Simonsbath, maintained his actions were covered under the law's exemptions, allowing two hounds to be used to flush out the fox until it was practical to shoot it.

The RSPCA claimed the conviction sent out...

> '...a clear warning to all hunts that the exceptions of the Hunting Act do not provide an excuse to continue to hunt wild animals.' August 11th 2006.

But the Countryside Alliance said that Mr Wright would appeal against the judgment, saying,

> 'No right minded person thinks that Tony Wright should have been branded a criminal.'

The police said that they would review their policy on illegal hunting, in the light of the Barnstaple judgment, and six months later, in October 2006, they prosecuted their first case in court, against the Master of the Devon & Somerset Staghounds, Maurice Scott, and a hunt servant Peter Heard.

Hunt supporters were angry at the alleged treatment of the two accused. Tom Yandle, speaking on behalf of the Masters of Deerhounds Association said

> 'We are upset and disgusted that a young hunt servant and a senior master of the hunt for 25 years, whose family farmed the Brendon Hills for generations, should have the indignity of being locked away in a cell reeking of vomit and urine for two and a half hours while the police discussed their future.' October 27th 2006.

While this case was adjourned for a later hearing, the two cases had stirred up passions. Hundreds packed the Memorial Hall at Exford for a meeting called by the moorland activists, Endangered Exmoor, to confront the police with their concerns. Chaired by Baroness Ann Mallalieu, the Labour peer and president of the Countryside Alliance, the meeting was told by one angry hunt supporter;

> 'Rural policing only works when the rural community works with the police and I think the police are now realising this (prosecution) has opened up a can of worms.' November 3rd 2006.

After many months, both cases were dismissed: Tony Wright, the first huntsman in the land to be prosecuted, finally won his case at the High Court in February 2009, three years after the first hearing at Barnstaple.

The Countryside Alliance welcomed the High Court's decision; chief executive Simon Hart noted that there had been only five successful convictions so far, and claimed;

*'The Hunting Act is an increasingly pointless piece of legislation…it is now a question of when, not if, the Act is appealed.' February 6th 2009.*

The League Against Cruel Sports welcomed what they called the court's clarification of the law and said the way was now clear for further cases to come to court. Six weeks later, in light of the High Court decision, the police dropped their case against the D & S Master Maurice Scott and his hunt colleagues.

───────── ❖ ─────────

By the end of 2007, the *Free Press* was running front page headlines declaring that the West Somerset Council was in deep trouble.

In the May local elections, the Conservatives who had held power for the past eight years had lost control of the council: the new Independent/Labour/Liberal coalition claimed that the authority faced a financial and a managerial crisis. They said there was not enough money in the council's coffers, nor sufficient staff in their offices, to run a proper service for the ratepayers.

Outside experts were summoned to help, both from a local government agency, and from neighbouring Sedgemoor District Council. The move reflected a long-running debate about how the council, with so few ratepayers scattered across such a wide area, could fund the urgent needs of its ratepayers.

Precious public projects were scrapped. Minehead's Aquasplash gym and swimming pool had been closed for months after the pool sprang a leak; there was now no money to repair and maintain the pool, and despite a fervent public campaign, it was demolished.

The council had planned to replace the pool with a new facility as part of an ambitious £51m New Horizons development off Minehead's Seaward Way. This was to have been a national pioneer project, bringing together on one site the district's new hospital, a 'health-plex' that combined swimming pool and leisure centre, and a skills and enterprise centre.

And this was no vanity project: the district needed it. New Horizons was designed to address some of West Somerset's pressing social problems highlighted in recent government surveys – below average earnings, with pockets of real poverty; a fragile local economy, where a higher proportion of school leavers failed to find employment; and house prices, in proportion to income, being the highest in the country outside of London.

The hospital and the skills and enterprise centre were to escape the council's financial cull, but much of the wider project would now have to wait.

───────── ❖ ─────────

In the autumn of 2008, a political storm blew up out of nowhere that for many summed up the divergence of views on the real nature of living on Exmoor. The Exmoor National Park Authority had in 2006 bought an old herdsman's bungalow at Blackpitts, just off the B3223 near Simonsbath, to prevent the potential 'urbanisation' of the moor.

It was nothing to look at, with its tin-roofed barn, but many believed it was the last remaining link on the moor with the huts where shepherds sheltered during the great reclamation of the moor in the nineteenth century. (Most of the others had been blown up in the Second World War by American troops using the buildings as target practice.)

But in September 2008, the Park Authority voted narrowly to demolish the cottage and outbuildings, to 'rewild' the landscape, and to build a new agricultural tenancy elsewhere. This caused a howl of protest, led by the Revolting Exmoor Peasants Party which had formed to oppose the demolition. (The Revolting Peasants soon renamed themselves Exmoor Uprising.)

Meetings were held and a 2000-name petition was delivered to the House of Commons. In the end, it appeared that 'people power' paid off; in December, the Park Authority reversed its demolition order and agreed to spend up to £100,000 renovating Blackpitts. The Park Authority said they feared the issue was distracting everyone from its wider work and endangering future working relations with the moor community.

# Staghounds charges dropped

A LENGTHY three-year legal battle has finally come to an end for three members of the Devon and Somerset Staghounds who had been accused of breaching the controversial Hunting Act.

All charges have been dropped against joint master Maurice Scott, huntsman Donald Summersgill and whipper-in Peter Heard after the Crown Prosecution Service (CPS) decided not to pursue the case.

The decision ends a three-year nightmare for the men, whose arrest sparked outrage among members of the rural community when it was revealed Mr Scott had been arrested and locked up in a urine-soaked police cell.

The three were charged in 2006 follow-ing as a whole," he said.

"We were always convinced that what we were doing was legal and, while we all hope that the Hunting Act does not last much longer, the Devon and Somerset Staghounds will be able to continue some form of hunting and deer management until it is repealed."

It is the second time in recent weeks that the CPS has backed down against a huntsman, having decided not to challenge a ruling that found in favour of Tony Wright of the Exmoor Foxhounds.

Mr Wright became the first huntsman to be prosecuted and convicted under the Act but subsequently had his conviction quashed.

He maintained he had simply been using two hounds to flush out foxes to be shot,

'The blur of Lycra and the whirr of wheels' swept across West Somerset in September 2008 when 100 top international cyclists competed in the South West leg of the Tour of Britain cycle race.

———— ❖ ————

While the decommissioning of the old Hinkley A nuclear reactor continued apace, renovation work in 2007 on the newer advanced gas-cooled Hinkley B had extended its generating life by a further five years until 2016, despite scares over age-related cracks in its boiler tubes and in the graphite blocks housing the nuclear core.

And again there was talk of a new Hinkley C plant, reviving the project that had been mothballed back in 1989. But unlike the first two plants, which had been sponsored by the state, Hinkley C was to be a private venture, and the French power company, EDF, was already buying up land around Hinkley to position itself for the next wave of nuclear build.

In September 2008, EDF bought the Hinkley B plant in a £12.5bn deal and immediately applied for planning permission for subsoil exploration to the west of Hinkley B, the site for a possible new reactor.

A year later, in November 2009, Hinkley was named by the government as one of ten sites in the UK approved for the next generation of nuclear power stations; with new fast-track planning processes in place, it was reported that Hinkley C could be operational as soon as 2017.

West Somerset Council was starting to think what it could do with the 'windfall' millions of pounds it might receive through planning fees, rates, services and the boost to the local economy.

———— ❖ ————

By late 2008, the Bearland Ventilation Flue, in Chargot Woods near Luxborough had been restored by the West Somerset Mineral Railway Project, with the help, among others, of local school children; the chimney had been built in 1860 to remove the foul air surrounding the iron ore miners working hundreds of metres below.

The project had won Lottery funding in 2007 to restore three structures that survived from the Brendon Hills' mining industry that had flourished in the mid nineteenth century; the Ventilation Flue, the Langham Engine House and the Comberow Incline – that magnificent example of Victorian engineering that hauled wagons up a 1 in 4 gradient onto the Brendon Ridge.

One of the early editions of the *Free Press* had described the incline as '....the grandest piece of work of its kind in the United Kingdom.'

The *Free Press,* which like the Bearland Flue had first appeared in 1860, had reported the early development of the Brendon Hills mines, their heyday in the 1870s and eventual decline in the mid 1880s; here in 2009 the paper brought to a new generation of readers news of the exciting restoration of the area's industrial legacy.

# Postscript

IN THE LAST WEEK OF July 1860, Samuel Cox and his three staff gathered in their cramped premises in Long Street in Williton to launch their new venture. They worked in relays around a hand press; one inked the flat beds of hand-set type, another cranked the handle to impress the paper onto the inked type, and the other two removed and stacked the printed pages.

Between them, they printed two pages of local news and adverts for that first edition of the *West Somerset Free Press.* Another two pages of national and international news had earlier in the week been printed in London and despatched first by train to Bristol and then on to Williton by stage coach.

On Saturday July 28th 1860, about one thousand copies of the first edition of the *Free Press* were distributed around the district, selling for three half-pence, the equivalent today of about £2.70. Within six months, the paper was to double in size to eight pages.

Samuel Cox had called the paper the *Free Press* not as a badge of political neutrality – although the paper has never followed any party line – but to denote that the paper, like many others that sprang up around the country at that time, was finally free of the punitive taxes on newspapers and on advertisements that had priced newspapers far beyond the pockets of the vast majority.

And since that first edition, it has been a proud boast of the paper that it has never once missed an edition, despite desperate staff shortages during two World Wars, and the challenges of industrial strikes and mechanical breakdowns.

The *Free Press* was printed in Williton for almost 130 years, before moving to contract printers elsewhere: pictured here on the last Williton print run in November 1989 are George Blake, Maurice Chidgey and Roger Willis.

(One edition in July 1948 looked doomed when the gas engine driving the printing press broke down on print day; the paper finally appeared after  Messrs Gliddons connected a belt from the drive shaft of a Ferguson tractor to the main shaft of the Cossar printing press and slowly the presses rolled once more.)

Week in and week out, the *Free Press* has faithfully reported both the 'big picture' events that have shaped the district we see today, and the notable triumphs and tragedies of those living in the area.

In researching this book, I have read every edition of the paper and it has been a privilege to be given both the access and the time to follow the progress of the paper and the district over the past 150 years.

But reading the back editions has also been a constant reminder of the irreplaceable role of the local newspaper in the community. The local paper is the only permanent forum for local news and opinion, the only permanent record of the developing history of a community.

The ubiquity and convenience of the Internet now threatens the economic base of all newspapers – national, regional and local – and throughout the country, we need, in particular, to treasure our local papers, the community's storehouse of local events and characters. We take them for granted at our peril.

In 1860, Samuel Cox faced serious competition of his own, and his conviction of the need for a good, truly local paper is as valid today as it was then. He wrote in his first editorial:

> 'We do not undervalue the various county and district papers which circulate among us, some of which are conducted with considerable ability, but still there are local interests, manifestly growing from year to year, of sufficient importance to justify far more than a few paragraphs occasionally appearing in the provincial press.

> 'To meet this want, the West Somerset Free Press has been originated, and puts forward its claim for support and patronage.' July 28th 1860.